THE ENVIRONMENT OF LEARNING

THE ENVIRONMENT OF LEARNING

Conflict and Understanding in the Secondary School

ELIZABETH RICHARDSON

WEYBRIGHT AND TALLEY
NEW YORK

Published in the U.S.A. by
WEYBRIGHT AND TALLEY, INC.
3 East 54th Street, N.Y. N.Y. 10022

Library of Congress Catalog Card Number 68–10528

Printed in Great Britain by
WESTERN PRINTING SERVICES LTD BRISTOL

Contents

Contents

Preface

I began to write this book about ten years ago, when I was becoming interested in the growing body of research into the problems of human relationships in clinical, industrial and educational settings. In 1959, when I took up my present post in the University of Bristol, I was given the opportunity to attend the second of the residential conferences in inter-personal and inter-group relations, run jointly by the University of Leicester and the Tavistock Institute of Human Relations. This experience influenced my ideas about school life in a fundamental way and enabled me to see both my own past experiences as a secondary-school teacher and those of the students I was working with in the Bristol Department in a new light. The whole character of the book changed radically as a result of this. I am most grateful to the University of Bristol for enabling me to go to this and later conferences, and to the members of the Leicester-Tavistock Executive Committee (Professor A. J. Allaway and Professor J. W. Tibble of the University of Leicester, Dr A. K. Rice of the Tavistock Institute and Dr P. M. Turquet of the Tavistock Clinic and Institute) for giving me the chance to carry this work further in subsequent years.

At about the time when I formed these new contacts, my reflections upon the problems of the secondary school were already being affected by the exciting work I had seen going on in a number of primary and secondary-modern schools in the West Riding of Yorkshire during the late 1950s. To the heads of these schools and to all the teachers with whom I was able to have discussions, and to Sir Alec Clegg who arranged for me to visit the schools, I should like to extend my warm thanks. I am also indebted to many members of the Standing Conference for Amateur Music, whose annual conferences I have attended as an observer during the last six years, for stimulating conversations about music in schools and youth groups, and for opportunities to see and hear about new developments in this field.

Their deliberations about the special problems of musical education and the experimental work which they are promoting reinforce what I have tried to say about the more general problems of teaching and learning, and have directly influenced one particular section of this book.

Since the present chapters began to take shape I have been helped in formulating my ideas by many people. Dr Ian Michael and Mr Herbert Gross read a very early draft and offered me helpful comments and criticisms. Professor Roger Wilson has given me a great deal of support and encouragement, writing extensive and detailed comments which were invaluable to me in the most difficult stages of construction, and discussing the ideas with me on many occasions. I should also like to thank Miss Edith Cope, Mrs Margaret Hinton, Mr Christopher Holtom, Mr Lewis Hull and Miss M. McNab, who read the completed MS and helped me in making final revisions.

To Professor A. V. Judges I owe a special debt of gratitude. He knows better than anybody how much this book has changed in the process of writing. It was thanks to him that I was able to make the transition from merely reporting other people's work to the much more difficult task of reflecting, in the light of other people's work, upon my own personal experiences in schools. He has given me what every writer needs—astringent but kindly criticism—and he helped me a great deal when I was reshaping the book and deciding what was relevant and what must be jettisoned. His suggestion that I should prepare it as a contribution to this educational series was in itself an important factor in these decisions.

Finally, I should like to thank the many past students of the Bristol Department who may recognize themselves in some of these pages. Their willingness to talk frankly with me about problems encountered in the classroom, and their ability to respond creatively to these problems, have contributed immeasurably to my own learning.

J.E.R.

CHAPTER ONE

Human Relations in the School

I. IMAGES AND STEREOTYPES

As teachers, we are divided between the desire to rule our pupils and the desire to be accepted as one of their society. This conflict finds expression in the precepts sometimes offered by experienced teachers to an inexperienced colleague: 'You must show them straight away who's boss'; 'You must try to get down to their level'; or, more cynically: 'If you can't beat 'em, join 'em!'

In fact most teachers avoid these extremes. But the imagery of levels and circles tends to persist in conversations about schools, as though the teacher must, in the last resort, choose between two equally unsatisfactory roles. Is he, then, to see himself as occupying a higher plane, revolving in a remoter orbit, than his pupils? Or is he to identify himself so closely with them that he almost renounces his adult status and his staff-group membership? Perhaps this overstates the problem. Yet it is not easy for any of us to accept the reality of our situation—a reality that places us neither wholly inside nor wholly outside any class that we teach. Unless a teacher accepts membership of the group as part of his role, he can do little more than offer instruction, give information, issue orders, and make assessments; at the same time, unless he accepts his special role as the leader of the group, he can do little more than watch the disintegration that will result from his abdication. And the matter is further complicated by the fact that the class, no less than the teacher, shrinks from the reality of this 'member/not-member' paradox. Yet it is as important for the pupils as for the teacher that the relationship between them should be right.

Most of us escape from the dilemma by accepting a compromise. In class we maintain the traditional role of the teacher who makes most of the decisions, hands out most of the information and gives most of the orders. Outside school hours—on picnics, perhaps, or at Christmas parties—we unbend and allow liberties which we should not dream of tolerating in the class-room. A young schoolmistress takes her class of eleven-year-old boys for a cycling expedition, submits herself to a perilous ride down a steep hill on the back of a tandem, and allows herself to be thrown to the ground by three members of the class during a rough game of 'Kick the Can' in the open field where they subsequently picnic. The following Monday morning she and the boys revert to their usual friendly, but fairly formal relation-ship as though neither of these comic incidents had ever happened. A young schoolmaster who is a keen rugby foot-baller finds himself playing nearly every Saturday at a local club, which includes among its members several sixth-formers from the school where he is temporarily teaching. He allows these boys, along with adult members of the club, to use his nickname, and on several occasions he drinks beer with them at the local pub. After some weeks one or two of the boys begin to cause him some embarrassment by carrying over this behaviour into school, greeting him by his nickname when they meet him in the corridors. He is uncertain what to do about this. Even-tually he contrives to have a few words with the whole group about it one Saturday on the club premises, and the matter is cleared up. It is recognized that his role in the football club is not the same as his role in school. The boys continue to enjoy an adult relationship with him on Saturdays; during the week they remember that he is a teacher and that they are still 'schoolboys', in a school where it is customary even for a sixth-former to call a master 'Sir'.

What does this curious splitting of the self into 'teacher' and 'not-teacher' really achieve? And why are children and young people so ready to accept the duality that it implies? Is this situation inevitable? In the small village school described by Mrs Sybil Marshall[1] such a splitting of roles could hardly have existed at all. The Sybil Marshall who read to the children, helped them to paint, studied the history of the village with them, and devised all kinds of experiments with them, was part and parcel of the whole life of the village, and the children probably treated her exactly the same in school as out of it. Indeed, as so much of the learning was conducted outside the

1. Marshall, Sybil (1963) *An Experiment in Education*, Cambridge University Press.

school building it must have been difficult to say where the boundary between school and village was or where school life ended and home life began.

These were young children, between the ages of five and eleven; the whole school was about the size of the average secondary-school class; Mrs Marshall was indeed simultaneously the head of the school and the teacher of all its pupils. Difficult as it must have been to attend, single-handed, to the needs of a group with such a wide range of age and ability, there were some problems (inevitable in large schools) from which she was wholly free. It is significant that the pronoun 'we' as used in her book always means 'the children and I': the group was self-contained and, within the school, had no rivals, although this is not to say that rivalries did not exist within the group. For the teacher herself, there was no staff–group membership to complicate her relationship with the children. Equally, there was no escape, for her or for the children, from the reality and closeness of that relationship.

In a sense the very size and obviousness of the age gap between child and adult makes it easier, in a primary school, for such close relationships to be achieved. There can be no doubt on either side that the group consists of so many children and one grown-up person. In the middle and upper forms of a secondary school the situation is very different. The age gap between a sixth-former and a young teacher may be as little as four years, and in a secondary-modern or comprehensive school it is possible for a young man or woman of barely twenty years to be teaching fifteen-year-old boys and girls in their final year at school. In such a classroom, teacher and pupil may be said to belong to the same generation; indeed, each may see in the other an older or younger brother or sister, or even perhaps a possible marriage partner, rather than a parent or child. Even as the gap widens, the irony of the situation still persists: the teacher, whether young, middle-aged or elderly, is an accepted member of the adult world; the pupils, who for the most part no longer look or feel like children, are still shut out of the adult world. In a school run on traditional lines there is little substantial acknowledgement that a fifteen-year-old is more mature than an eleven-year-old, or likely to be so. We are told that more and more young people are staying on at school beyond the statutory leaving age; but side by side with the figures which

disclose this trend, there are others, about which we ought not
to be so complacent, which show a serious wastage of ability
among those who leave at fifteen.[1] Some, it is true, go to colleges
of further education, where they can pursue their studies as
members of more adult communities. But these institutions,
which were in any case not cast for this role, have by no means
succeeded in salvaging all those school-haters who could benefit
from a higher education.

It is now a well-established fact that the boys and girls whom
we are urging to extend their period of schooling are maturing
much more rapidly than were their predecessors thirty years
ago.[2] Yet the schools have hardly begun to meet this change in
the situation. School furniture, school uniforms, school rules
and patterns of classroom relationships have changed remarkably little in the past thirty years, although, admittedly,
methods of handling subject matter have probably changed a
good deal. Grammar-school teachers of today are, generally
speaking, treating their pupils of fifteen, sixteen and seventeen
in much the same way as they themselves were treated by their
teachers ten, twenty or thirty years ago. There are exceptions.
From time to time we hear of schools where the senior pupils,
with staff support, are undertaking adult responsibilities, by
offering social services in the community, and are given a
significant amount of responsibility in the running of their own
internal society inside the school. But, for the most part, young
people who are still at school are living under a benevolent
autocracy.

The occupants of our fifth and sixth forms thus find themselves subjected to two kinds of pressure. On the one hand there
is the pressure to join the struggle for higher learning at the top;
on the other hand there is the urge to escape from a school
system that seems bent on pushing them back into childhood.
The academic learning that is demanded too often seems to have
lost touch with the emotional learning that is such a central
concern for the adolescent, whatever kind of adult work he

1. See, for example, Douglas, J. W. B. (1964) *The Home and the School*,
London: MacGibbon & Kee; *Higher Education* (Robbins Report), (1963)
London: H.M.S.O., Appendix One, 'The Demand for Places in Higher
Education'; Elvin, H. L. (1965) *Education and Contemporary Society*, London:
Watts, pp. 39–44.
2. Tanner, J. M. (1961) *Education and Physical Growth*, University of London
Press: Chapters 7 and 8, pp. 113–26.

will be taking up as an adult. Small wonder that teachers are constantly lamenting that their fourth forms are at best politely unresponsive and at worst openly rebellious, while their sixth forms, particularly if they are on the arts side and more particularly if they are girls, are apathetic, inarticulate and apparently without opinions or convictions. How can we get behind the barrier to the feelings that are undoubtedly there to be released? What can we do to ensure that growth and learning enrich each other?

The task is not easy, for in both teacher and pupil there are forces working against the very change that both so earnestly desire. Every good teacher wants to help his pupils to grow up and become independent of him; but because so much of his joy and satisfaction come from his consciousness of their need of him, he is painfully inhibited from standing back. It is hard for him to withdraw support and withhold information. He must lose his pupils in the end; but he need not start losing them yet—or so he thinks. The pupils, too, have conflicting feelings. At the conscious level they want to be given more adult roles. They would like to be rid of their school uniform, their school desks and their school note-books. They would like to engage in sophisticated discussions with their teacher. But let him make any move in this direction, and they will probably recoil in alarm, fearful of putting themselves and him to the test of a genuinely adult relationship.

What happens, for example, when a teacher tries to reduce the distance between himself and his class by proposing a change in the seating arrangements, substituting a circle of chairs for rows of desks? In one term three attempts to do this were reported to me: the first teacher was working with an upper-sixth-form group in a girls' grammar school; the second with a lower-sixth-form group in a mixed comprehensive school; the third with a day-release group of seventeen-year-olds in a technical college. In the three schools the process of adjustment to the new idea was remarkably similar. The first reaction to the teacher's suggestion was, in each case, open-mouthed surprise, followed by a rather sullen compliance; all three teachers reported that the pupils, having recovered from their indignation, seemed slightly better able to exchange ideas and respond to one another than when they had sat at desks. But in each case the sequel was the same. The following lesson found the pupils defiantly back in their normal places. Two of the three teachers were too intimidated by this retreat to press for a repetition of the furniture-moving; the third calmly requested the group to sit as they had done the week before, and they moved into the new positions after considerable delay and much grumbling. With the other two teachers, who returned to the attack in the third lesson, much the same thing happened. Yet, in the end, all these classes admitted that they preferred the new arrangement, and all three teachers noted a steady improvement in the quality of the discussion.

It seems, then, that along with the wish to be treated as an adult by the teacher, and indeed in vigorous conflict with this wish, there is a subconscious need to keep him in a visibly recognizable position of authority. It could almost be said that, unless the teacher resists the temptation to accept this authoritarian role, his pupils' fear of growing up will overpower their desire to grow up. It is, on the face of it, remarkable that pupils of this age should put up such a powerful resistance to a simple change of this kind in the seating arrangements. The truth is that the apparently simple shift of furniture symbolizes a radical and evidently frightening change in the pupil–teacher relationship. Once they have moved out of the classroom structure (symbolized by the rows of desks *facing* the teacher) into a seminar structure (symbolized by the circle of chairs *including* the teacher) the pupils have to enter into a totally new kind of situation. They are now face to face with each other, as well as with the teacher. As persons, they feel more exposed and vulnerable, for it is far less easy, in a circle, to remain anonymous. Furthermore, it is far less easy to go on preserving a fantasy image either of the teacher or of the other members of the class. It is this first step towards a situation in which reality must be tested that is so feared and resisted, both by the teacher and by his class.

If this is so at the top of the school, where the pupils are studying their chosen subjects and already, at best, share with their teachers certain intellectual interests, what is likely to be the outcome of similar attempts to push down the barriers in the lower forms? What will happen, say, at third or fourth form levels? Here numbers are greater, seminar learning (though not group work) is out of reach, and no class will contain more than a handful of future specialists in the particular subject under consideration. This is the age group that comes in for the heaviest fire in the public press. Doomed to carry the guilt for the rising (if still small) proportion of delinquents, even those who are not delinquents turn against a disapproving adult world by setting up their own culture, and almost defy any adult to share their tastes. The teacher who enters this world of pop music, beatnik clothes and curious hair styles with any suggestion of going slumming or pretending to be one of the younger generation, does so at his peril. His only right of entry is as an adult who is genuinely interested in them as people— interested enough to want to know how they really think and feel, and sincere enough not to pretend to share tastes and enthusiasms that he does not really share. Children will ruthlessly test the integrity of a teacher who tries to penetrate their ranks in this way. And sometimes they will contrive to push out an adult whose motives have been entirely genuine.

Mr A., a young teacher, who had a taste for Flamenco music and was a competent guitar player, used this talent in a boys' grammar school as a bridge towards a closer relationship with his pupils. He spent some of his lunch hours playing to groups of third and fourth year boys in the school hall, and found that, down there, they talked to him naturally and appeared to be enjoying his music. But one day he came into the classroom to find a sentence scribbled across the blackboard: 'Guitar man— go, go, go!' Immediately, he was on the defensive, sensing that the boys were challenging his role as a teacher. Fearing what might happen if he treated it as a joke, he retreated into the conventional schoolmaster's behaviour, and rather irritably told a boy to clean the board. How consciously contrived, one wonders, was the ambiguity of the message behind those scribbled words? Did the class intend Mr A. to take it as a jocular invitation to 'get going' on his guitar—to bring the informal situation into the lesson and give up the pretence of being a teacher? Or was he to take it as an overtly hostile injunction to clear out and stop trying to push his way into their society? Almost certainly the latter. For the teacher's part, was his quick spurt of alarm prompted by a fear that one of his colleagues might have seen the message and that the class had deliberately set out to damage his relations with the staff group?

I heard of a class of girls in another school who tested out a young music teacher (Miss B.) in a rather more sophisticated way. This teacher was convinced that there must be some mutual interchange of opinions on the subject of music, and that she could not hope to broaden the musical interests of her pupils if she made no attempt to listen to the music they enjoyed. Whereas the Flamenco player, not being a music specialist, had to go outside the classroom to make his personal contacts with the children, Miss B. was able to build her relationships into the fabric of her lessons. Just before the end of the term, knowing that she would not be returning to the school, the members of one class, with whom she had exchanged lively arguments, presented her with a record token, which carried two conditions: she was to choose one of three records they recommended, and she was to bring it to their last lesson, listen to it with them and tell them honestly why she had chosen it. Both these conditions she accepted: and it would seem that for this class she passed the test.

It is interesting to speculate what might have come to light if the guitar player had dared to explore with his class the motives that had prompted them (or one of them) to write the ambiguous and disturbing message on the board. As it was, they succeeded—whether they had consciously wished to or not—in maintaining the split between the 'teacher' who took over their geography lessons in the classroom and the 'human being' who played the guitar to them in the hall after lunch. And so they were able to preserve on the one hand the fantasy of the authoritarian figure whose word was law in the classroom and, on the other, a quite different fantasy of the 'guitar man' who was not really a teacher at all.

This splitting up of relationships enables the child (and indeed the adult) to come to terms with conflicting feelings about the same person by establishing two distinct situations; but in doing this he undermines the totality of personality. Sometimes it is not the individual person that we split, but the group we have to relate to. When we look back to our earliest school-days we seem to see our teachers as falling into two distinct categories: there were the good-looking, well-dressed, kindly, efficient teachers whom we loved; and there were the sour-faced, drab, malicious or merely incompetent teachers whom we hated or despised. Yet could they really have fallen into such strongly contrasted groups? Is it not more likely that the majority of those who taught us in our earliest years were neither wholly good nor wholly bad—neither the angels nor the monsters into which our fantasies have turned them—but fallible human beings with fluctuating moods and variable talents? Indeed, we must all remember occasions in our childhood when our rough and ready divisions of the staff into the 'kind and unkind' or into the 'strong and weak' proved suddenly inadequate, or when our previous estimate of a teacher as 'lovable' or 'unlovable' was suddenly revealed as an over-simplification.

Take, for instance, Mr C., who taught me history when I was about nine years old. He was a big fat man whom we feared and hated. Our history lessons (or so it seems in retrospect) consisted of oral tests on the pages of the history book that we had read for homework; he would rap out questions, and we would stand up in turn to answer, moving up or down the class according to the correctness or incorrectness of our answers. One day, at the end of the morning, I found myself seated at a lunch table surrounded by girls from the senior school. It was about five minutes before it dawned on me that I had come to the early lunch by mistake and should at that moment be in Mr C.'s history class. Terrified, I rushed to the room, knocked on the door and stood shivering in front of him trying to explain why I was late. I will never forget the astonishment I felt when, instead of roaring angrily at me, he smiled gently and said: 'Well, well! I made that very same mistake one day last week! Come in and sit down.' I think that was the only time I ever saw him smile; but I never forgot that there was, under the mask of the ferocious history master, a gentle, friendly, understanding human being.

We had another master, Mr D., who taught me science some years later. He was not in the least intimidating. In fact we exploited mercilessly his inability to stand the sight of a girl crying. He was renowned for the speed with which he would give us 'order marks' (which had to be reported to our form mistress) and for the ease with which he could be persuaded to let us off. One day, however, he found me reading a novel under the desk and took the unusual and quite irreversible step of sending me to the headmistress. The next morning I was punished by being publicly reprimanded by her in front of the whole class and was ordered to apologize formally to Mr D., who was standing at the side of the room looking the picture of misery. At that moment, lacerated as I was by the denunciations of the headmistress, who had exposed me as deceitful, lazy and utterly contemptible, I was astonished to find myself pitying the poor master even more than myself. For the first time I saw that what I had dismissed as mere weakness of character was also something lovable. And yet, recalling the incident with my classmates afterwards, I scoffed at his tender-heartedness just as they did, as though I had never felt that momentary liking and sympathy for him.

It was easier for us as children to see Mr C. as hateful and Mr D. as despicable than to entertain the notion that our feelings towards them (and theirs towards us) might be more complex. In a way, I suppose, we made Mr D. pay for our sufferings with Mr C. by playing on his weakness and fear as his more masterful colleague had played on ours. Any suspicion that the history master might have been more afraid of us than we were of him, any pang of guilt towards the science master for the misery to which we constantly subjected him, were firmly suppressed, since to acknowledge such uncertainty about the quality of our relationships with these two masters (and about the quality of the work we did with them) would have been to face uncomfortable conflict. And so we hugged to ourselves the conviction that the one was so cruel that history was torture, and that the other was so laughable that science was unimportant. Meanwhile, of course, other subjects in the curriculum were being identified with the 'goodness' and 'badness' of other teachers. And so it continued over the years, with some modification of the crude divisions of childhood, but with little understanding of the central ambivalence of the teaching–learning situation.

What effects do these highly coloured memories of our own early experiences as pupils have when we ourselves become teachers? Clearly, we do not wish to emulate either the tyrants or the fools. And so we try to steer a safe middle course between the way of dictatorship, which would make healthy argument impossible, and the way of anarchy, which would destroy the very foundations of co-operative work.

In reality there is no such thing as a safe, standard, middle course. Teaching is compounded of successes and failures, of eloquence and verbal clumsiness, of benevolence and malice, of altruism and self-seeking. Most of us care about our pupils in the present and are prepared to devote time and energy to them; yet most of us have ambitions for ourselves in a future that has

no place for the pupils we are concerned about today. As for
these pupils, they are neither angels nor devils; sometimes we
love them and sometimes we hate them, and when we hate them
the fault may not lie in them only. There is something of Mr C.,
probably, in most of us, and something of Mr D. too. And Mr
C., after all, had his tender side, as Mr D. had his stern side.

In the last resort what children respond to is a total personality, with all its imperfections, its weakness as well as its
strength, its bad temper and irritability as well as its tenderness
and good humour. A description of a teacher who won this kind
of response was written for me some years ago by an American
student who intended himself to become a teacher. He described
a woman who had taught him English in his high school when
he was about sixteen. He offered no idealized portrait but
presented her as she really was—strong, courageous, imaginative, often fallible, often guilty of poor judgement, frequently
ruthless and seldom tender, fiercely determined to make her
students self-reliant and self-respecting, slow to forgive any sort
of humbug but quick to encourage initiative and industry. He
presented her, in fact, as she probably would have wished to be
presented by one of her pupils. In doing so, he conveyed, un-
forgettably, the quality of the relationship that must have
existed between this teacher and her classes. And this was what
impressed me. The following extract is worth quoting because
it illustrates both her integrity and the ability of her students to
recognize and value that integrity.

Interaction among the students was particularly good in this
teacher's classes. She encouraged us to criticize each other. We
formed groups, reformed them, evaluated each other, and tried
again. Miss E. was always authoritarian in her discussion groups,
but she made the question live for each student. Frequently she
would draw shy ones into the talk by a direct question. Often her
questions were embarrassing, even humiliating, and I have no doubt
that she did some students some harm by pointing class attention to
them. But she did inestimable good for some of us, by forcing us to
think when we were 'on the spot,' by making us defend and support
our statements. . . .
She had courage. She was never afraid to try a new teaching
technique, one she had read about, one she had seen demonstrated
at conventions, or one suggested by a student. She was not afraid to
fail. She failed miserably in front of us several times, but she went
right on trying. I can recall one lesson she gave on the importance
of the impression a person gives simply by his manner of walking.

She had several students demonstrate how to walk and how not to walk; they didn't do it to please, and she made them do it again. Over and over again, the students tried the same walk over a twelve-foot space. The class began to laugh at her. She regained control, and tried again by having the entire class, walk together. For eleventh graders, this was truly ridiculous. Miss E. tried fervently to save the situation, but failed, and we never heard anything more about how to walk. This must have been a devastating blow to her own ego, but she was able to overcome this.

She never took revenge on us for the way we had acted. Fully as important, she never apologized for the lesson. It was simply chalked off as a failure. . . .

Mary E. never made me feel that she liked me personally. But she did demonstrate a real and vital interest in all her students. She went straight to the heart of any matter, forced the students to clarify and organize and qualify what they thought and said. She developed in us a real ability to discriminate in our thought and reading between the logical and the emotional.

Teachers often speak as though they cannot be other than what schools allow them to be. In a sense, of course, this is true. Every teacher has to accept a framework, and the framework is more rigid in some schools than in others. Yet, at the same time, every teacher has a certain amount of freedom; and for the most part, within his classroom, he can, indeed must, teach in the way that seems best to him. Within any school, teachers will claim large or small areas of freedom in proportion to their own courage and initiative. Miss E. would probably have gone her own way in any school, on either side of the Atlantic. Schools are quick to seize on such people and set them apart as cranks, to be tolerated, laughed at a bit, and admired in a guarded sort of way.

In the same way, society labels certain schools as 'experimental'—a label that carries a particularly dangerous mixture of adulation and contempt. These schools, which are more often than not privately run establishments with relatively small numbers of pupils, have influenced fundamentally our concept of the ideal pupil–teacher relationship. But because they can be put aside as exceptional, they have had little effect on general practice within the state system of education. By mildly approving such ventures, we can convince ourselves that we have ideals, while continuing to conform to more conventional patterns of activity in our own institutions.

We need to know a great deal more about these powerful

unconscious motivations that enable us to resist even the changes that we consciously wish to bring about. Too much of our thinking is ineffective because it is divorced from feeling. Conversely, too much of our feeling works destructively because, being unacknowledged, it lies beyond the control of our thinking. Behind that fourth-form rebelliousness and rudeness there may also lie positive feelings; behind that sixth-form apathy there may be a passionate belief in causes. How can we, as teachers, reach through the negatives to the positives, and meet the personal needs of our pupils?

2. PERSONALITY AND GROUP BEHAVIOUR

Much of the negative behaviour that we find so baffling in the middle years of the secondary school arises from what Professor Erikson calls the 'adolescent crisis of identity'.[1] Other writers have referred to this as the 'search for the self'.[2] One describes it as the struggle to escape from being a mere satellite—revolving first round one's parents and then, in early adolescence, round one's contemporaries—so as to become a person in one's own right.[3]

Erikson's account of the phases of human development, from infancy to old age, helps us to understand how this 'identity crisis' reaches its height during the teens and how its successful mastery prepares us to meet the successive crises of later life. To understand how the adolescent meets his problems, we have to consider how he has coped with the earlier crises of growth. For behind the identity crisis, or below it, there is a whole series of other conflicts that have led up to this one—conflicts about trust in others, about belief in one's own autonomy, about one's courage to use initiative, and about joy in industry. All these are gathered up into this central conflict of adolescence—the search for one's own identity.

Basically, the earlier conflicts are resolved in infancy and in early and middle childhood. If early mothering has been good, the child will have emerged from the struggles of infancy with

1. Erikson, Erik H. (1959) 'Growth and Crises of the Healthy Personality', in *Identity and the Life Cycle*: International Universities Press.
2. Jersild, A. T. (1957) *The Psychology of Adolescence*, London: Macmillan, and (1952) *In Search of Self*: Columbia University Press.
3. Ausubel, D. P. (1954) *Theory and Problems of Adolescent Development*, New York: Grune & Stratton.

a basic trust in other people. If, in the stormy days when he began to walk and had to learn to be clean, he was handled with tact and patience, he will have emerged with a basic belief in himself as an autonomous being, capable of learning to control his own body and regulate his own life. If, as a talking. questioning five-year-old, he was able to deal with his conflicting feelings towards his parents and learned to accept the reality of their relationship to each other as well as their relationship to himself, he will have emerged from the pre-school years with confidence to use his own initiative. If, during the primary-school years, he had plenty of experience of being successful, he will have emerged with a basic enjoyment of work, and a belief that he will one day be a productive and useful adult.

Between the ages of about seven and twelve, then, the child has been relating himself to society by learning to do the things his parents and other adults do. But in adolescence his greatest need is to discover and come to terms with himself. It is during the secondary-school years, particularly the middle and later years, that he is striving to discover his own separateness and uniqueness as a person. And so, imperceptibly, his attitude towards school is bound to undergo some modifications. The search for a personal identity involves some degree of withdrawal from parental domination; and because, inevitably, this changing relationship with parents is projected into the school situation, the teacher may no longer seem so acceptable for the child to model himself on, particularly if the teacher represents for the child that very competence that, in the eyes of society, the child does not appear to have.

What is the significance for English children of Erikson's diagnosis of the central conflict of the pre-adolescent years—the crisis of 'industry versus inferiority'? Are the majority of our pupils able to emerge from the primary-school years with a basic belief in their own competence? Unfortunately, we have to acknowledge that our educational system presupposes a qualitative difference between those who are considered to be 'grammar-school material' and those who are not. And the stark fact is that those in the second category far outnumber those in the first.

The boy who comes up from the primary school labelled as an academic success may accept his secondary-school work, on one level at least, as something that he needs to get him to a university. He will be prepared to work for his 'O' and 'A' levels. But in the process, this side of his development—the intellectual side—is in danger of becoming split off from the personal side. His teachers may come, more and more, as time goes on, to appear in his eyes as people who are, in a sense, unrounded. They are, he may think, 'not quite human': they are different, somehow, from other adults he knows; they have to be addressed differently; there may even be some suspicion that they do not live normal adult lives. Needless to say, unmarried women teachers are in even greater danger of being so labelled by the girls they teach, since marriage and motherhood are, rightly, seen by girls as the natural culmination of the growing-up process.

If the splitting apart of the emotional and intellectual aspects of growth and learning happens even in the grammar school, where work can, at least by the ablest pupils, be seen as relevant to future professional pursuits, how much more is this likely to happen in the secondary modern schools and even in the lower-ability groups in the comprehensive schools? The young people who inhabit these forms are carrying into their adolescent years a conviction, not that they have proved themselves competent, but that society has labelled them as failures. For the members of IIIG in the comprehensive school or even for IIIC in the grammar school, industriousness may be felt not as something that brings satisfaction and joy but as something that brings only boredom and frustration.

The whole problem of the split between emotional and intellectual learning is exacerbated for secondary-school teachers by the compartmentalization of learning into subjects, by the piecemeal pattern of the time-table and by the visual symbolism of most classrooms. At the age of five, emotional learning is part and parcel of all the learning a child does; and if he is in a good infant school, a concern for human relationships is at the heart of what goes on in his classroom. In many junior schools this continues, so that personal initiative and the willingness and ability to co-operate in joint enterprises develop side by side with the mastery of skills, materials and ideas. But as a child moves into adolescence it seems that his teachers expect less rather than more initiative from him. And so he himself begins to make compartments for his learning: intellectual learning belongs to the classroom and the laboratory; he learns the virtues of team-work on the games field; he picks up his social life around the lunch table; and emotional learning looks after itself as best it may.

It is not that teachers wish to evade the task of educating the emotions as well as the intellect. Many contrive to find ways of doing both; and most teachers are aware of a conflict between the two kinds of obligation they feel towards their pupils—to provide discipline for the mind and freedom for the growth of personality. But the school as an institution almost forces the separation of these. Professor Gardner Murphy finds the same problem in American schools. His thinking leads him to believe that 'the nurture of rationality may perhaps lie in other efforts than the sheer encouragement of rational thought; indeed, that the rational may best continue to grow in the instinctive soil in which it was engendered, and that too clear and sterile a surgical separation of thought from its ancestral and parental roots in love and impulse may threaten its viability'.[1]

What is the solution to our dilemma? We need to think a great deal more about the relation between what our pupils are learning consciously in the classroom and what is going on at the feeling level—often unconsciously—in the group situations in which the learning is done. At the heart of every teaching–learning situation there is a problem of relationships with authority—one that will be found to have roots going right back to infancy. The teacher brings his own personal assumptions to his solution of it, assumptions that may change as his experience helps him to redefine the problem. If he is a good teacher he will be able to recognize in the group or classroom situation both the cohesive effects of his own influence as an adult with whom the children feel they can identify (as with a good parent), and the disintegrative effects of the rivalries that will be going on within the group itself (as between brothers and sisters). It follows that he must be able to accept and contain strains within himself that are comparable to those felt by a parent. In other words, echoes from the family situation will be at work, if only at the subconscious level, in every teacher–pupil relationship and, by implication, in the relations between the pupils themselves.

1. Murphy, Gardner (1961) *Freeing Intelligence through Teaching*, New York: Harper & Row, p. 22.

This is not to say that the role of the teacher is to be a parent substitute. Indeed, if he is to help his pupils to grow up and learn independently of him he must resist the temptations that may be held out to him by his pupils when they want to set him up as a parent figure. What it does mean is that the importance of the inter-personal relationship in the learning situation is central—a point made strongly by Professor Ben Morris in his paper, 'How does a group learn to work together?'[1] He draws attention to the transference of feelings and attitudes from the child–parent relationship into other situations (a phenomenon first discovered by Freud[2] in the doctor–patient relationship) in order to make further assertions about the nature of leadership. He distinguishes between the authoritarian leader who, like the over-dominant parent, expects the members of the group to identify strongly with him to the point of sinking their own opinions and not daring to criticize him, and the weak leader with whom no identification, and therefore no sense of security or common purpose, is possible. He sees 'optimum leadership' as 'something qualitatively different from either authoritarian or weak leadership', depending not on whether 'more or less authority' is exerted, but rather on 'the qualities of relationship existing within the group'.[3]

Many teachers resist the implications of Freud's discoveries about the transference phenomenon; others accept the idea without working out the essential differences between the roles of parents and teachers, talking vaguely about 'father and mother figures' as though it were a question of simple substitution. The effects of an over-eager acceptance of the psycho-analytic view of the teacher's role on the part of some teachers may be that others become unduly suspicious of it and hostile towards it. This in its turn may lead to an over-valuation of the intellectual aspects of learning at the expense of the education of the emotions. Professor Peters, for example, in his inaugural lecture, said: 'There has been too much loose talk about the dimension of the personal in teaching. Indeed, one often hears that "the enjoyment of good personal relationships" with pupils is in

1. Morris, Ben 'How does a group learn to work together?', in Niblett, W. R., (ed.) (1965) *How and Why do we Learn?* London: Faber & Faber.
2. Freud, S. (1921) *Group Psychology and the Analysis of the Ego*, London: Hogarth Press, Vol. 18 of the Complete Works.
3. Morris, p. 112.

danger of becoming a substitute for teaching them something'.[1]
The warning is salutary. But the implications of his general
argument seem to be that the teacher's task of 'initiation' must
be seen, not in the framework of multi-dimensional relationships between persons engaged in various learning experiences,
but in the framework of a known world of knowledge and ways
of thinking.

For Professor Morris, personal relationships are fundamental
to all learning. The whole teaching–learning enterprise, he
believes, depends on the ability of the teacher to be sensitive to
these relationships with pupils and to their emotional implications. If the group's identification with him is 'positive but
relatively mild', and if he accepts the ambiguity of being 'both
separate from it and a member of it', he will be able to 'guide
without domination, because the group is not afraid of him
and he is not afraid of the group'. All this implies that we cannot
fully understand what it means to be a teacher without understanding, at the feeling level, what it means to be a member of
a group engaged in a common task with a leader. The examination of this kind of experience, through membership of a group
that accepts as its task the study of its own relationships, has
been made possible for teachers and other people in leadership
roles by the pioneer work of Dr W. R. Bion[2] and by his associates
at the Tavistock Clinic and the Tavistock Institute of Human
Relations, much of it through the residential conferences
organized by the Tavistock Institute in collaboration with the
University of Leicester.[3]

My own experiences with small groups, since attending one
of these conferences seven years ago, has inevitably affected the
way I think and feel about education. It is in the light of that
comparatively recent experience that I find myself looking back
on my own teaching in secondary schools before 1950 and trying
to understand the situations that I now see students handling
during their school practice. The illustrative material used in

1. Peters, R. S. (1964) 'Education as Initiation', *Studies in Education*, Evans
for the University of London Institute of Education. See also, review-article
by Professor Reid, L. Arnaud (1965) in *British Journal of Educational Studies*,
XIII, ii, pp. 192–205.
2. Bion, W. R. (1961) *Experiences in Groups*, London: Tavistock Publications.
3. Trist, E. L. and Sofer, C. (1959) *Explorations in Group Relations*, Leicester
University Press, and Rice, A. K. (1965) *Learning for Leadership*, London:
Tavistock Publications.

this book has been drawn from both these sources. Some of my examples are taken from small groups and others from classes of between thirty and forty. We should note that the occurrence of the small classroom group, even below the level of the sixth form, is not so rare as it is conventional to assume. And it may, in fact, increase; for if schools develop team teaching, the class of thirty will no longer be the norm. Already many schools are experimenting with sixth-form general courses in which lectures given to a large group of up to sixty are combined with discussion periods with groups of about a dozen; and many teachers are responding to the opportunity offered by the presence of students in the schools to divide classes into smaller groups that can be taught concurrently, the student taking over one sub-group while the regular teacher takes the other. Moreover, the emotional processes we can learn to recognize in the small group are also going on in the large group, where they are, undeniably, a great deal more difficult to work with. The two kinds of situation are not so totally different that understanding gained in the one is irrelevant to the other, as some work going on in Leicestershire is beginning to show.[1]

Those of us who have withdrawn from schools to take part in the education and training of teachers are sometimes asked whether we 'miss teaching'. To be sure, our students in the colleges and departments of education are a good deal more mature than those we used to teach in schools. And yet, basically, we are still engaged in a teaching–learning situation—a partnership in which we learn as much from our students now as we used to learn from our pupils in schools. Much of what happens in the day-to-day relationship and interchange of experiences in an education course illumines, if we care to examine it, the problems being faced by teachers in schools every day. Privileged as we are in teaching our students in small groups at least part of the time, we have the chance to observe and reflect upon items of behaviour which, in more crowded classrooms, we could easily either fail to observe at all or find completely overwhelming.

In a student discussion group much may come to the surface that, in a more tightly structured situation, would remain hidden. If such a group accepts, as part of the task of people who intend to be teachers, some responsibility to look at the way

1. Grainger, A. J. (1965) 'The Bullring', *New Era*, vol. 46, No. 9, pp. 209–17.

work is being done as well as at the work itself, strange and sometimes disquieting things can happen. We begin to discover that intellectual learning and emotional learning are more interdependent than we have supposed. And if we dare pause from time to time deliberately to look at what is happening in the group, we learn that emotional conflict is better handled if it is exposed and examined than if it is suppressed and denied. It is startling to discover how the furniture and equipment in a tutor's room can come to symbolize strong feelings of anger or affection, how the lateness or absence of a member may be interpreted and used by the group, how relationships can suddenly be disturbed by matters relating to assessment of work in the course as a whole, how much people resent returning to the department as students after spending a whole term taking the roles of teachers in the schools, how much a group may be affected emotionally by the prospect of ending the joint enterprise begun some weeks before.[1]

Now all these are school problems too, though often not recognized as such. Are sudden changes in the time-table just administrative matters, or do they have emotional repercussions which, when observed critically, can be seen to be affecting learning? What does a class really feel about a child who is habitually late for lessons or plays truant, and what are the effects of his attitudes on their commitment to the work in hand? What about the competitive struggle for marks and good examination results all the way up the school: can we disregard the effect of this struggle on the group's emotional life and on the capacity of its members to learn? Are we right to ignore the conflict our sixth-formers must be facing when they return to school after the summer holidays, knowing that many of their contemporaries have seen the last of school? What hidden forces and reactions should we have in mind when we handle the ending of the school year, or the loss or disintegration of a particular classroom group?

This book is really about personal relationships in the secondary school and about the way emotional undercurrents affect the work that any teacher is doing with his classes. Underlying

1. See, for example, Richardson, Elizabeth (1963) 'Teacher–Pupil Relationships as Explored and Rehearsed in an Experimental Tutorial Group', *New Era*, vol. 44, Nos. 6 and 7; (1965) 'Lateness, Absence and Withdrawal', *New Era*, vol. 46, Nos. 9 and 10; (1965) 'Personal Relations and Formal Assessment in a Graduate Course in Education', *Education for Teaching*, No. 67.

all the arguments and every use of an actual occurrence is my belief that we have to learn to recognize and use these undercurrents instead of trying to go on teaching as if they did not exist. Sometimes an unexpected and apparently irrelevant incident may be a more fruitful learning experience, for both teacher and class, than some of those for which the teacher has consciously and carefully planned. It is not without significance, I think, that the incidents I remember most vividly from my own teaching in schools are those that highlighted something in the personal relationship between myself and my pupils, whether they were directly concerned with work or not. Indeed, the point I am trying to make, throughout this book, is that the building of relationships is part of the work of every teacher, essential if he himself is to develop as a teacher, and if his pupils are to grow up into sensitive and intellectually competent adults.

CHAPTER TWO

The Teacher and the Form or Tutorial Group

1. THE CHILD'S PLACE IN THE SCHOOL

In the great majority of English day schools, the 'form' unit is still regarded as the natural centre of a child's school life; and the most important pupil–teacher relationship is still that between a child and his form master or form mistress.

For the pupil, this convention has its roots far back in childhood. At the age of five he had to take the enormous step from the private and protected living space of his home to the public and exposed living space of the classroom. Here the 'form mistress' or 'class teacher' quickly became for him one of the most important adults in his life. For a considerable number of hours a day she was, indeed, a substitute for his mother. Moreover, through her, he found his range of experiences suddenly widening, suddenly opening up all kinds of new possibilities for exploration and growth; while in her charge he learned to cope with new kinds of conflict and frustration and found himself experiencing new satisfactions. And then, probably after only one year, he had to lose her and adapt himself to a new teacher.

For some children this first transition from one teacher to another is fraught with difficulty. And something of this pain in ending one relationship and embarking on a new one must be present all the way through school life. For a long time to come this first teacher—if she has been loved—will be the model against which the child will measure all subsequent teachers. The remark of a six-year-old girl, who had recently moved up into her new form and had not yet quite adjusted herself to her new teacher, was a touching reminder of the kind of fantasies a child may have in facing a new and unpredictable situation. She explained to us solemnly that she and her class-mates had been told that they must say 'good afternoon' to the teacher whom they found in the cloakroom at the end of the day and shake hands with her as they went out, whichever teacher it was. She went on: 'I had hoped it would be Miss F. [her previous form mistress], but it turned out to be Miss G. [the headmistress], so I had to shake hands with her.' She paused, then added, with a faint note of pleased, yet grudging surprise: 'But it was quite pleasant really.'

It is easy for any adult to be sympathetic about the foolish dreads of a child as small as this one, and to accept the fact that a loved first teacher will be mourned for some time to come. But how much credence are we prepared to give to the notion that much older children may view with some trepidation the onset of a relationship with an unknown teacher, one who may prove to be a poor support in times of difficulty, or, worse, a threatening authority figure? As the child goes up through the school, and certainly by the time he reaches his secondary school, he is learning to take such changes as they come, to some extent. But the process of embarking on a new relationship with a new form teacher will not in itself become progressively simpler. As the years go on he will be forming attitudes towards all his teachers, and he will be indulging in a good many fantasies (and also learning some facts) about what it is like to have this one for a form master and what it might be like to have that one. Whichever member of staff he faces over the classroom desk when he returns to school at the beginning of a new school year, there will be certain feelings with which he will have to come to terms: feelings of disappointment, maybe, that he is not to be in Mr X's form this year, feelings of relief that he is not in Mr Y's, feelings of delight at finding himself in Mr Z's, feelings of uncertainty if the form master turns out to be a new member of staff whom he has never before seen. If he is elated, it will be difficult for him not to idealize the situation to such an extent that he is bound to experience a let-down sooner or later, since all gods turn out in the end to have feet of clay; if he is disappointed it will be difficult for him to see anything good in the situation at all.

And what of the form master's feelings? With the memories of last year's form still fresh and insistent, he will have scrutinized the new list of names. And now he faces a group of thirty or so pupils, each of whom will be entering the situation with some kind of expectation and with a set of prepared emotional attitudes. Moreover, unless he has been given a first form, he is entering a group that already has a history and an established pattern of relationships and rituals, some of them observable, some of them hidden. If the form is orderly, docile, apparently a mere aggregate of quiet, biddable schoolboys, waiting for the usual rituals of the opening day of term to get under way, the master may safely assume that more trouble lies below the surface than can yet be seen. Conversely, if the form is rowdy, hostile and openly destructive of order, he may be helped in gaining their co-operation if he can persuade himself that there is a reverse side to their present aggressiveness, and that they need the very relationship that they are now so vigorously resisting.

Even for an experienced teacher there is something curiously embarrassing in this opening form meeting of a new school year. It is possible that he will feel almost shy as he enters his form room, even if the form is one he has already taught. There is a sense, on both sides, that this relationship that is just beginning holds something unknown, unpredictable. No matter how many times he has 'had a form' before, this first form period of the year seems an entirely new and unrehearsed occasion. And so indeed it is. He may be prepared for the role that he is to take as form master, but he cannot predict on the basis of his experience with last year's form how this group of children will behave with him. For every group, like every individual, is inescapably unique. When, in years to come, he looks back at his experiences as a form master, he will be unlikely to find himself confusing this form with any other. Certain faces and voices and personalities will cohere in his memory; they will persist as persons who were members of a particular group, and were associated together in certain unforgettable incidents—some funny, some sad, some pleasurable, some exasperating, some elevating, some humiliating.

The initial attitude of the form to the new teacher will contain elements of dependence on the one hand and of rebellion on the other. Which of these emotions holds sway at the time of the first meeting will depend partly on whether the group has already had a life of its own or is meeting for the first time, and partly on the kind of experience its members (separately or together) have had with other teachers before meeting this one. Thus in a school or neighbourhood where relations between pupils and teachers are generally hostile, a class may greet a new teacher with naked and frightening aggression, as though fully expecting to drive him out of the school or into a nervous breakdown within a few weeks. Much more commonly, a new teacher—even a timid one—will be surprised to find the class behaving very meekly for the first day, perhaps for the first week, and only later trying to arouse his temper or fray his nerves.

In both kinds of situation the teacher's natural reaction is to fall back on his authority, to talk a great deal and to take advantage of the fact that he has in his classroom, provided he can exploit it, a captive audience. And so, out come his administrative announcements, his brisk arrangements for the group's future work, perhaps his first attack on the subject the form will be studying with him. The new time-tables are stuck on the insides of desk lids; form officers are elected; name tabs on clothing may be inspected. By the end of the period the form members know little more about the teacher as a person and he knows little more about them as persons. Anonymity—that most popular of protective devices—has been successfully preserved.

There is a common assumption about the reassuring effects of a display of administrative efficiency at the beginning of any relationship that has a tutorial function. But it is very much open to question whether the reassurance is for the benefit of the group or for the benefit of the teacher. In fact we all, as teachers, repeatedly discover that instructions and explanations, however carefully communicated, are frequently misunderstood or incompletely assimilated on first hearing. 'They just don't listen', we complain, when we should perhaps be asking ourselves why our students, whether they are twelve or twenty-two years old, do not appear to hear what they are being told however intently they may appear to be listening. It seems that what people are attending to on the first day of a school or university year is something quite apart from factual information about courses of work, though at one level of consciousness such information may seem to be the important thing to take away at the end of the day. It is impressions about people that are the felt experiences of such a day—impressions about teachers and impressions about fellow students. The verbal messages about time-tables and courses and requirements may carry very little weight; but the non-verbal messages that people convey to each other by their ways of behaving carry a great deal of weight.

Perhaps IIIB's new form master should resist the temptation to do most of the talking in that first form meeting and should take the enormous risk of adopting the role of a listener. But he must offer a framework, or he may find that he has merely replaced his benevolent autocracy by a destructive anarchy. Adult groups of a dozen or so, meeting in a tutorial or seminar situation, sometimes solve the problem of the opening session by exchanging mutual introductions. Clearly this procedure is hardly appropriate to a class of thirty or more children, particularly if they are already half-way up the school and know each other quite well. Yet the principle behind the mutual-introductions session is applicable to any age group. If the teacher can create a situation—right at the beginning of his association with the class—that forces them to communicate with one another as much as with himself, he demonstrates his belief that their thoughts and opinions are worthy of attention. Moreover, he enables them to emerge as persons, rather than remain as masked, anonymous members of a class.

Thus, children in a first-year class, meeting their form teacher for the first time, might be encouraged to exchange information about the primary schools from which they have moved, and even perhaps to say what they feel about coming to their new school, be it grammar, modern or comprehensive. A second-year class might discuss what it feels like no longer to be the youngest children in the school and what were the best and worst things about the year now past. Fourth-year pupils, facing changes in the spread of subjects in their time-table, might consider the implications of having dropped some subjects to take up others. Fifth-formers, surely conscious of the fact that their contemporaries from neighbouring schools, or from other classes in their own school, or even from their own class, have already left, might be encouraged to talk about the problems of staying on at school beyond the statutory leaving age. A sixth form might consider the nature of the transition to sixth-form studies and what are likely to be the rewards and difficulties of working with a smaller range of subjects and with more free periods on the time-table.

An opening session of this kind sets a pattern for future exchanges by freeing the pupils to talk about the matters which are important for them in the present. The teacher at the very outset demonstrates his willingness to listen, even if he has to hear things that are not particularly complimentary to himself. He may find himself discussing openly with the children their disappointment at losing contact with a teacher from whom he has taken them over, both as form master and, say, as their French or mathematics teacher. He may have to listen to complaints about the irrelevance of his own subject to their real concerns as growing people. In days to come his ability to accept and tolerate the reality of the children's feelings may turn out to be close to the heart of the relationship that develops between himself and them.

2. THE BUILDING OF POSITIVE RELATIONSHIPS

When we consider how little time is actually allowed in most schools for this special 'form' relationship to grow, it is remarkable that it should acquire as much importance as it does. A form period on the first day of term; ten minutes at the beginning of the morning and afternoon sessions throughout the year for filling in registers, collecting dinner money, checking the numbers of milk drinkers, inspecting name tabs on clothing, satchels and purses, dealing with complaints from other teachers and so on; a form period on the last day of term for clearing up: this is the usual ration of time. And perhaps the dislike so often expressed of the administrative chores such as marking the register is not so much a protest against having to do these jobs as a protest against a system that seeks to reduce the form teacher's relationship with his form to this kind of level. Yet even these brief and rather frustrating registration periods seem in some inexplicable way to add to the ordinary teaching relationship an entirely new dimension. What, then, is the nature of these feelings that are bound up in the terms 'my form', 'our form master' and 'our form mistress'?

In the first place, it does normally include a teaching relationship. And it is very important that the form teacher should have the chance to do with his own form the kind of teaching that he does best; he should not be saddled with English or mathematics or religious knowledge, whether or not he feels competent to teach them, simply because they have come to be regarded as 'general form subjects'. It can hardly be less than disastrous for him to be teaching his own form less effectively than any other that he takes. The work that is done with the form teacher, whatever subject label it carries, is part of the foundation upon which the whole relationship rests. If the members of the form sense that this work is less important to him than, say, the work he does with his sixth form or with a parallel form that he takes for some other preferred subject, he will never really know his form as he wishes to do; nor will he ever feel that they really know him. Conversely, a teacher who is able to share with his form a genuine enthusiasm—whether it be for science or painting, for mathematics or music, for history or for home crafts— may find that this mutual interest in some shared activity leads to a deepening of mutual trust and confidence and a new kind of knowing of each other.

This was clearly perceived by the members of the Newsom Committee when they were preparing their report, *Half Our Future*.[1] They have proposed that teachers should be encouraged to strengthen their contacts with their own forms, not by taking on one or more of the so-called 'general subjects', but by combining with their own special subjects one or two allied activities towards which they have natural leanings. Thus, an English specialist may elect to teach his form English, drama and art, a biologist may wish to combine biology with rural studies, a scientist who is a married woman may feel perfectly competent to combine her subject with housecraft, a second English specialist may combine hers with religious knowledge and social studies, and so on. Such groupings, by ensuring that every form sees its form teacher in more than one kind of learning situation, enables both staff and pupils to see beyond the artificial boundaries separating 'academic' from 'non-academic' subjects. And as these boundaries begin to thin out, so do those between work and leisure, so that activities which start as work assignments in laboratory, workshop, housecraft room or art studio may develop imperceptibly into hobbies and voluntary enterprises.

If the 'form' has a real identity apart from its register and the administrative tasks it has to perform from day to day, there will be an interdependence between form-room activities and those connected with the subject or subjects taught by the form teacher. Two examples may serve to make the point clear. Some years ago a physicist was taking up a post in a school where his pre-

1. (1963) *Half Our Future* (The Newsom Report), London: H.M.S.O. pp. 100–2.

decessor had yielded to pressure and allowed the physics laboratory to be used as a form room. He was viewing this situation with considerable apprehension. Greatly to his surprise, however, he found as the first year went on that he was not merely tolerating the arrangement but was actually beginning to like it. The relationship between himself and his form seemed to be acquiring depth and meaning from their joint responsibility for the care of the laboratory. A contemporary of his, a biologist, later reported a similar experience from a different school. He too had to use his laboratory as a form room. After a year or two he was given a particularly difficult fourth-year form. As time went on he found that some of the toughest characters in this form were the very ones who would stay on after school talking to him and helping him in his laboratory and showing an active interest in biological ideas.

Who can say whether, in such situations, the spontaneous interest in the subject or the wish to seek out the companionship of the teacher is the motivating force for the pupil? The important thing is that the relationship itself develops in such a way that the teacher as a person and the person as a teacher become for the pupil more recognizably the same human being.

Yet the situation holds the possibility of danger too, for in encouraging the growth of such personal relationships with certain members of his form the teacher may unconsciously be jeopardizing his more complex and difficult relationship with the whole group and thus with other individuals within that group. How is he to resolve this dilemma?

Perhaps it can never be resolved—only understood and tolerated. Perhaps the tension between each child's need of a close, unshared relationship with the form master and his need of acceptance by his form mates is an inevitable one, dangerous if it remains unrecognized, but a source of important learning if it can be brought out into the open and acknowledged. For this is a basic human conflict that will occur again and again for everyone—not only while he is at school but after he becomes an adult. Whenever he belongs to groups which have accepted leaders—in work and leisure situations alike—he will experience this kind of tension between his need to have the leader to himself and his need to maintain his membership of the group. Sometimes he may feel that if only the other thirty or so were out of the way, he might get to know his form teacher better.

Similarly his teacher, as a student, may once have wished his fellow students out of the way so that he could get to know his college tutor better. Yet neither the child in the school nor the student in the college could really tolerate the loss of those rival claimants for the attention of the staff member: child student and adult student alike must come to terms with the necessity of sharing the staff member with other people and must tolerate and control jealous and possessive feelings. Equally, the teacher in both situations must control, while acknowledging to himself, his own desire for closer relationships with preferred pupils. He must always ensure that privileges offered to one pupil are at least available for all, even if not accepted by all. He must guard against unwittingly creating a specially favoured inner circle.

This problem is really part of a wider one. For in many other ways, too, the forces that bind the group together as an entity are in conflict with those that urge every member to preserve his own separateness. The children in IIIB, like the students in any university tutorial group, need at times to assert their individuality, to demonstrate their indifference to the group, to withdraw from it in some way. Yet the longer the form or the tutorial group has been in existence, the more difficult it is for any member to do anything that might really encompass its destruction. The group itself comes to matter. And the members discover a need to preserve the group.

The strength of the affection that most teachers come to feel towards their own forms can be readily observed in any school. 'Nice little lot, aren't they?' one young English master remarks to me, as his very backward but warmly co-operative first-formers troop out of a classroom, smiling at him as they pass him in the corridor. I have just been watching them in a lesson taken by one of my students, and as I endorse their form master's comment, I find myself reflecting that the eager friendliness I have just been witnessing in his absence may not be unconnected with the quality of their relationships with him and their consequent feeling of trust and security in the school.

On another occasion a considerably older teacher is standing with me outside his classroom, very early in the autumn term, as his fourth form are going in. Watching them speculatively and rather sadly as they slouch and swagger into the room, he says to me: 'This is the toughest lot I've ever had. I'm not going to say I will never hit one of them. But if I ever do, I shall know that I have failed.' Later that morning I see that already, in various subtle ways, he is making them feel responsible for their own behaviour and is turning acts that are potentially disruptive into socially approved and constructive group enterprises. Already, by the simple expedient of initiating a private reading ritual at the beginning of every morning and afternoon session, he has stopped them from clattering into the room and banging desk lids up and down with deliberately hostile intentions. Already these rather loutish boys and distinctly provocative girls are beginning to sense that their tough-looking form master is really on their side, and at the same time that he is prepared to make demands both on their intelligence and on their good-will.

Sometimes this essential quality of affection, lacking the equally essential quality of detachment, can turn into a smothering and somewhat ludicrous possessiveness. This is a danger to which women, particularly childless women, are perhaps more susceptible than men, just as mothers, by the very nature of their role, are more often over-possessive than fathers. The over-possessive form mistress becomes unnecessarily boastful about her form's virtues and unnecessarily defensive about its shortcomings. A self-protective note creeps into her voice when any children in her form are being discussed. She implies that they can do no wrong and that any criticism of them is by implication a criticism of her. And so indeed it may be, though not quite in the way she imagines. For she is in a sense a member of her form, and must therefore accept a share of any criticism that is meted out to them. There will be times when her membership of her form will inevitably conflict with her membership of the staff group. Nevertheless it is essential that the second should never be seriously threatened by the first, for if that happens she will have so allowed herself to be absorbed into her form that she has weakened her role as a teacher.

We often speak as though the need for a close relationship were a one-way matter: we assume that it is only the children who have need of the care and affection of a teacher. But this is not so. The need works in both directions. The teacher, too, has need of the affection of his class, or, failing that, of their docility and obedience. If he exploits their affection, he will create a mutually dependent relationship: if he exploits their docility, he will be creating a potentially explosive situation, since a submissiveness founded in fear is bound to contain hostile elements.

By demanding that his form satisfy his own need to be either loved or feared, he thwarts their growth. If, on the other hand, he is able to put the children's interests before his own, he will realize from the very beginning of his relationship with the group that his real task is to help them to use his leadership in a mature, responsible way, so that they can ultimately become independent of him. The first kind of teacher will try to keep his form dependent on him, either by pampering and over-protecting them or by establishing a sort of reign of terror. The second will hand over more and more responsibility to the form, while remaining in the background as a dependable adult whose help can be sought in times of crisis.

Once the form or tutorial group has acquired a kind of emotional cohesion, the staff member may find himself facing a new temptation—the temptation to exploit any situations of rivalry that arise between his form and someone else's. Inevitably the rivalry will be there, both among the children themselves and in the staff room. In other words, the teacher must recognize the existence of an inter-personal rivalry between himself and his colleagues and also the existence of inter-group rivalry between his own and other forms. It almost seems that, having once discovered its own identity as a group, the members of a form may seek to preserve that identity by belittling or in some way rejecting other groups. This kind of process can occasionally take quite dramatic forms, both in schools and in adult institutions.

I recall an instance in a boys' school, where I was teaching English. At the time this episode struck me as amusing and even appeared to me to have been educationally valuable. Now I find myself wondering what role I was unconsciously playing and whether the effects were as simple and as harmless as I thought them at the time. The episode concerned my own form, a bright second-year group of about thirty boys, and a far less bright group of about fifteen fourth-year boys. I took both forms for English. On the day in question there was some crisis of organization in the school, the details of which I have forgotten. As a result of this, I found myself volunteering to combine these two groups for a period, despite the difference in age between them. As it happened, I had recently been working with the fourth form on letters of application, and these older boys had actually written answers to an advertisement in the local paper, which they had already handed in to me. When the forty-five or so had somehow crammed themselves into my room I proposed that a committee drawn from my second form should interview the writers of the letters of application.

Six of the younger boys were quickly appointed to take on this task; they seated themselves at my table and proceeded to examine and discuss the letters, to the great amusement of their form mates. About half a dozen of the fourth-form boys were then interviewed. The contrast between the bright efficiency of the second formers in the roles of secure and confident employers and the slouching embarrassment of the fourth formers in the roles of applicants for jobs was striking. The younger boys enjoyed the situation enormously, and did not hesitate to reprimand the prospective employees for untidy dress, poor deportment or casual speech and attitudes. Surprisingly, perhaps, the situation did not get out of hand. I left the 'lesson' feeling inordinately pleased with myself and with my own form. But it may be significant that I can remember nothing at all about my relations with the fourth form after that episode, although the name and face of the 'chairman' of that interviewing board are still fresh in my memory after the passing of over twenty years. Why, I now wonder, did I not question at the time my motives in deliberately placing my own form in such an advantageous position in relation to the older boys? Was it, perhaps, a possessive ownership of (and pride in) the more junior form that lay behind my action, rather than the simple wish to extend the reality of a written exercise, which served for a rationalization at the time?

If it is hard for a teacher not to misuse her 'ownership' of her form, it is equally hard for her not to feel flattered if her form demonstrates its ownership of her. She may feel flattered, for example, if the members of her form express a strong need for each other in a slightly unusual situation, since she can interpret this as a sign that she has created a united group. Another incident, this time from a girls' school, comes to mind that illustrates how a group needs to protect its own identity once it has found it. The whole upper school was being organized into groups for a theatre party, and it was necessary for some forms to separate, as the seats were in blocks in different parts of the theatre. My form of fourth-year girls found, to their consternation, that they had to divide into two groups. To my surprise and amusement they reacted to this news with cries of dismay, protesting that they were far too united a form to tolerate being split up on an occasion like this. I remember that I teased them for making such a fuss and that the division into two sub-groups was in the end settled fairly easily. It seemed that we all recognized that their display of indignation had really been a bit of an act— flattering and reassuring both to themselves and to me.

3. CRISES IN THE RELATIONSHIP OF FORM AND FORM TEACHER

Not all events remembered from past experience with this form and that, however, fall into this kind of category. For along with the demonstrations of support and unity, there are many acts of hostility and various kinds of testing-out situation that must also be part of any teacher's record. It is perhaps not without good reason that we tend to associate such clashes, not with groups that were our own forms, but with groups with whom we had only a teaching relationship. Is this due to a trick of memory —an unconscious desire to suppress the negative side of our relationship with those 'special' forms? Or was it in fact more possible to come to terms with the difficulties between ourselves and the children when there was an acknowledged personal bond, over and above the teacher–pupil relationship, within which those difficulties could be contained?

Most of us can recall hours or days of crisis when it seemed that the whole form was testing one's dependability as an adult. Often such a test would concern one's ability to cope with the deviant behaviour of one member of the form without destroying her membership of the group. Two examples stand out vividly and painfully in my memory. One involved recurrent cheating, the other recurrent stealing, in two different third forms in the same girls' school. In both situations, it was evident that the group had been carrying the burden of knowing that these things were going on and suddenly came to a decision to involve me, as the form mistress, in the conflict caused by this knowledge. In both situations it became evident that the feelings of the other girls towards the guilty member of the form were unbearably complicated. They wished neither to condemn the person nor to condone the action.

The cheating was brought to my notice towards the end of the week of school examinations. The staff as a group were already concerned about the amount of cheating that had been going on and had arrived at a decision that each of us, as invigilators, should immediately write 'cancelled' across the paper of any girl found cheating in an examination. We all acted as invigilators with our own forms. On the Wednesday afternoon I found that a girl at the back of the room had written some notes on the back page of her rough note-book and was using these in her French paper. I acted in accordance with the staff decision and cancelled her paper.

The next morning the form captain and another girl came to the staff room and asked for me. When we had moved out of earshot of other girls or staff, the second girl said to me, somewhat sternly: 'Mary was cheating in a little way yesterday, and she was caught. But there's someone else in the form who has been cheating in a big way for a long time, and we think it's time *she* was caught.' It seemed to me that in this communication there was a striking lack of vindictiveness: nor was it only the sense of a miscarriage of justice that seemed to have prompted the girls to give me this information, although that was certainly a factor in the situation. I had a strong sense that the decision had been prompted partly by a near-adult concern about the ultimate effect on the culprit of being able to go on living as dishonestly as she was doing. It was clear, in the little that the spokesman said, that 'a long time' meant a very long time, not merely the few days of the examination period. I was given no further information. And I was left with a strong feeling that, having been placed fairly and squarely into the conflict-ridden situation that the girls had been experiencing for some time, I was, in a sense, on trial.

The examinations continued for the rest of that day. I was aware, uncomfortably, of a strange sense of divided attention in the classroom. It seemed that it was immensely important to the form that I should not fail them now. In fact, I detected, rather miserably, another slight instance of cheating, and I was told fiercely afterwards by the same spokesman that, once again, I had caught the wrong girl. It was only the evident seriousness of the whole matter to the form as a group that now prevented it from becoming laughable. She added, even more fiercely: 'You walked straight past her when she had the paper screwed up in her hand. I could have kicked you, Miss Richardson!'

By Friday I was beginning to feel out of my depth. I decided to consult the headmistress. And hard on the heels of my action, news came from one member of the staff that one girl in my form had come out of the examination with an alarmingly high mark that bore no relation whatever to the quality of her work during the year. Later that day it was discovered, by the distasteful method of inspecting this girl's desk during the lunch hour, that she had systematically prepared for nearly every examination a set of useful notes on the preceding examination paper, written skilfully on small areas of the papers so that they could be held folded in the hand and surreptitiously examined in the course of the examination. The headmistress's action showed a human and touching concern for the feelings of the girl who had now been exposed. She asked her to come to her room, inviting her to bring a friend along with her for support. The culprit was one of the most timid members of the form, the last person anyone would have suspected of duplicity; the friend who readily accompanied her to the head's room was one of the more prominent and sociable members. The relief in the form was almost palpable.

The other episode was even more painful, and it, too, led to a search of desks, but this time the search was public. For some time a girl in my form had been suspected of kleptomania. The head had on several occasions found her wandering round the cloakroom, apparently feeling in coat pockets, when she should have been in class. But she had never been actually caught stealing. One day two members of my form came to me when the others had left at the end of the morning, looking slightly flushed and not a little worried. They began by half-apologizing for what they were about to say, and went on to disclose that one of them had missed her purse that morning, that they had both 'looked in Dorothy's[1] desk', though they realized that they should not have done this, and that they had found, not the purse they were looking for, but one belonging to a girl in the form next door. It was evident that they were only too aware that the matter had suddenly expanded to frightening proportions, and that they needed to get rid of the responsibility they had found themselves saddled with. And I in my turn unloaded the responsibility. Once again, as in the matter of the cheating the year before with a different form, I fled to the headmistress.

1. The name is fictitious, as are all names of children used in this book.

The matter was dealt with immediately. The head came along to my form, told the girls in my presence that a purse was missing (a fact of which, of course, they were all well aware) and asked their permission to carry out a search of desks. They agreed with enormous relief. I began to go through the desk nearest the window, and two minutes later I heard the head saying quietly that we need search no further. When I turned round I saw that there were seven purses lying on the table. The form, without a sound, had watched these being removed one by one from Dorothy's desk. Dorothy was sent along to wait outside the head's room. And the head talked quietly to the rest of the form, explaining to the girls that anyone who stole as Dorothy was doing was, in a sense, ill and needed help, and appealing to them not to ostracize her or to victimize her in any way because of this incident. As the weeks went on I never saw any sign that Dorothy had become an object of hostility.

It seemed that in each of these incidents the form as a group felt, along with their resentment against the deviant member, a sense of responsibility towards her and a dim understanding that the staff might find it possible to be on the side both of the group and of this member. Moreover there was evidently a sort of parallel ambivalence in the attitude of each of these forms towards me as its form mistress. I must be placed in an impossible position: I was to identify a girl who had succeeded, as it turned out, in deceiving teacher after teacher for about two years, cheating systematically in homework, tests and examinations and getting away with it when less skilful and more ingenuous cheats were caught and punished; or I was to expose a girl as a thief without descending to the action of rifling her desk in her absence as two of her form mates had done. Thus the form had to test out my omnipotence: and inevitably, and necessarily for their own growth, they had to find out that in such a situation I, too, was helpless. I, too, had to turn to a higher authority.

Perhaps, however, by accepting the need of help and by recognizing that the problem was a community problem—the sort of problem, in fact, that occurs from time to time in most schools, and that was particularly liable to occur, even in the most stable school communities, during the unsettled post-war period of which I am writing—I did in the end demonstrate a kind of dependability. On each occasion the culprit was exposed, as she had been all along to her classmates. But, because of the action taken by the headmistress, the group was able to adopt a therapeutic role in relation to the exposed member rather than to use her as a victim and turn her into a scapegoat.

A teacher may be forgiven much provided she is basically dependable. The girl who informed me (twice) that I had missed the real culprit during the cheating episode had had occasion, earlier in the year, to remind me, with equal asperity, that I had broken a promise made to this form. On this occasion I had been prompted by something that had arisen in an English lesson to suggest that the girls should write and produce a play and had been somewhat taken aback by a cold lack of response. When I enquired whether the idea appealed to them, their spokesman said pointedly: 'Yes—if it comes off this time, Miss Richardson.' With a pang of guilt I recalled that I had made a similar proposal to them about a year before to which they had responded with alacrity: I had encouraged them to start working on a project, and had then failed to see my part of the plan through. This reminder was a salutary warning to me that children do not easily forget—if indeed they ever forget—a betrayal of that kind.

It is not easy for children to distinguish between a teacher's dependability and a teacher's determination to maintain a dependent group. Indeed, it is not easy for adults to make this distinction. Even a group of university students will discover only with considerable struggle whether a tutor or a lecturer who appears to be withdrawing from a leadership role is really abdicating or is simply resisting the temptation to do for the students what they can do for themselves. Every group has a right to expect that the leader will be dependable; but equally the leader has an obligation to provide situations in which the group can ultimately achieve independence.

This is a process that requires time. And the need for time implies the need for continuity and growth in the relationship. Before leaving this subject we need to pay a little attention to this problem of continuity.

4. CONTINUITY AND ROLE DIFFERENTIATION

I have used the form rather than the tutorial group as the focus for this chapter, though clearly much that has been said of the one can also be said of the other. The emergence of the tutorial-group system in the large comprehensive schools is an interesting variant on the older system, and may prove to have certain advantages.

The tutorial system lays more emphasis on the need for continuity on the one hand and for heterogeneity of membership on the other. Some tutorial groups contain not only a wide ability range but also a wide age range. Children coming in to the first forms thus find themselves mixing with near-adults at the top of the school. Such a group, by its very nature, foregoes the advantages of being taught—as a group—by its tutor. What does it gain?

Probably it will gain by having unprogrammed time on the time-table, since it cannot be assumed, as it can with the form system, that some of the 'getting to know' is happening in scheduled lessons. Also, it is likely to be a somewhat smaller group than a form that is also a teaching unit. A tutor who has, say, two twenty-minute periods a week with a tutorial group of about twenty-five pupils, drawn from various classes, may find that it is a positive advantage not to be associated, for these particular children, with lessons on a time-table. His tutorial periods may come to be regarded as little islands in time—bonus periods that can be used for unstructured discussions about any problem the children have on their minds. A sensitive tutor, who is alert to the significance of the topics that the children spontaneously raise, may be able to provide for them the opportunity so many of them need—the opportunity to talk together openly, in the presence of an adult who can be unjudging and tolerant of differences, yet is felt to have won through to a personal philosophy of living himself.

There is something in these all-age tutorial groups, provided they have time for more than registration and the collection of dinner money, that is akin to the relationship between the members of a house in a boarding-school. The house unit that is also a living unit has something of the dynamic structure of the family group, in that it contains an age-range similar to that found in a large family. Consequently the society within the house must face and deal with conflicts that are not basically unlike those that arise in the family. The housemaster, like the parent, must balance the claims upon him of boys who are nearly adult with those of boys who are barely emerging from childhood. Unlike the parent, however, he must maintain relationships with several at each age level. The younger boys in his house, like the younger children in a family, have to accept the presence of older and more privileged siblings. But unlike the younger children in the family, they will experience, as they move up the school, not only a change of age, but also a change of position; and as they themselves become the older brothers, they will discover, as their predecessors did before them, that privileges carry responsibilities and that rights involve duties.

To some extent this may also be true of an all-age tutorial group in a large day school. Such a group also invites comparison with the now almost obsolete one-teacher village school, where children could experience both continuity and change, both possession and deprivation, in such a way as to learn something about the problems of living. An all-age tutorial group will be continually changing at its extremities, as older pupils leave and younger ones enter the school. Facing this kind of loss and renewal every year, its members will be learning to reconcile the pain of ending old experiences with the stimulating effects of embarking on new ones. The loss of a tutor must also be experienced from time to time, as staff changes occur; and here the continuity of the group itself provides a stable framework in which such loss can more easily be tolerated.

However, this kind of tutorial system presents administrative difficulties, particularly in schools that are operating in scattered buildings. And some have actually abandoned it in favour of tutorial groups based on single age groups. But the ability range can still be very wide. And it may be that some of the tensions caused by streaming and setting, by the allocation of pupils to subjects and teachers, even perhaps by decisions about which forms are to take G.C.E. and which C.S.E., can be openly discussed in these groups, if tutors are bold enough to face the conflicts and sensitive enough to help children to deal with them in an increasingly mature way. It may be that, being less tied to teaching relationships, which, as we have seen, are an essential part of the traditional 'form' situation, these groups can be freed to undertake some of those elusive tasks of growing-up which, in secondary schools, can so easily be submerged beneath the demands of the curriculum and the time-table.

There is, however, one serious danger in the tutorial system which we should not ignore. It may come to be used defensively as a means of creating even more of a dichotomy than already exists between those functions that are labelled 'pastoral' and those that are tied to the 'teaching of subjects'. A teacher who takes a form up the school for his particular subject and is also their form master for their first, second or third years in the school, finds that the effects of this deepened relationship are not lost, even after he ceases to be the form master, although there may be a temporary deadening of their warmth towards him for a term or so after the change. Conversely, if he becomes their form master in the fourth or fifth year, having already taught them for two years, there is a basis already laid down for the new kind of relationship that is starting. A tutor, on the other hand, can hardly avoid being faced, sooner or later, with the difficulty that he teaches certain members of his group and not others; and the emotional divisions this sets up between the members may seriously disturb his relationship with the group as a whole. If he can help the children to face and accept the rivalry problem, and to recognize that there are both advantages and disadvantages in belonging to the sub-group that is also taught by him, this in itself can be a learning situation for the whole group. But it does involve some difficult changes of role for the teacher, with the result that the roles may be separated out more rigidly than they really ought to be.

CHAPTER THREE

Patterns of Leadership and Control

I. LEADERSHIP AND THE CULTURAL PATTERN

So far, in examining patterns of behaviour in the form, we have been focusing attention mainly on the relationship between the group and its teacher. But the teacher is not the only leader in the group. And, indeed, unless he is able to recognize the leaders within the group and can help children to use them in an increasingly mature way, his own leadership will be of little avail.

In any group of thirty or so children there are many potential leaders, and the roles these individuals take or have ascribed to them by the group will depend partly on the group culture that is already in existence before the teacher arrives, partly on the culture of the school itself and partly on the culture of the neighbourhood which the school serves. But it will also depend on the attitudes adopted by the teacher himself, on his skill in relating himself to his pupils and on his ability to tap interests and emergent talents which will vitalize the work he wishes them to undertake. Let us consider an example, from a secondary-modern school in a northern industrial city.

I am sitting at the back of a classroom, watching Mr H., an experienced teacher, at work with his own form—a fourth-year class of very backward boys, all due to leave school within two or three months. They are poorly dressed, inarticulate and loutish in their general appearance. It is obvious that they have enormous difficulties in handling their own native language, both in speech and in writing. Yet with this teacher they are friendly, in their own rough and ready fashion, co-operative and willing to try to learn. During the first half-hour or so Mr H. talks with them about the lay-out of a steel mill, using a coloured diagram that he has drawn out on the blackboard, and helps them to think about it, interpret it and ask questions about it.

A bell rings. There are noises of classes moving round the building, doors opening and shutting and so on. He brings this lesson to an end and gives the boys two minutes to talk and stretch their legs.

As the noise outside dies away, the boys inside the room settle down and look at the master to hear what he is about to say. He reminds them that they have still some work left over from a current-affairs lesson, and that they ought to do some English fairly soon: which, he asks, would they prefer to do today for the rest of the afternoon? There is a general demand for English. He smiles, moves away from the front of the class, and sits down somewhere near the back. Two boys come out. The sliding blackboard is pushed towards the middle, and each boy draws a large object out from behind it. The first turns out to be a ship in a bottle, the second a couple of live pigeons in a basket. Both objects are placed on the table, and the first boy proceeds to describe how the model ship was made and how it was possible to get it into the bottle, demonstrating the second part of his talk by drawing the ship out of the bottle and re-inserting it. This talk—with questions—lasts for about ten minutes.

And then the other boy, grinning slightly, shambles over to the table, pulls his basket of pigeons towards him, uncovers them and takes one out, and begins to talk. He is a tow-haired youth with dirty hands and a grin that I find hard to interpret. His speech is, to me, almost unintelligible. He obviously knows a great deal about pigeons and keeps the class enthralled for forty minutes. Somewhere in the middle of this, the master interrupts him, with a polite apology, to ask him if he will show me what he is showing the class. The boy strolls over to where I am sitting, holds out the pigeon, spreading its wing, and points out some marking which, I now gather, indicates something about its age. He jerks his head forward, saying 'D'yer see? D'yer see?' I ask him a question to satisfy myself that I have understood what he has just been explaining to the boys. He then returns to the front of the class and goes on with his lecture, pausing now and again for questions. When the bell rings one has the feeling that he could go on for another half-hour and that the form would go on listening to him and questioning him.

Afterwards I ask Mr H. the two questions that have been forming themselves in my mind as I watch this remarkable performance. How low is this boy's I.Q.? And what is his normal pattern of behaviour outside in the street? Is he the kind of boy who kicks other people into the gutter, or is he the one that gets kicked into the gutter? I learn that in the society of the street he is the one who kicks others about, and I learn that he has an I.Q. of about 78.

Here, then, was a potential wrecker of any form and of any work situation—a boy of very low intelligence and very high destructive impulses. Yet this teacher had been able to mobilize this boy's leadership in such a way that the form accepted him in a role that was not unlike that which the teacher himself had been taking in the earlier part of the afternoon. Here was a boy who, in many classrooms would have been leading the fight against the adult (or, to put the matter in a different way, leading the flight from the work of the classroom); but here, he was actually taking charge of the class in an adult way and was teaching them, out of his own experience, how to breed and care for pigeons. Mr H. had in fact brought into play the creative side of his nature, though the world beyond the classroom saw a good deal more of its destructive side.

Now, although when the bell rang at four o'clock he and his audience still looked good for another half-hour, it is in fact doubtful whether he could have held this particular situation for very much longer. Mr H.—as the man ultimately responsible for what happened in the classroom—had timed things wisely. The bell intervened at a point where the boy's leadership was still being accepted. Had the lesson gone on very much longer, there might have been a swing of feeling against him—a move, perhaps, to have 'Sir' back in the leadership role, or a bid for power by some other member of the form.

This teacher had established with this potentially turbulent class a culture in which work and cooperation were possible. How is this kind of relationship achieved with young people whose interests and value systems do not, by and large, corres-pond with those of the school in which the law compels them to stay, well beyond the time when they still feel like children? How is the 'Let's fight the staff' culture changed?

Again, a specific example may illuminate what happens when such a change is actually in progress. This class, also, is a fourth-year group, not educationally backward as the other one was, but well down the scale in a streamed comprehensive

school, and notorious for its resistance to work and its hatred of
authority. This time the teacher (Mr J.) is young and inexperienced. The form is one of the two (the other being a bright
first form) whose work in English he has been allowed to take
over completely for one term. He is, in fact, in the middle of his
professional post-graduate training, and taking over this particular form is regarded by the school as his baptism of fire. The
first time I see him he is struggling to work through a fairly conventional comprehension exercise. Although the subject of the
passage is an exciting one and although he tries to tap the class's
interest by drawing out comparisons with contemporary events,
he never really manages to break through the barrage of noise
and confusion, until the last ten minutes of the lesson, when,
surprisingly, most of the class settle down and do some quite
good written work for him. Even when the noise is at its height,
I see little sign of personal ill-will towards him; and indeed
various monosyllabic responses to his questions are shouted to
him cheerfully through the noise. But the culture is anarchic.
Real work, as long as there is any sanction to talk at all, is
impossible. Mr J., it seems, has only two choices available to
him: either he accepts the leadership of the more powerful boys
in the form and abandons all attempts to work; or he challenges
this leadership and becomes the enemy, drawing the destructive
fire upon himself by taking aggressive retaliatory action. As an
observer I can see that this young man has a sensitive enough
approach to his subject to become a very effective teacher. In
my indignation about the behaviour of the class I am inclined
to think that he should adopt a somewhat more aggressive role,
though not necessarily a punitive one. But he opposes this, on
the grounds that a show of aggression with a form like this, bent
on living up to a bad reputation, will be likely to increase rather
than reduce their hostility. Equally he has no intention of going
into collusion with the form by joining the flight from work. So
we discuss a third possibility—finding some framework within
which the form leaders, at present operating negatively, can be
induced to operate positively.

When I visit this class again about three weeks later, with
a colleague, the situation is changing dramatically. It happens
to be the week of the fight between Sonny Liston and Cassius
Clay, which has been hitting the headlines for some time. The
members of IVG have done some research on this and have

come to this lesson prepared to report on various aspects of the event. During the first ten minutes of the lesson, Mr J.—working against considerable shyness and resistance—manages to collect a panel of six members, including two girls, one of whom joins it only on condition that her friend accompanies her to give her support. The six are given seats at the teacher's table, where they sit, half-pleased, half-embarrassed, waiting for the word to begin. Mr J. stands over by the window. The rest of the form are still talking, shouting and shuffling among themselves, but he remains friendly and unruffled, in spite of the fact that he has two visitors from the university sitting at the back of the room. He asks for silence so that the first member of the panel can give his talk—on the events leading up to the fight. Miraculously, as he turns towards the panel, a hush descends on the room. The boy heaves himself to his feet and struggles through his prepared speech. The form listen to him in complete silence. Bedlam breaks out again as soon as Mr J. suggests that the form discuss the points the speaker has raised; yet he continues to treat all the pupils, whether members of the panel or not, with the same unfailing courtesy and respect, showing an interest in the ideas that are struggling to find expression and actively helping people to conduct an adult, sophisticated discussion.

Half-way through this a boy comes into the room, swaggering slightly; he shuts the door rather more noisily than he need, strides across the room to his desk by the window with no more than the merest glance at the teacher, and begins a conversation with the boys near him as he sits down, throwing his satchel on to the floor. Mr J. takes no action, but continues to play his part in the discussion, sometimes from a standing position, sometimes sitting over by the window. As the lesson goes on, the other speakers give their prepared contributions. Each of them speaks to a silent, attentive audience. When the girl stands up to make her speech, last of all, the latecomer—by now fully involved in what is going on—calls for silence for her, almost unnecessarily, as it happens, since the rest of the class are already settling down to listen to her. The discussion following each contribution from the panel continues to be turbulent and difficult to control; but the quality of the comments improves steadily; boys who in the earlier lesson seemed capable only of shouting monosyllables, are beginning to conduct conversations with the teacher and with each other. Most significantly of all perhaps, the swaggering latecomer is twice heard appealing to Mr J. to get the class to listen to what he is trying to say.

This lesson might by some standards have been described as a shambles. In the total context of this form's reputation it was very remarkable indeed. What we observed was a process of change from a situation in which the only acceptable leadership was destructive, anti-adult and anti-work, to a situation in which leadership was shared between the teacher and certain members of the form. The culture in which, it might have been supposed, the adult had to choose between adopting an oppressive, authoritarian role and going into collusion with an adolescent gang that was refusing to work, was yielding to a new culture. And this proved to be one in which the pupils could learn how to accept an adult relationship with a teacher and, in doing so, improve their own social and conversational skills.

2. LEADERSHIP ROLES AND PERSONALITY TRAITS

Much of the turmoil in difficult classes arises from the fierce competition for leadership. For a classroom, like any society, becomes anarchical and destructive if leadership is ineptly handled. This kind of conflict is not peculiar to adolescent groups; we have only to recall the struggles within political parties during the last few years, following the death or retirement of a leader, to remind ourselves that rivalry is always present in the human group, however primitive or sophisticated its method of handling the conflicts.

The importance—for children and for adolescents—of the presence of an adult society to act as a holding institution for these violent antagonisms has been illustrated powerfully in William Golding's novel, *Lord of the Flies*[1]—the story of how a group of children, who find themselves alone without adults on a remote Pacific island after a 'plane crash, struggle to set up a civilized and unified society, only to live through a terrifying process of degeneration into savagery. To teachers, who never quite lose their fear of the destructive potentialities within the classroom, this book carries a profound message. Of all the novels about children that are recommended to intending teachers, it seems the most widely read and reread.

1. Golding, William (1958) *Lord of the Flies*, London: Faber & Faber.

In this novel, the two boys Ralph and Jack represent, we may say, the powers of good and evil. But together they represent the need in every human being and in every human group to reconcile the good and bad parts of the self. It is the failure of the two boys—and of the society that contains them—to come to terms with their own rivalry that leads to the tragedy. Yet at the beginning of the story they try to do this. Ralph, having summoned all the children together by blowing on the conch, is faced by a rival leader, Jack, who arrives with his choir marching in order behind him. Ralph, however, is acclaimed the leader. Immediately he bestows upon Jack the task of organizing the 'hunters', thus handing to him the kind of physical and destructive power that leads in the end to the collapse of the forces of order within the group. Yet in this raw and naked situation of rivalry, Jack and Ralph, we are told, smile at each other 'with shy liking'. For a while they succeed in preserving a balance of power, but in the absence of a stable adult society to contain the destructive forces, the partnership breaks down and Jack, unable to tolerate his own frustration, breaks away and establishes the outlaw society which finally overcomes the law-abiding one and leaves Ralph alone and completely vulnerable. Yet at the moment when Jack breaks with Ralph, there are tears in his eyes—tears of humiliation because the group has just refused to depose Ralph and raise him up as leader, and tears for the loss of friendship with the very rival against whom he will later declare war.

The society described in Golding's book exists in a cultural vacuum. It needs only the appearance of two adults on the scene for the dangerous, ruthless savages suddenly to reappear as little boys, playing at war. Yet, ironically, the adults themselves have landed from a battle cruiser and are in naval uniform.

In school the conventions are normally preserved and emotions are held in check to such an extent that we may not even recognize their existence. Yet the forces of destruction are there too, in playground and classroom, as anyone who has taught in the kind of school usually described as 'tough' well knows. We have all read half-serious, half-comic accounts of classroom situations in which the teacher's authority is continually being undermined either by the most aggressive bully in the form or by its most neurotic and dependent member.

These situations are far from funny either for the teacher or for the group, however skilfully an amusing writer can turn them to comic account. Why, then, does the group tolerate such destructive leadership? And how can the teacher work with the forces that give rise to it?

The problem of leadership has always exercised educators at all levels, and will always continue to do so. What have psychologists and psychiatrists to say about it that can be helpful to teachers in schools?

During the last thirty years or so there has been a definite swing away from the older tendency to look for 'leadership traits' in individuals. It is now recognized that leadership must be regarded as a role rather than as a cluster of personality traits, and that we must look in the group as well as in the leader himself to discover why his leadership takes the form it does. In a school classroom, or in an out-of-school club, or in the playground, children of very different temperaments may at different times take over the leadership of the same group. The 'natural' leaders are not always those whom we would expect to take this role; sometimes, when events in the group seem to be getting beyond the adult's control, we do not even know who the leaders are.

A new approach to the question has been opened up during this period in the research that goes by the name of 'sociometry'. As its name suggests, this branch of social psychology is concerned with attempts to measure social relationships. Understandably, it has had a considerable appeal to teachers, particularly to those who look for ways of organizing small groups within the classroom and of encouraging the emergence of internal leadership. The sociometrist focuses his attention on the actual choices that children make when they seek companions in work and play. In fact, he goes further and asks them to state in advance what their choices are, and he then uses this information when he constructs his groups. Needless to say, the more genuine the 'criteria', or choice situations, he uses, and the better persuaded the children are that he will at least try to meet some of their wishes when he allocates them to small working groups, the more valid will be the information they give him. The pattern of relationships that emerges from such an enquiry is bound to throw some light on the problem of leadership, particularly if the testing is carried out as part of a continuing programme of group activities that demand the exercise of leadership.[1]

Teachers who use this procedure soon discover that popularity is not necessarily synonymous with the kind of leadership that they are trying to cultivate in their classrooms. A pupil who shines in class when all thirty or so are operating as a dependent group is not necessarily the most effective member of a small group; a quieter, more self-effacing child may turn out to have more skill in drawing the best out of his companions. The star on the sociogram may be the most disruptive member of the class, or he may be one of the most co-operative. A child who appears on the sociogram as a relative outsider may yet influence the behaviour of the class at a given time.

The sociometric technique was invented by Dr J. L. Moreno, who first used it on a large scale and over an extended period with the help of Dr Helen Jennings in a residential training school for delinquent adolescent girls at Hudson, New York.[2] They themselves very soon began to emphasize the impossibility of correlating leadership with any particular traits or clusters of traits. In fact, if we study the personality profiles both of overchosen and of underchosen children, we soon discover that very different individuals with very different personality characteristics may be equally well regarded in the community, and that similar personality characteristics, superficially observed, may appear in individuals who occupy the most favoured and the least favoured positions in the choice distribution.

Sociometric workers, whether they are teachers with leanings towards psychological investigation or research workers with an interest in schools, direct their attention mainly to the influences that individual people have on one another. They are interested in identifying networks of mutual attraction in the group or community. In organizing small-group work in a classroom, they will be concerned with the development of leadership potential in children who have not, in the large group, emerged

1. See Northway, Mary L. (1953) *A Primer of Sociometry*, University of Toronto Press; Jennings, Helen H. (1959) *Sociometry and Group Relations: a Manuel for Teachers*, American Council for Education; Evans, K. (1962) *Sociometry and Education*, London: Routledge & Kegan Paul.
2. Moreno, J. L. (1961) *Who Shall Survive?* (revised edition), New York: Beacon House, and Jennings, H. H. (1950) *Leadership and Isolation*, New York: Longmans, Green.

as leaders, and they will study the sociograms for evidence of a growing cohesion in the working groups or for signs of tension between one group and another. All this is likely to have an important effect on the teacher's attitude towards his class. His powers of observation are likely to be sharpened, and he may find himself handing over more and more responsibility as children show themselves increasingly capable of exercising it.

But—like all techniques—this one carries a danger. The teacher, if he becomes more interested in the technique than in the purpose for which he is using it, may find himself turning imperceptibly into a social engineer, manipulating children's choices for his own purposes rather than to further their growth. The sense of power wielded by the sociometrist is insidious. It is hard to say at what stage 'classroom organization', aided by sociometry, becomes 'manipulation'. Furthermore, in his enthusiasm the teacher, turned sociometrist, may forget that the information the sociogram gives him is at best limited. It gives him a pattern of expressed choices for a particular activity at a particular time, and nothing more. It tells him nothing about the motives underlying these choices, nor indeed has he any guarantee that the choices are genuine, or, if genuine, that they will outlast the day on which they are committed to paper. Within these limits it tells him a good deal about the interpersonal affinities in his classroom—who is attracted to whom; and it gives him an overall picture of the cliques and divisions, the probable centres of influence and social success and the probable centres of pain and social failure.

Thus far, so good. But of the fluctuating moods and emotional needs of the group as a whole or even of the small sub-groups he forms on the basis of the choice pattern, it tells him virtually nothing. For this, and for an understanding of the corresponding leadership needs of his class, he must use other resources. These resources lie far more in the felt emotional consequences of his own leadership role in the classroom than in his technical ability to manipulate the potential work-leaders in the class.

3. HARNESSING THE EMOTIONAL FORCES IN THE GROUP

As the over-all leader in the work situation, the good teacher will have one main objective: to help his pupils to learn for themselves. For the one inescapable truth about the whole educational enterprise is that every child must, ultimately, accept responsibility for his own learning, whether he is an acknowledged leader in his form or its most retiring member. As individuals, the children in our classrooms want to learn. They want to acquire the skills of the adult world and to experience the excitement of discovery. Certainly, by the time they reach the higher forms of the secondary school, and probably by the time they enter the first form, they are aware that the kind of life that will be available to them as adults will depend on the use they can make of the opportunities the school gives them to do this growing and learning. Yet, as members of groups, their behaviour is continually dominated at the primitive, unconscious level by emotional needs that may have little to do with growing or learning.

I suggested in the last chapter that the relationship between the teacher and his own form was in essence a mutually dependent one, and that a form teacher's role as the leader of a dependent group carried with it all the pains and anxieties as well as the pleasant characteristics of the dependent group culture. We must now ask ourselves whether the teaching–learning situation, too, depends on the ability of teacher and class to use this dependent culture in a sophisticated manner, or whether another kind of relationship must be sought.

Certainly, if the teacher is not dependable, his pupils will not learn. Conversely, if he sees himself as omniscient, believing that all knowledge must emanate from him and merely be transmitted to his pupils, they will eventually become restless and frustrated. And here is the paradox. Children will submit for a long time to teachers who dictate notes to them or write notes up on the blackboard to be copied into note-books; they will accept P.E. lessons that resemble army drill, demanding the same responses from everybody; they will allow a science teacher to organize their experimental work for them down to the last detail, and to impose on them set models for the writing up of the results; they will take for granted that they should all be given identical tasks for homework. It seems that, provided the teacher plays this kind of role efficiently, the class will submit to any amount of such spoon-feeding, preferring safe and easy security to the possible pains and uncertainties of learning by their own efforts and mistakes.

However, in time, such a routine produces its own difficulties and frustrations. Where everybody is expected to make the same responses, rivalries are bound to spring up. Not everyone can please the teacher equally. The children find that they cannot easily share his attentions. And so rivalry and mutual antagonisms begin to disrupt the group. Bill Green, who can always answer the teacher's questions, becomes an object of hostility. Maggie Brown, who is more bored and restless than most, and is falling behind in her work, becomes the centre of tittering attention. And suddenly, from leaning helplessly on the teacher and competing for his good opinion, the class finds a new kind of unity by combining against him and against the frustrations imposed by his method of teaching. The culture has changed from dependence to something quite different.

Before we look at this new, aggressive and potentially destructive situation, let us consider another kind of pupil–teacher relationship which appears at first sight rather like the dependent one but turns out to be something else. Probably many teachers would agree that the ideal teaching–learning situation is one in which the teacher works with one pupil. For the master teaching the pupil, we substitute two scholars, one more experienced than the other, but both partners in an enterprise of which the outcome remains unknown. This pairing relationship or working partnership is the essence of the university tutorial situation. But it has its counterpart, certainly in the sixth form, and less obviously in classrooms lower down in the school. Every time a teacher sits down by a child to work through a mathematical problem, or to talk with him about a picture he is painting or a poem he is writing, or to discuss what is happening in a scientific experiment, he is using a pairing relationship. But, since he cannot do this with more than a handful of the members of a class in any one lesson, he must also make it possible for the children to pair off with each other.

Clearly this procedure, if work goals are unclear to the children, can degenerate quickly into chaos and confusion. For in a group that has broken up into pairs there is no visible and tangible leader. The controlling factor is something in the future—the hope of a worthwhile product from each pair. The danger is that the situation becomes too competitive, or that the group will settle into lethargy, leaving it to one pair to do the real work. And so the success of the pairing activity is likely to depend on the teacher's ability to make his class feel that the contribution of each pair is essential to the success of the final product. This product may be the creation of a wall newspaper or a magazine, or the mounting of an exhibition, or the staging of a dramatic sequence; or it may be something as abstract as the mastery of a new kind of mathematical problem or of a new scientific concept or the greater understanding of the human problems in a novel.

I have been trying to apply to the classroom situation a theory of group behaviour that was worked out in the late 1940s and early 1950s by Dr W. R. Bion (mentioned in my opening chapter) on the basis of intensive experimental work with small groups. Some of these were groups of patients in a therapeutic situation at the Tavistock Clinic in London; others were training groups at the Tavistick Institute of Human Relations— people in responsible positions in industry and education, including some members of the staff of the Tavistock Institute itself. Unlike many other psychiatrists doing pioneer work in the field of group therapy, Bion strove to avoid the temptation of merely treating his patients as individuals in the group. Similarly, with the training groups, he avoided personal contacts or exchanges with any individual members and confined his interpretative observations to matters that concerned the group as a whole. Over and over again he found that the underlying emotional processes in the group were both antagonistic to and essential to the conscious and sophisticated purposes of its individual members.[1]

At times his groups were dominated by their need for one person on whom to depend; and they would try to set up this person as omniscient and infallible. At other times they appeared to be relying on a pair, as if in the hope that this pair might produce the new magical leader in the future. And at other times they were concerned only to preserve their own identity by fighting something or running away from it. The real problem for every group seemed to be to learn to recognize these unconscious needs, or 'basic assumptions', and to become capable of mobilizing the one that was most appropriate for the task they were met to perform.

Now we can, I think, find parallels to these kinds of phenomena in our school classrooms. Bion's theory helps us to understand the difference between the helpless dependence that saps

1. Bion, W. R. (1961) *Experiences in Groups*, London: Tavistock Publications.

real work and the intelligent use of the basically dependable teacher. It helps us to see the difference between the group that escapes into fruitless pairing situations and the group that consciously uses pairs to bring a planned project to fruition. It helps us to see the difference between the destructive fight–flight culture that leads to anarchy or to apathy, and the healthily aggressive relationship between teacher and class that promotes learning through the dialectic of discussion and argument.

The fight–flight culture can take one of two forms. If antagonism is open, it will take the form of noisy rebellion, and the leader will be the most openly aggressive boy or girl in the class. If the antagonism is concealed, it will take the form of a massed flight—not necessarily a physical flight, though this frequently happens when the bell rings at the end of a tedious lesson, but more probably a flight into silence and apathy. In such a situation it is hard to detect where the leadership lies. The one certain thing is that it is no longer invested in the teacher, however strenuously he goes on trying to teach. And apathy can be just as hostile and nearly as exhausting in its effect on the teacher as open rebellion.

From the point of view of the group, the fight–flight culture is no more satisfactory than the dependent culture. If the leader of the dependent group has to be infallible and omniscient—the perfect teacher in the classroom, who never puts a foot wrong—the leader of the fight–flight group must be invincible, or so swift in retreat that no one can catch either him or the group that follows him. So the hostile class, which is trying to ensure its survival by fighting or running away from the teacher, needs a child who is brave enough to defeat the teacher or cunning enough to lead the group right out of the situation. This may be possible in fantasy. But in reality the whole organization of the school, and of the society that the school serves, is there to prevent the success of either fight or flight. Moreover, any child who leads such a fight exposes others as well as himself to the punitive powers of the institution. And as casualties mount, it becomes more and more evident that this culture will not ensure the surivival of the group either. And the class may collapse suddenly into its former docility, returning helplessly to the dependent culture.

A vivid example of this kind of abrupt switch of the emotional temperature from aggression to submission was brought back some years ago to a tutorial-group discussion by a graduate student after the term of school practice. Mr K. told us how he found himself teaching a first form that had had a succession of teachers, of whom he was the eighth, for French. It was regarded as a difficult form; and there was in it one particular boy who was a persistent trouble-maker. After a long series of lessons in which this boy had been thoroughly disruptive, Mr K. gave him some lines as a punishment. When he brought them the next day, Mr K. noticed that he had written "ABK is mad" across the paper. He decided to ignore this and merely dropped the paper into the waste-paper basket. About half-way through the lesson the boy started misbehaving again, so he brought him out to the front, and presently noticed that he had written 'ABK is mad' on the blackboard. He then sent him outside the door, and subsequently discovered that he was writing the same message on the dusty corridor window, to the great amusement of those still inside the room. Mr K. told this story with considerable humour, but without disguising the difficulty he had been faced with in trying to deal with the boy. It was also evident that, exasperated as he had been, he had found the boy attractive.

This part of his story had a distinctly comic flavour; the sequel, which he divulged later in the tutorial-group session, was unexpectedly moving. Asked what further steps he had taken, he replied sadly: 'Well, I pushed it still further out.' He had finally reported the boy to his form master, with the result that he was given a beating. Mr K. added even more sadly: 'This had a shattering effect on the class. For a whole week they were struck dumb. So I was able to get on with my teaching. But they were quite unable to learn.' The group received this in a stunned silence, evidently as much affected by Mr K.'s complete honesty as by his concern about the effect his action had had on the class.

The discussion that arose in the tutorial group after Mr K. had told us this story threw an interesting light on the problem. One member of the group remarked that perhaps this boy had only been putting into words something that most children feel at times about most teachers. From that it was an easy step to consider that the tutorial group had sometimes regarded me as slightly mad, and indeed sometimes still held this opinion. They agreed, but Mr K. reminded me with a smile that the message had not yet been written on my carpet.

Reflecting on this incident from the safe distance of a private study, one wonders whether it might have been possible to treat it as a group phenomenon rather than as a personal display of impertinence to a teacher. For in a sense, this particular boy was acting as a spokesman of the group. By throwing the impertinent comment back to the class, almost as a counter-joke, and asking whether the rest agreed with his opinion, the teacher could have taken the sting out of the attack and at the same time made a little legalized aggression against him possible.

It is a question of distinguishing between behaviour that springs from a personality defect in the child and behaviour that is expressing something on behalf of the group. It may be that a child's persistently aggressive behaviour can best be met by recognizing that he is being allowed to carry a good deal of the aggression for the group, and by trying to use this group aggression in some positive way. Most teachers come to recognize, as Mr K. did, that sending the fight–flight leader out of the room is very rarely a solution to the problem. Too often the rest metaphorically accompany the banished offender, even if he does not find such a vivid way of keeping attention focused on himself as this particular boy did. If, on the other hand, the punishment, or the sequel to the punishment, is too drastic, the form is crushed to the point of helplessness.

There is, however, a form of retaliation that is a great deal more dangerous to the group than the removal and punishment of a ringleader; and that is for the teacher himself to walk out. By doing this, he himself becomes the victim of the aggression he arouses in the group, leaving behind him as an uneasy sense of loss and guilt. It occasionally happens that a teacher who has antagonized a class of children allows himself to be driven out in this way. If ever a class provokes a teacher to these lengths, its members are left feeling that they have been collectively guilty of a sort of murder. If their mood turns to remorse they will seek to make amends. If their mood turns to ridicule the damage to themselves may be very much greater, since they may set out to test all subsequent teachers to the limits, and may come to boast of their talent in destroying their teachers in this way.

The ultimate test of any member's ability to take the group's hostility, whether this member is the teacher or one of the pupils, is his willingness to stay in the group. Now in the classroom the teacher is both more free and less free to leave than anyone else. He is more free because he is an adult. But he is less free because he is bound to the group by ties of duty and responsibility; and the pupils know this. And so, if he leaves for no reason except to punish them, he is abandoning them. The primitive fear of the loss of the supporting mother is thus reactivated in the pupils. And so, surprisingly, such an exit is likely to be marked not with a howl of delight but with a sudden shocked silence. The expected triumph turns abruptly to dismay. When the class fools the teacher to the top of his bent, what they are really testing is his ultimate concern for them. If he cares for them more than for his own dignity, he will stay. If he 'teaches them a lesson' by leaving he expresses his ultimate, perhaps irredeemable, hostility: he abandons them.

In such a withdrawal, there is also, for the teacher, an element of defeat and even perhaps of self-punishment. He himself is bound to be left with an overwhelming sense of inadequacy, which will have to be lived through when he next encounters these same people, and even others who, he feels, may have heard about the incident. His pupils will probably sense his predicament too. And so, along with their own feelings of guilt, there is the anxiety arising out of his defeat. For they need to feel that he is somehow indestructible.

A class who, in Bion's terminology, is dominated by the fight–flight basic assumption, needs to be helped to face and master its own dangerous aggression. It may be that children who find themselves in this situation consciously fear their leaders even while they allow them to lead. Teachers who are prepared to admit that they have been faced by such group behaviour will sometimes report that individual children have said to them privately, or even openly in class: 'Why don't you keep us in order, Sir?' Perhaps the real plea is: 'Why won't you help *us* to keep *ourselves* in order, Sir?' The difference in wording is significant.

Certain members of the class begin to dislike the anarchy that is created by their own disruptive leaders. They find themselves longing for a teacher who will establish himself as a dictator and bring order out of chaos. Yet merely to substitute an authoritarian régime is not really a solution to the problem. For the group will just as easily fall a prey to the next disruptive leader that comes along. The aggression has to be used rather than merely suppressed for the time being.

I suggested earlier that the group that has taken flight into apathy is just as hostile as the openly rebellious group and can be nearly as exhausting to the teacher. In the hostile class, the object of attack is the teacher, and his best solution is somehow to direct the aggression against the difficulties in the work situation. In the apathetic class, everyone is trying to run away from the demands of the work situation; and the problem is to bring the disguised hostility out into the open in such a way that fight, in the form of an attack on difficulties, takes the place of the wish to run away from the difficulties.

Again, an example may make the point more clearly. It is 11.20 a.m. I am sitting at the back of a classroom in a girls' grammar school. Miss L. is reading a selection of Keats' poems with a fourth-year class—the A stream. Nothing she can tell these girls about Keats' life, no question she can ask them about the poems they are reading succeeds in bringing a flicker of a human expression to their faces, let alone a spontaneous comment to their lips. They watch her politely, appear to be listening, or stare unseeing at the books in front of them. What are they really thinking? What sort of revelations would the teacher get if she threw her prepared lesson aside and challenged three or four of them to say what was really in their minds or what they would consider a reasonable topic for poetry in the 1960s? How might their attitude change, I wonder, if she were to come down from the teacher's high desk that dominates the room from one corner, and if, for once, the school convention that compels even these tall, well-developed girls to stand every time they answer a question or offer a comment could be waived.

Afterwards we discuss the problem. Miss L. is in despair about this class, for she knows that the girls are intelligent and is perceptive enough to realize that although in her lessons their faces may look empty their minds certainly are not. She decides to try shock tactics. In her next lesson she asks them what they would consider important enough to be a subject for poetry— what they themselves would choose to write about if they had to write poetry. At first, suspecting a trap, they give her the answers they think she wants them to give. Challenged further, they begin to bring real enthusiasms out into the open, and they also begin to test her out by trying very mildly to shock her.

Now this lesson, although at the time it could not have been said to have much advanced the cause of Keats versus the current pop star, did ultimately affect their whole attitude to poetry. They found that they did not have to pretend with this teacher that they liked everything she read them; at the same time they found that, if she was prepared to allow them to be aggressive in expressing their opinions, she also expected them to produce reasons for those opinions. When eventually I saw this class again, Miss L. began by reading with them a poem by Robert Frost, with a few preliminary remarks to put it into a context. The girls discussed it with some heat, and then, with the help of provocative interjections from the teacher, began to thrash out what it was that made poetry distinguishable from prose. What astonished me was the way in which this roomful of extremely reserved young women, whose thoughts could not have been guessed at from the mask-like faces they had showed before to their teacher, had been transformed into a number of vivid and distinct personalities, expressing at first quite crude and naïve ideas, but gradually, under the pressure not only of the teacher but also of the group, tightening up their choice of words and phrases and trying to communicate clearly to one another what they were struggling to think out.

During the weeks that had intervened between the two lessons I saw, Miss L. had been able by degrees to dispense with all the meaningless formalities I had noted in the earlier lesson. The girls now spoke spontaneously, without raising their hands; they did not stand while speaking, but sat as any group of adults would sit while conducting this kind of discussion; and they addressed each other, turning round in their chairs to do so, almost as often as they addressed the teacher. Yet there was order in the proceedings. They were sensitive to one another's impulses and were prepared to listen as well as to talk.

This teacher had succeeded in turning a situation which had degenerated into a flight from the task into something more like a pairing culture. She had effected this change by first bringing out the hostility concealed behind the politely bored, resolutely expressionless faces in her classroom, inviting the girls first to direct this against herself in the form of an open rejection of the materials she had been using with them, and then channelling it into the intellectual task of determining what really constituted poetic expression in any age.

4. LEADERSHIP RE-EXAMINED

At the beginning of this chapter I described two classroom situations: in the first, an experienced teacher created a situation in which a potentially disruptive boy of very low ability took a leadership role in a work situation, keeping a class of very backward boys absorbed in a lecture on pigeon breeding; in the second, an inexperienced teacher with a noisy and apparently uncontrollable class launched an exercise that turned anarchy into something approaching an organized, adult discussion about a topical event. We are now in a position to look back at these examples and see whether Bion's theory throws any light on what the two teachers described in these incidents were able to do.

It is significant, I think, that both these teachers used pairing situations. Mr H., when he withdrew to the back of the room, was replaced by two boys, giving their talks independently it is true, but operating as a pair in taking over the leadership for the rest of the lesson. Mr J. had prepared for a similar take-over by giving the members of the class different aspects of the same topic to prepare, and his panel could have been described as three pairs rather than as six individuals. In fact, it will be recalled, the one girl who spoke on this panel joined it only on condition that her friend accompanied her to the table. In this way both teachers eased their classes into a situation that enabled them to look for leadership to a pair rather than to the fantasied omniscience of the teacher or to the fantasied invincibility of the aggressive rebel. The first teacher handed over to a pair, following a period in which the class had been fairly dependent on himself; the second created a situation in which he sought pairing relationships with several members of the class in turn, and at the same time encouraged them to operate in pairs instead of merely relying on or violently opposing himself as teacher. Thus both teachers gave the potential fight–flight leaders in their classes leadership roles in co-operative, work-centered situations.

Let us now try to put Bion's ideas together in the framework of the school classroom.

In the dependent culture the danger for the group is that it relies too implicitly on the leader and becomes frustrated because the leader cannot rise to the expectations people have of him. And so the teacher, as the dependent leader, must contrive to be reliable while continually urging the class to question his omniscience, challenge his opinions and realistically accept his human limitations. And at times he will create situations in which members of his class take his role, and become accepted as alternative leaders in a basically dependent culture, using their own expertise as he uses his when he is the accepted leader.

In the pairing culture, the danger is that the group rests in the lazy hope that two members will continue indefinitely to carry responsibility; individuals then become frustrated because their hope of some perfect product from these two is never realized. Here the teacher's role is to break up the task and give each pair or small group a manageable part of it to tackle. In this way achievement becomes possible, because no-one any longer supposes that one pair can be left to produce the magic solution.

In the fight–flight culture the danger is that the group will either destroy the teacher or itself by the unleashing of its own hostile impulses or withdraw from the situation altogether. And so the role of the teacher is to channel the aggression into an attack on ignorance and apathy, so that the class rediscovers its powers of cooperation in a learning situation and uses its leaders in a constructive way.

Thus when one kind of basic assumption threatens to overwhelm the group and make work unproductive, the teacher has to try to find ways of mobilizing another, so that new forces can come into play and be used by the group in an increasingly mature and responsible fashion.

The leadership of the children or young people in changing classroom situations now comes to be seen as intimately bound up with the kind of leadership the teacher himself chooses to use. And as the class grows more mature as a group, and better able to handle its emotional needs, so its members will discover that leadership can be exercised in many different ways and by many different individuals.

But it is not leadership roles only that are taken by members of the class. Just as a confident child will exercise a natural wish to dominate others and will be encouraged and even compelled by his classmates to take this role, so the timid child will be used by the group as a scapegoat whom it is safe to ridicule, or—less obviously—as someone who can safely be ignored and left to be ineffective, and so carry the problems of being ineffective for everyone else in the group. Of all the ship-wrecked boys on William Golding's island, Piggy was the wisest and most sane. But because he was fat, wore spectacles and had asthma, he could be jeered at and pushed aside, even by the good Ralph, who knew how many of his best ideas he owed to Piggy. And most classrooms have their scapegoats, just as this group of shipwrecked schoolboys had theirs. We must now, therefore, devote some thought to the roles carried for the group by the lonely, isolated or rejected children in our classrooms.

CHAPTER FOUR

Loneliness, Isolation and the Fear of Rejection

I. THE TEACHER'S DILEMMA

Probably most of us, at times, see in our pupils shadows of our former selves. This can be both a help and a hindrance to us in doing our jobs. If a teacher has an image of himself as a child hovering on the edges of groups, neither wholly inside nor wholly outside them, he is likely to notice and sympathize with a pupil who appears to be having similar difficulties. An episode observed in the present may recall an episode experienced in the past. But if he champions this former self too obviously he may damage rather than repair the child's tenuous relationship with his classmates.

As a young woman in my early twenties, temporarily teaching in the Midland school where I had myself been a pupil, I became involved in just such a situation. I had first arrived in this school at the age of thirteen, having moved south from Scotland with my family. In my new environment I soon became somewhat painfully aware of my Scottish accent and was particularly teased about my pronunciation of the word 'Latin'. Only in French lessons was my accent an advantage, since I had little difficulty in pronouncing the pure vowels without diphthongizing them as the other children tended to do. I was aware, also, that I was known in the school as 'the girl with the back-bag'; and although in Scotland I had thoroughly approved of this kind of receptacle for school books, since it left one's arms free and kept the weight well distributed, in my new school I found myself growing ashamed of it. Yet another source of embarrassment was the fact that I, like the Scottish girls of my generation, continued to wear my school uniform, black stockings included, after school hours, whereas my new companions never lost any time in changing out of their uniforms as soon as they got home. Within a few months I had persuaded my parents to buy me a case for my books, and had accustomed myself to this new and far less convenient way of carrying them to and from school. It took a little longer to persuade them to let me wear light stockings (the hall-mark, then, of adult status) after school hours. And it probably took longer still to get rid of my Scottish accent.

About ten years later I found myself teaching for a few weeks in the same school. In one of the forms I took there was a new girl who had recently moved with her family from London. She had a marked Cockney accent. One day, when she was reading aloud, I became aware that the rest of the class were exchanging glances and that some of them were tittering. I said nothing at the time, but something in my angry glance round the room pushed the ridicule underground. A few days later, when the London girl happened to be absent, I talked to the others about this incident and tried to make them understand that their attitude to her had been snobbish and unkind, and that any of them—deposited in a London school—might find herself feeling as much like a fish out of water as the newcomer was probably feeling in this school. Later still, in a French lesson, I found myself drawing the attention of this class to the ease with which the London child was mastering the pronunciation of a sound which the others were finding difficult.

I do not recall that I was aware at the time of the similarity of this girl's predicament to my own in the same school ten years earlier. And I assumed, optimistically, that I had by this prompt action enabled her to become fully accepted in the group. Now, more than twenty-five years later, I find myself wondering whether, by fighting this girl's battle for her, I may not have contributed to her isolation. I had no evidence about what subsequently happened to her in the school playground, or about the extent to which she was being received into children's homes. And I now wonder whether the battle I thought I was fighting for her was really my own one, in a new guise.

Should I, then, have turned a blind eye to the unkind exchange of glances and a deaf ear to the unkind tittering? Surely not. But problems like this are delicate to handle; and openly championing the outsider may not, in the long run, be the wisest course to take, even if it appears to produce good results in the short term. Moreover, there may be other forms of exclusion—simple neglect, for example—which can do more lasting damage than teasing and ridicule. For teasing can, in certain situations, turn into more positive and kindly attitudes, if the object of the teasing is allowed to handle it in his own way. But neglect leaves the victim feeling that there is nothing to handle and that he has nothing of value to contribute to the group.

The problem of loneliness is deeply rooted in human personality. It has its positive as well as its negative side—a fact which is reflected in the language we use when speaking of it. Sometimes we think of the state of being alone as a precious right: at such times we call it 'privacy'. At other times we feel it as a painful deprivation and call it 'isolation'. The infant who has reached the stage of crawling likes to test out his own physical separateness by getting out of his mother's sight at times; yet his greatest fear is that she will stay out of reach of him when he needs her and that he will be left alone and abandoned. The adolescent needs a room of his own and times of seclusion so that he can test out his personal separateness and come to terms with an identity that is his and no-one else's; yet this struggle to free himself from his childish dependence on adults is so painful that he has to seek a kind of interim shared identity with young people of his own age. He dare not, any more than his former infant self, be too much alone. And so, for a while he is afraid to be different, though ultimately it is his uniqueness that he will have to face and accept.

This shared fear of being different and therefore isolated can very easily turn into a need to be identified with the group in persecuting anyone who can be readily labelled and set apart as odd and laughable. If twenty-nine children can unite in finding the thirtieth absurd, the twenty-nine can convince themselves that they are normal. Furthermore, by labelling this one 'odd' child as the outsider, they build up their defences against their own fears of isolation. Inadequacy as a group member is safely projected into one individual; and as long as the twenty-nine continue to find reasons for excluding the thirtieth, so long does the thirtieth carry on behalf of the others the feelings that they are striving to be rid of—the fear that they, too might be in this situation because of some other kind of inadequacy or peculiarity. It may almost be said that every group seems to *need* someone to take on the role of the isolate.

Teachers are apt to protest that the cause of this problem of the isolated child in the classroom lies in the present size of teaching groups. There is a partial truth in this. It is difficult for the adult in charge not to lose sight of the outsider—not to take part in the acts of exclusion, in fact—when the group is as large as thirty or forty. And it is correspondingly easy for the other children in the class to avoid facing their own share of responsibility for what is happening to the outsider. Some of the evidence from sociometric studies seems to show that the provision of opportunities for working together in small groups of six or eight gives the more timid children the chance to establish friendships and find their level in the total group. But we should not lose sight of the fact that the problem of exclusion occurs even in quite small groups and that it can manifest itself in different ways.

How, then, can we as teachers help children who find themselves in this painful situation? Are we to seek the cause of the problem in the personality of the rejected child, in the structure and leadership of the group, or in some unconscious côllusive process that makes each play into the pattern of the other? I hope to show that the third approach may be the most fruitful in the long run.

2. THE ISOLATE IN THE SOCIOGRAM

Sociometric studies of this problem have frequently been concerned with the first kind of enquiry—attempts to identify personality traits or behaviour patterns that are found in disliked or socially neglected children. We read detailed descriptions of children who appear with low scores on choice lists and (where dislikes are also recorded) high scores on rejection lists. These case studies may be accompanied by written comments from other children, giving reasons for their attitudes towards their rejected fellow-pupils.

Repeatedly, the authors of such studies admit that the evidence points to considerable variety of personality characteristics in the group of children who are labelled 'isolates' or 'outsiders'. Mary Northway[1] at first identified only two categories: the shy, withdrawn or 'recessive' children who were neglected rather than actively disliked, and the thrusting, interfering 'aggressive' children who were openly rejected by their classmates. It was apparently possible for children to

1. Northway, M. L. et al. (1947) 'Personality and Sociometric Status', *Sociometry Monographs*, No. 11, New York: Beacon House.

feel some pity for those in the first category, but not for those in the second.

At a later date, Northway suggested that three categories could be identified: 'recessive' children, 'socially uninterested' children and 'socially ineffective' children. She implied that those in the first and third categories were neurotic or delinquent (the most severe cases being near-psychotic) whereas those in the middle category had their own particular strengths and talents and were on the fringe of groups from choice rather than from necessity.

Follow-up studies of children placed in each of these categories showed that teachers had been unable to do very much to help those who had been described as 'recessive', since many of them had turned out to be almost psychotic and had had to be referred for psychiatric treatment. Those in the second and third categories, however, had proved amenable to help. The 'socially uninterested' could be encouraged to use their talents within the group instead of only outside it and to take part usefully in projects, so acquiring value in the eyes of their classmates. The 'socially ineffective', many of whom were hostile and disruptive, were gradually helped to acquire more insight into their own behaviour and to replace their uneasy attempts at self-advertisement with a more genuine self-confidence.

Now the children in Northway's study were identified as outsiders in the first place because they were 'among the least accepted fourth' of their class groups. The basis for this grouping was a fourfold sociometric test, in which each child was asked to name his first three choices of companion in four actual school situations. The choices were weighted according to order of preferences to produce a score for each child. These were plotted on a circular diagram with the help of three concentric circles; the children whose scores were in the highest quartile appeared in the centre and those whose scores were in the lowest quartile appeared on the outside of the diagram. Northway admits that some of these 'outsiders' received as many as fourteen choices, while others of them received none.

In another study, however, we find that 'popular' and 'unpopular' members of a class were identified from sources derived from a somewhat different type of sociometric test.[1] These

1. Bonney, Merl E. (1947) 'Popular and Unpopular Children: a Sociometric Study', *Sociometric Monographs*, No. 9, New York: Beacon House.

children were asked to give the names of those they would prefer as companions in the various activities described. Choices were unlimited, and were given in order of intensity. By implication, all those who were not named on the lists were unwanted. This, then, was a slightly more direct and certainly less tactful method of inducing children to make negative as well as positive choices. In still another study, this process went even further, the children being invited (though not instructed) to name those they positively did not want to have with them.[1]

Here, then, are three quite different categories of 'social unacceptability'. And in the three studies, the children are being asked to admit to three different levels of dislike. The first might be called 'indifference' or 'neglect', the second 'relative unpopularity' and the third 'outright rejection'. We must assume that the communication of these feelings from children to investigators must have been accompanied by corresponding degrees of guilt and disturbance, at least for some of those tested.

The sociometric worker is liable to fall into certain traps in his attempts to objectify his evidence about interpersonal relationships in his classroom. In the search for data that can be subjected to some kind of statistical analysis, two important matters are liable to be completely overlooked. First, little account is taken of the emotional effects on children of writing down for an adult's scrutiny the names of liked and even perhaps disliked classmates. Secondly, even less account is taken of the fact that a relationship of some kind exists between the children and the adult who asks for this information, especially if this adult is the teacher. These two kinds of feeling, both largely ignored by the sociometrist, are closely entangled with one another.

The person who does the testing, and who does or does not act upon the information he is given, is in fact the isolate *par excellence* in the group. His name appears on no choice list and on no sociogram. He is, apparently, above choice. At the same time he becomes the possessor of information about the group which both isolates him and gives him power. Whether the power is benevolent or sinister may, for the children, depend on whether he intends to use the information to further the well-being of the group or merely to hoard it for his own purposes. When

1. Jennings, pp. 32–3.

the subjects are adolescents or adults it is doubtful whether any good intentions can save the investigator from appearing sinister. How then can we be so naïve as to imagine that this relationship, which must be felt by every member of the group as a powerful factor in the situation, will have no effect on the behaviour of the members towards one another, including the way they rate each other in the sociometric test?

In studying a situation like this we have to take account of a complex pattern of guilt and responsibility. The child may feel burdened with what he has committed to paper; at the same time, consciously or unconsciously, he will be concerned about how he is perceived as a member of the group by his classmates and by his teacher. The adult is burdened with the knowledge of what the children have revealed; yet he is by no means sure what these revelations mean. He cannot necessarily assume that the giving or withholding of a choice (or 'vote', as it may appear to the child) means what it seems to mean—that the person chosen is regarded by the chooser as a compatible companion for the activity in question and that, conversely, the child who has not been chosen will prove incompatible with those who have passed him by. At the same time, because he has all the information at his disposal, the class may expect him, magically, to create happy, tension-free working groups.

One unexpected result of my own use of these techniques in a girls' school remains obstinately in my memory and now seems more significant to me than some of the other evidence that impressed me more at the time.[1]

One girl (Brenda) appeared on my chart at one stage of the experiment not as an isolate but as an apparently unrealistic chooser of companions. The girls whom she named belonged to a fairly close-knit group, and none of them had indicated any interest in her in making their choices. However, there were two girls in another group who had named her on their choice lists, although she had not responded by choosing them. After consideration, I placed her in the group where it appeared that she was wanted—that is, with the girls who had actually named her on their choice lists. And what happened? Instead of settling down to the work they were supposed to be doing, these girls

---

1. 'Classification by Friendship: Sociometric Techniques Applied to the Teaching of English', in Fleming, C. M. (ed.) (1951) *Studies in the Social Psychology of Adolescence*, London: Routledge & Kegan Paul.

amused themselves by attacking Brenda. The more she protested about the way they were wasting time, the more they used her as a target for abuse and ridicule. Eventually, at her own request, I transferred her to the group towards which her own choices had been directed. I feared that she would fare even worse among classmates who were indifferent to her and well adjusted to one another. But to my surprise they accepted her easily, and she herself began to relax in their company and, later, in the form as a whole.

Looking back on this episode, I now ask myself whether it was my attempt to create congenial groupings or the nature of the group experience itself once the groups were formed that was the more important for these children. Inevitably, conflicts arose, and would have arisen, however planned or unplanned the grouping had been. Equally, some girls were bound to become more effective, merely because they were given the chance to work in face-to-face situations, and this would have been so even had I not been at such pains to create congenial groups. I now believe that my real task as a teacher was to enable my pupils to face the implications of what they did to each other rather than to strive to reduce the chance of uncomfortable friction. Perhaps one real opportunity for learning of this kind was missed when I transferred Brenda from her 'friends' to the children who apparently did not care whether they had her in the group or not. Undoubtedly, by removing her from the disruptive group I robbed those girls of the chance of working through their difficulties with Brenda and of making amends to her for what they had done to irritate and disturb her. In a sense, I allowed this group to kill her off, and then gave another group the satisfaction of resuscitating her. The apparent improvement of her status in the form may have been bought at a higher price than I realized at the time.

And now another piece of evidence comes back to my mind, forcing me to ask a further question about what had been happening to my relationship with this form during the first eighteen months after they entered the school.

When these children were about half-way through their second year, about three months before the episode just described, a decision was made at staff level which concerned them, along with the rest of the school. This had to do with the arrangements for school dinner. The meal was eaten in a large, prefabricated building, the girls sitting at fairly long tables, each table accommodating eight and each supervised by a ninth senior girl from the fifth or sixth year. Hitherto the children had sat down wherever they happened to arrive as the queue moved round, with the result that the heads of tables had no chance to get to know stable groups of children. It was decided, accordingly, that the table groupings should be made permanent. As I was at the time engaged on an experiment in group work and was already using sociometric techniques, I offered to arrange the table groupings for the twelve forms in the first, second, third and fourth years. This I did on the basis of sociometric tests, asking every child who stayed for school dinner to name four others, in order of preference, with whom she would like to be placed.

For me, the most striking piece of evidence that emerged from this survey was that one form had a very much higher proportion of isolates than any other: namely, IIC, the form that contained Brenda. Now, IIC was one of the two second-year forms I was teaching at that time. I had each of them five times a week for English. Both were involved in my experiment, but had been given very different roles. IIC, in fact, were not as yet taking part in the experimental group work, but were acting as my control group and were therefore still being taught, in my lessons, by the familiar, conventional methods. I had, at the outset, been as frank with these girls about the whole situation as possible, and had undertaken to work with them in a similar fashion after the experiment had been going for a year—a promise which I honoured when the time came. Yet the fact remained that for the past two and a half terms IIE, the parallel form next door, had been having experiences in their English lessons which, for IIC, would have to be postponed for yet another term. At the same time the girls in IIC, like their rivals next door, had been asked to submit at intervals to various kinds of tests, including occasional sociometric ones.[1]

And now, on this new sociometric test, which unlike the others was to have an immediate meaning for them as well as for IIE, a startling pattern revealed itself. Out of the thirty-four girls who stayed to school dinner and who were therefore

1. These two forms were, in fact, parallel forms in an unstreamed three-form grammar-school entry. In my contribution to C. M. Fleming's book (op. cit.) I referred to the experimental group as 'Class-group E' and to the control group as 'Class-group C'. I have retained the letters 'C' and 'E' for convenience in cross-reference.

eligible to be chosen as companions, six received no choices at all and one other received only third and fourth choices. In IIE, on the contrary, there was no girl who was unchosen, and all but one received at least one first or second choice. At the time I was unable to attribute this startling difference entirely to the beneficial effects of the small-group experience, enjoyed by IIE but denied to IIC. For I had the further evidence from the other seven forms which I had tested in the course of replanning the seating in the dining-room. And in no other form was the proportion of unwanted children so high.

In retrospect, it now occurs to me that the pattern reflected something more than a mere set of choices for lunch companions. I believe that it also reflected something about the form's feelings towards me. During the first period of the experiment, while IIC remained my control group, I had (naïvely) been reassured by the fact that they had never outwardly complained about what was happening. Today, being a great deal less sanguine about the reality of such apparent reasonableness, even among adult students, I am fairly certain that they must have been suffering from quite strong feelings of deprivation, anger and frustration. If this was so, they must have felt that I was rejecting them in favour of the other form. Is it fanciful to suggest that they may have reacted to the situation by unconsciously projecting their own feelings of unworthiness into one another, so becoming divided against themselves?

Strangely enough, my conscious reason for deciding to use the other form (IIE) as my experimental group had been the very reverse of what, as I believe, the girls in IIC may have suspected. For in the early weeks of that first year it was IIC (then still IC) that I had found the more attractive to teach. IIE had seemed, in that first term, to have an unusually high proportion of silent, unresponsive members, and for this very reason I had decided to use this form for the experimental work in the first place. By the end of the year, IIE had strikingly reduced its number of unchosen members. But even more significant is the fact that my own attitude to the form had completely changed. Because of the experiences I had shared with them, I was now finding them increasingly attractive to teach. Had this form's gradual absorption of its lonely members been made possible by its own growing image of itself as my preferred group as well as by the opportunities offered by the group work? And conversely, can the high proportion of unwanted members in the other form (IIC) be seen as a consequence of that group's growing image of itself as a group that I perhaps no longer enjoyed teaching?

I have dwelt on this example at some length because I believe that the problem of the lonely child in the classroom cannot be studied without reference to the total surrounding context—a context that includes the relationship of the class to the teacher. Certainly the cold-shouldering of about one sixth of this form by the remaining five sixths could not be accounted for in terms of the personalities of the children concerned. Of the outsiders in this form whose faces and personalities I can still recall clearly, only one seems to have behaved in a way that, in any situation, would probably have earned her some dislike. But let us take a glance at some of the others. There was Elinor, who was quiet, withdrawn, shy, but not obviously unhappy—a comparative stranger to the form: she had been transferred from another school as a result of a family move, and even now her home was far beyond the boundary within which lay the other children's homes. The girls did not appear to dislike her. They simply failed to notice her. There was Daphne, who was eager to please, fussy in her movements, inclined to giggle, full of superficially bright ideas but incapable of carrying any of them through. There was Pauline, a tall, rather languidly pretty girl with charming manners but little drive or persistence and apparently nothing to contribute to a discussion. And there was Brenda, whom events showed to be more of an outsider than the sociograms revealed. Are we to suppose that they revealed any truer a picture about the other four?

The problem of isolate behaviour must be seen, even by children, as a problem of the group. That is to say, the isolated individual, whether he withdraws partially or totally, or whether he assaults the group in a self-advertising manner, is making some kind of communication to the other members and is responding to some kind of communication from them. If the lonely or rejected member is to be helped, the teacher will need to create a situation in which the other members of the group will become more sensitive to one another's needs. And it is possible that they will be able to do this only if they are also prepared to communicate more honestly with the official leader, even if that official leader is the teacher of the group.

3. ISOLATE BEHAVIOUR AS PART OF A TOTAL SITUATION

In taking this question further it may be helpful to consider three degrees—or categories—of isolate behaviour that an individual may exhibit. First, there is behaviour that is adapted to the group at a highly sophisticated level, involving a temporary and deliberate drawing apart as a necessary prelude to a full and effective participation in the life of the group. Secondly, there is behaviour that is the outcome of special circumstances that set the individual concerned apart accidentally, forcing him into a role that is unlike the kind of role he usually finds himself taking in groups. Thirdly, there is what may be described as fringe behaviour, springing from some kind of personal difficulty in handling human relationships, and used by this group to satisfy certain unconscious purposes. Sometimes this fringe behaviour can become hostile and damaging, culminating in a complete repudiation of the group.

These categories of behaviour are not mutually exclusive. One may shade into another, as a result of events in the group. A child may find himself behaving differently in different groups, or in different phases of the same group. Too many, however, appear to be stuck permanently in the third category; and as long as we fail to pay attention to the role the group is playing in keeping a child there, so long will he continue to behave as the group wishes him to behave. But let us consider these three categories separately.

In the first, the individual is content to be isolated because he sees this state as a necessary preliminary for what he wants to do in the group. This need to pause and, as it were, guard one's privacy during a period of transition into a new situation is well illustrated by Mrs Lois Murphy in her book *The Widening World of Childhood*.[1] This is a part of every child's experience, when he is beginning to emerge from the seclusion of his home into the social world that surrounds his home. And it is an experience we all re-enact whenever we have to penetrate the ranks of a new group. It is not a process that can be hurried. Mrs Murphy and her colleagues describe the behaviour of pre-school children in various new situations, including a party. And as we watch

1. Murphy, Lois B. (1962) *The Widening World of Childhood*, New York: Basic Books.

these events through the words of the observers and through the interpretative commentaries, we find ourselves distinguishing between those children who, like Elinor, paused rather too long and the more secure, sturdy children who insisted on taking their own time about joining in the games, deliberately isolating themselves for a while, but then took part with confidence, buoyancy and enjoyment.

Teachers who use discussion and activity methods will readily recall examples of pupils whose style of entry into a new group is cautious, controlled and non-committal at first. Such people very often become highly effective members of the group, earning more approbation, in the long run, than do the more obvious leaders. They are likely to be told that they are envied for their capacity to listen and then unexpectedly to put their finger on the important point in the discussion. Their contributions often have to be waited for; but when they do come they are felt to be helpful because they grow out of what other people have been trying to say. These are the apparent isolates who turn out to be closely in touch with the feelings of the group.

Anyone who accepts a leadership role in and on behalf of the group must also accept a measure of loneliness. Headmasters and headmistresses know this only too well. This is so even if they work with rather than merely through their staff, and however accessible they make themselves for discussion and consultation. In a sense, a head must be all things to all people and cannot allow himself the luxury of any especially close relationship with any individual colleague that might threaten his working relationship with the group. Moreover, he must accept the burden of ultimate responsibility for the work of the institution. We shall have more to say about this in a later chapter. Here it is perhaps enough to remind ourselves that even the youngest child, once he is asked to carry out any special responsibility on behalf of the group, may have to learn to handle not only power but the loneliness that goes with power.

There is another kind of necessary period of isolation which most of us have to bow to at times. This is the moment of pause as we enter a new and strange society. Dr Paul Halmos says: 'An Englishman, an American or a Russian is anxiously lonely in a manifestly un-English, un-American or un-Russian world.'[1]

1. Halmos, Paul (1952) *Solitude and Privacy*, London: Routledge & Kegan Paul, Introductory Note, p. xvi.

This is an example of what he calls the second problem of loneliness—man's 'in-group' loneliness, which springs from his emotional dependence on the groups, sects, nations and races into which he has organized himself. Thus the personal or 'social' loneliness that cuts the individual off from other members of the group (even of the group he knows well) is reinforced whenever he is among strangers by this second-level loneliness caused by his separation from his membership or reference groups.

We have already had some examples of this 'in-group' loneliness in this chapter: Elinor in IIC, who had been transferred from another school and lived a long way from her present one, the London girl whom I taught in her new Midland school, and myself as a child in the same school newly arrived from Scotland. All these belong to my second category of isolated children: for all these were placed by accident of circumstances on the outskirts of the group, at least for a while. Elinor, though she did not have the extra complication of a strange accent, probably fared the worst of the three, for she was crippled by shyness. And so for her, Paul Halmos's two kinds of loneliness reinforced each other: it was hard for her to handle simultaneously her social loneliness (stronger for her than for most of her classmates) and her in-group loneliness as an exile from the old familiar school community. And so, where a less timid child would have paused just long enough to give the group time to assimilate her, this one waited too long. Only very gradually was she able to start functioning as a member of this new class. And in doing this she was undoubtedly helped by learning situations that enabled her to work closely with a few other members of the class at a time.

Sometimes this kind of circumstance leads to a different kind of isolation—a curious feeling that one is being used as a mascot. Perhaps I was treated as a kind of mascot when I first arrived in my new English school, with my Scottish accent and my back-bag. The feeling of being a mascot was not without its pleasurable side, since it involved attention. Yet I longed to escape from it and be accepted as myself. So, perhaps, a coloured child who is over-protected and almost petted by his white classmates may really long to be taken for granted, to be allowed to get into scrapes like the rest, even to be scolded by the teacher. Making allowances for people can be a form of exclusion.

It is touch and go whether a child who is singled out because of some immediately observable difference (in size, age, colour, or voice) is turned into a mascot and cherished by the group or pushed out of the group with or without active ill-treatment. The very small boy among rapidly growing thirteen-year-olds who is nicknamed 'Tich' may rejoice in his title and become popular, or may hate it passionately and become an outcast. The eleven-year-old girl who seems like the baby of the class may be encouraged to act out the part, or she may be cold-shouldered and ignored. It is difficult to say which is the worse treatment, ultimately, for the physically or mentally immature child. Certainly it is more comfortable to be treated as a mascot. But as long as child and group continue to go into collusion over this relationship, so long does immaturity remain a bar to more lasting satisfactions. Moreover, the mascot behaviour will not last for ever. Sooner or later the child will find that he is no longer a mascot. He has imperceptibly become an outsider.

What, then, of the child who is more intellectually mature than his classmates? What is likely to be his role? Again, it seems that the group may hover between two entirely different courses. They may put him on a pedestal and idolize him, as did Whyte's street-corner boys with the older and more experienced Doc.[1] His survival will then depend on his ability to maintain his superiority in the activities most valued by the group, for example, in games or in motor-cycling: if he excels at these as well as at science or English or mathematics, his success in work will arouse admiration too. On the other hand, a class may see the superior achievement of one member as a kind of threat, both to their own self-image and to their relationship with adults: the boy who excels at science may seem to be identified more closely with the science master than with his classmates. This is a dangerous position to occupy.

We are now moving into our third category of isolate behaviour. For the very fact of being set apart from the group in some way is likely to give rise to defensive and somewhat neurotic reactions from the individual concerned. The clever child allies himself with the teacher, for protection, maybe, and unconsciously develops a style of behaviour that the form regards

1. Whyte, W. F. (1943) *Street Corner Society*, Chigago University Press. Discussed in Homans, G. (1951) *The Human Group*, London: Routledge & Kegan Paul, pp. 156–89.

as supercilious. The over-anxious child becomes more anxious as a result of what the group does to him; and since anxiety and hostility are never far apart, this behaviour makes it easy for the other children to project more and more of their own hostility into him. And so, by identifying himself more and more with their image of him, he comes to behave more and more as the others expect him to behave.

Now this must be what is happening to many children in school classrooms and to many sixth-form pupils in small seminar groups, when they find themselves caught inescapably in a role which they and the group have woven for them—a role of silence and ineffectiveness, perhaps assumed to be hostile, perhaps assumed to be merely timid and self-effacing. At its most cruel, the situation may even be put into words by class-mates: 'Oh, he never speaks, Sir!' At its least cruel, it is merely a steady pressure, unconsciously exerted by the group and felt by the child to be the weight of his own inability to be interesting, coherent, or even barely articulate.

In the small group there is a chance for the pressure to change. Imperceptibly it may begin to appear to the child that the group is trying to force him, not to maintain silence, but to break through and speak. For along with the primitive need of the group to find some individual member to carry the stigma of ineffectiveness for everybody, there is also a need to stop hurting the part of the group that is being destroyed, to make amends for past unkindness and to find a more sophisticated way of dealing with the fear that gives rise to the unkindness. What can the teacher do to hasten this reparative process?

4. THE TEACHER AS AN AGENT OF CHANGE

A good deal can be done for the excluded child merely through the provision of opportunities for work in small groups, for here it is almost inevitable that some new facet of the child's personality will come into view. For the child himself, retreat into self-excluding behaviour becomes less easy, though we cannot assume that it will not still happen. It is a collusive process that has to be broken into. The isolate is not only being labelled by the group: he is also labelling himself. He, for his part, has to learn to see himself as less different from others than he has come to imagine himself to be; and his classmates have to learn to feel themselves into his position and understand that what they have helped to make him is what any one of them might have become if the circumstances had been different. Each is a potential isolate and has probably experienced temporary isolation.

We all display neurotic behaviour occasionally as members of groups. We indulge in angry, aggressive retorts, probably expressing our views with a great deal more heat than the occasion warrants; we demand more support from the leader than we really should expect as adults; we retreat into nervous silence when we ought to be meeting an intellectual situation with appropriate questions and comments. But some individuals —and children, who have not yet discovered their true identity, are particularly prone to this—find themselves taking one or other of these roles in every group. This child is always hostile; that one is always dependent and clinging; that other is always shrinking back into a frightened silence. Repeatedly, their fellow-pupils respond to such behaviour patterns by urging these children into their usual roles. And so the vicious circle remains unbroken.

In schools the obvious place for this kind of problem to be worked out is in the form or tutorial group, provided it can be given time to meet regularly without any fixed agenda. In other words, children have a great need for times when they can have free-floating discussions in the presence of their teachers. And there are tutors and form teachers, in schools where such time is allowed, who are enabling their pupils to let the barriers down in this way. With groups as large as thirty it requires great courage to abandon the props of organized lessons. We are accustomed, as teachers, to holding the reins. We fear chaos if we loosen our holds. Yet teachers who do this sometimes discover unexpected sources of control, strength and mutual concern among the children themselves.

But there are also indirect ways in which children can be induced to examine their own motives and feelings more honestly. The English teacher—through the study of literature and through the children's own personal, authentic descriptions of actual experiences—can do a great deal to bring these problems out into the open, without necessarily making any specific reference to the acts of exclusion that are going on in the classroom. We all use imagery a great deal more than we realize, and what we spontaneously choose to speak about, either in a

free and undirected discussion or in exchanging thoughts about
a play or a poem or a painting or even a piece of music, may
be reflecting some emotional problem that concerns our relationships with one another. This is the principle behind the psycho-
therapists use of projection techniques, and it may be operating
in a classroom discussion more strongly than any of us realize
and with a therapeutic effect of which we may or may not be
aware. This was brought out quite powerfully in a Canadian
National Film Board film *Shyness*, when, towards the end, an
eight-year-old girl who had, very slowly, been helped to take a
tentative and limited part in classwork, was enabled to take an
enormous step forward during a discussion period when her
classmates talked about fears. A wise and sensitive teacher had
seen that something more than small group projects, helpful as
these had been, was needed. And as the boldest and most confident members of the class stood up, one after another, and
admitted to various irrational terrors, this pathologically shy
little girl began to see her own kind of fear as something that
could be talked about and overcome.

Once such a fear is exposed it becomes more manageable,
not merely because the person concerned has dared to acknowledge it and look more closely at it, but also because those who
have unconsciously contributed to it become able to recognize a
need in a fellow human being. I once watched an English
specialist (Miss M.) taking a revision lesson on *Twelfth Night*
with a class of fifteen-year-old girls. They had read the play in
the previous term with another teacher, and for the first quarter
of an hour or so appeared to remember nothing about it at all.
Miss M. steadily resisted the temptation of offering them a
recapitulation of the events in the play, but continued to probe
into such vague recollections as they were able to produce.
Eventually, the theme of love emerged, and for the next quarter
of an hour this was explored in the context of the various
triangular relationships and the various levels of experience in
the play. But the most interesting part of the whole discussion
came when the role of Malvolio was examined and the motives
of those characters in the play who expose him to ridicule and
have him locked up as a madman. Miss M. engaged her pupils in
a quite searching argument about the ethics of this behaviour,
challenging their assertion that what happens in a play has no
relation to what happens in real life and making them examine

their cheerful assumptions about the feelings of excluded persons. Could we really assume that the outsider wanted to be an outsider? Could we really put our consciences to sleep by assuring ourselves that he (or she) probably had a circle of friends somewhere else? Could we really go on believing confidently that he had only himself to blame for his loneliness?

After the lesson was over, Miss M. told me that there was a girl in that form who was in just such a position, and that she—and, she thought, the girls—had been well aware that it was not just the isolation of Malvolio and the cruelty of his tormentors that were being talked about in that 'revision lesson on *Twelfth Night*'. I can well believe that the 'revision', if we must call it this, was all the more effective because it was vitalized by this real-life problem in their midst, and that some new insights into their own behaviour may have been gained from this rather unusual classroom discussion on the dramatic events in a Shakespeare play.

At a still deeper level, we have to recognize that the behaviour of children towards each other may be related in various unrecognized ways to their relationship with their teachers, particularly the teacher who is most closely associated with them in the life of the school as an institution. Earlier in this chapter I stated my belief that every group needs an isolate. A class of thirty or more children may, of course, contain more than one who could be so named. If my suspicions about the reality of the relationship between myself and IIC at the time of my experiment have any validity, it would seem that a high ratio of outsiders may indicate a high level of suppressed hostility against the teacher. Perhaps Elinor, Daphne, Pauline and even the aggressive Brenda could more easily have been assimilated if the form had not, at times, so strongly wished to get rid of me.

Now the relations between a class and its teacher are never simple—never either wholly positive or wholly negative. And the roles that certain children find themselves taking can sometimes arise out of this very complexity. There is, for every class, a basic problem of how to contain the apparently irreconcilable needs of the group: the need to preserve the teacher as the good object and to destroy him as the bad object. This conflict is implicit in all relationships with authority, and stems from the earliest feelings about the good and bad mother. Thus, in a class which has a basically good relationship with the teacher, the aggressive feelings may be contained and expressed on behalf of the group by the 'bad boy' in the class. Unconsciously, his classmates share some of the hostile feelings towards the teacher that he, as a person, has a need to express. But on the conscious level they dissociate themselves from his behaviour. It is easier to repudiate him than to admit that they too at times have antagonistic impulses against a teacher whom they basically like and so they project this unacknowledged hostility into the most aggressive member of the group. Conversely, in a class that has a basically hostile and destructive attitude to the teacher, it is not uncommon to find that there is one member who stands apart from the general attack and is allowed to do so. Thus, he carries for the rest the residual sympathy for the teacher that ensures the teacher's survival: but he has to pay for this privilege by being labelled derisively as 'the good boy' or 'the square' or the 'teacher's pet'.

There is no simple answer to the problems of isolation and rejection. We have to recognize that the causes are multiple. We have seen that some of our lonely pupils may be regarded as carrying for the group those universal feelings of inadequacy and isolation which writers like Erich Fromm[1] and Paul Halmos[2] regard as part of the human lot. We have seen that others— already by an unlucky chance set apart from the group in some way—may be pushed a little further out towards the boundaries of the group, perhaps as a substitute for the teacher, whom it does not seem expedient to try to exclude; or they may be used unconsciously as targets on which the hostile feelings towards the teacher may be displaced. And we have seen, lastly, that by an act of projection, a group may ensure that some member will express for the rest the feelings that seem out of tune with the dominant mood, and in so doing be partly dispossessed by the group.

These problems are rarely to be attributed totally to the personality of the child or totally to the unkindness of the group. It seems that there are certain individuals who have what Bion calls a 'valency' for flight, just as certain others have a valency for dependence or fight or pairing. The isolate repeatedly takes flight from the realities of the social situation around him, and

1. Fromm, Erich (1942) *The Fear of Freedom*, London: Routledge & Kegan Paul (paperback edition 1960).
2. Halmos, op. cit.

the group, while not actually expelling him, unconsciously or deliberately keeps him on the edge of things. In the long run, however, even children may come to have some perception of what they are doing to these only partially accepted fellow-pupils. Given time, in a teaching climate that is sufficiently permissive to allow the inner life of the group to develop, they will begin to feel concern for the lonely person in their midst, and will look for ways to make amends. And if this climate allows aggressive feelings to emerge in the context of work and through the relationship between teacher and class, the need for scapegoats is likely to diminish.

In a good primary-school the importance of personal relationships is often visibly apparent in the way the children are seated in the classroom; and because teaching is far less tied to special subjects, the primary-school time-table allows for similar flexibility in the use of time, We have to recognize that administrative arrangements play an important part in determining what kind of relationships can be developed, both between the teacher and the class as a group and between the children themselves. And the quality of these relationships affects, in its turn, the quality of intellectual learning that is going on. In the next two chapters we shall consider how the physical setting and the time framework are having their effects on the emotional and intellectual experiences of secondary-school pupils and their teachers.

CHAPTER FIVE

The Physical Setting and its Influence

I. THE CLASSROOM LAY-OUT AND ITS EFFECT ON LEARNING

The traditional image of the teacher dies hard. Certainly to most members of the public, and probably to most of his pupils, he figures as the person who should be the focus of all eyes, the central authority who tends either to be asking all the questions or supplying all the answers, the presiding adult through whom all communication must go. Is it the conventional arrangement of desks in straight lines that is responsible for the persistence of this image? Or is the teacher image responsible for perpetuating the desk arrangement? It is hard to say. The pattern has simply become familiar. Many teachers would feel lost without it; and the very pupils who most resent being penned in desks might resist most stubbornly any attempt on the part of a newcomer to change the convention.

Some years ago I heard a young American high-school teacher describing how she and her classmates in a twelfth-grade class (comparable to an English sixth form) set their faces against a young history teacher who tried to base his teaching on project work and arranged his classroom to facilitate group planning and discussion. So successful was their opposition that he soon felt himself obliged to admit defeat and resume the spoon-feeding to which they had been accustomed. On another occasion an English teacher recalled to me her experiences as a staff member in one of the Cambridge Village Colleges, during the war, where, among other innovations, an English room had been set up like a university seminar room: desks had been dispensed with entirely, and the chairs provided had extended left arm-rests to accommodate books and papers. Far from responding with pleasure to this unschool-like atmosphere, far from seeing the new-style chairs as symbols of their near-adult status, the pupils (who were in their mid-teens) saw them as objectionable and menacing, and complained openly, at first, that they did not like the room. To take a third example: a student who was doing her term's teaching practice in a small country grammar school was given permission to take a small fourth-year group into the sixth-form room in the new wing for a series of discussion lessons on twentieth-century war poetry. The room was attractively decorated and had been furnished with comfortable fireside chairs. The sixth form were delighted with it and proud of the status it conferred on them as near-adults, with something like a common-room of their own. But the fourth-form boys and girls who were allowed to borrow it, far from feeling relaxed and free to talk more spontaneously and naturally as the teacher had hoped they would, were for the first two or three periods very shy and ill at ease. It turned out that they had to *learn* to accept comfortable and grown-up-looking surroundings and to rise to the demands of a more adult relationship with a teacher.

How can we prevent the familiar visual image of the class-room from becoming so set in the pupil's mind that any departure from it will constitute a threat? Why, after all, should it be assumed than an arrangement of desks that is appropriate for the work going on in one room is equally appropriate for the work going on next door? Must all classrooms look exactly alike?

Consider how the variety of activity patterns in five first-year or second-year classes might be expressed visually in the arrangement of the classroom furniture. In Room 1, where a test is going on, the traditional arrangement of rows of desks will obviously be appropriate. In Room 2, however, where a class is working in groups, the desks have been pushed together in fours to make little tables, at which the children are seated face to face so that they can communicate with the minimum of noise and difficulty. In Room 3, a panel is presenting a pre-pared reading from a novel. Six members of the class are seated at the teacher's table as a platform party, while the others are sitting on chairs in a double or treble semi-circle, the desks being temporarily stacked round the walls. In Room 4, the desks have been arranged in a large, hollow rectangle, and the whole class is seated at this in council formation. One of the pupils acts as chairman, sitting at the middle of the top table, with a pupil secretary on his right; his job is to help the class arrive at certain decisions concerning the allocation of tasks for a history project.

In Room 5, a French lesson is under way. The chairs have been set out in lines, two down each side of the room facing inwards; the teacher is working from the back of the room with a projector and a tape recorder; the screen is at the front and there is plenty of space down the middle of the room. The children are seated so that they can easily look either at him or at the screen. Later in the lesson he will be calling members of the class out into the space near the front to carry out various actions in relation to each other and to him.[1]

Each of these arrangements presupposes a different kind of communication to be at the heart of the lesson. Moreover, in each the role played by the teacher is different. The teacher in the first is simply an invigilator. In the second there is no one leader, though the teacher is available to give help or advice to any group needing it. In the third room one group is responsible for communicating something of interest to the rest of the class, and the teacher is really part of this group's audience and, in fact, sits with the audience. In the fourth room the teacher is a committee member, working under the chairmanship of one of the pupils, though recognized as a member with special skills and knowledge of resources and with a special teaching role in the group. In the fifth room the teacher is himself communicating some new information to the class, helping them to increase their skill in a foreign language and using mechanical aids that will enable them to judge their own achievements objectively.

It is obvious that the actual process of communication between pupils, as well as from pupils to teacher, will be affected in some way by the physical arrangements in these different rooms. What, then, are the actual day-to-day effects of the conventional arrangement of desks on the children who occupy them? Being entirely teacher-centred, this arrangement impedes natural communication between pupils in different parts of the room. It almost encourages shy children to be inarticulate and to rely on the teacher to be their interpreter. The girl who answers a question or offers a comment from the front of the room may be quite inaudible to those sitting behind her, and she will certainly be unable to see their reaction to what she says. The boy who speaks from a seat near the back will probably be heard by the rest of the class, since he will have to use

1. As recommended in C.R.E.D.I.F. (1958) *Voix et Images*, Paris: Didier, p. xxx.

more volume in order to be heard by the teacher; but he will be little better informed than the girl at the front about the reactions of his fellow-pupils, since he will be looking, for the most part, at the backs of their heads. Some children enter cheerfully into the competition to secure the teacher's attention and approval. Others find the whole situation threatening and become intellectually crippled by it. Others, of course, prefer to form their own systems of communication in their own part of the classroom.

How many children are prevented from playing a full part in the classroom by sheer mistrust of their own verbal skill in these difficult circumstances? Even as adults, most of us experience these feelings from time to time, when we hesitate to enter a discussion following a public lecture or to express our views at a meeting. Now, an adult discussion can be facilitated to a remarkable degree by the simple expedient of rearranging the lecture room so that the usual rows of chairs facing the speaker give way to some kind of semi-circular or horseshoe formation, which enables members of the audience to face one another as well as the speaker. Yet the school classroom, in which most teachers are trying to encourage the articulate exchange of knowledge and ideas, clings to a physical arrangement that inhibits it.

Admittedly, rapid re-organization of a room is possible only if the desks are light, flat-topped and stackable. Admittedly, teachers have to work with the furniture they happen to have: and in some of the older schools they and their pupils are still having to struggle with old battered-looking desks, perhaps heavy with ironmongery, perhaps fastened permanently to benches, frequently cursed with sloping lids, and almost invariably so clumsy that children cannot easily move them from one part of the room to another. Even in the old buildings, however, rooms can sometimes be used to better advantage than they are. And in the new ones, where desks are a great deal more portable, the traditional arrangement in straight rows facing the teacher's table has changed scarcely at all. Sometimes the regrouping of a class does not call for any shifting of furniture, but merely for a slightly unusual use of the furniture as it stands. Opportunities can easily be missed, especially in a situation that does not at first sight look very promising.

In the examples that follow, we see a number of young teachers, engaged in a term of school practice, a little unsure of their right to do anything unexpected with furniture and anxious to conform to what is expected of them as students in training rather than as fully-fledged staff members. Sometimes, perhaps because of the uncertainty about their status, they fail to see how a class can be redistributed in a room or how a room intended for one kind of lesson can be adapted for another. Occasionally they do something that looks unorthodox and find that the action has surprisingly welcome results.

On one occasion I see a lower-sixth-form class taken by an English specialist in a rather large needlework room. Eight girls are assembled for a lesson on Sheridan's play *The Rivals*. Miss N., as any of us might have done, seats herself at the rather high teacher's desk, itself elevated on a platform. The girls are distributed between three of the six long heavy work tables, each of which has a sewing machine fixed to one end of it. Three girls are sitting at the second front table on the left, three at the second front one on the right, and the other two at the table behind that. It seems hardly possible for nine more or less adult people to be seated more awkwardly for any kind of discussion. Miss N. has to look from side to side as though she were umpiring a tennis match, and she can hardly avoid taking upon herself the task of asking all the questions and making all the decisions. After a recapitulation of events, the scene is staged in a narrow space between the side of one long table and the platform on which the teacher's desk stands. One of the girls has it in her to give a very spirited performance and obviously enjoys her role; but as she has had no chance to plan her entrance or any of her moves with the others, she can do little with the part except use her voice as effectively as possible.

Throughout this lesson the girls, who are all about sixteen to seventeen, show no overt reaction either to being kept at arm's length during the preliminary discussion or to being given so little say in how the acting itself should be tackled. Indeed, it is fair to say that since they have chosen to sit spread out in this way, they have apparently wished to keep the teacher at arm's length and to avoid energetic cooperation with each other. Yet, as I watch them, I have the impression that they are feeling slightly frustrated without quite knowing why. I find myself regrouping them in imagination. I see the eight girls, with Miss N., sitting close together at one of those long tables, facing each other across the length and breadth of it, and planning vigorously, as a production group, how this scene can be staged, how the available space and furniture in the room can best be used, which member of the group should be given this role and which that, who should be the producer once the scene gets under way, and so on. When, at the end of the lesson, I ask one of the girls who has taken no part whether she thinks such a piece of production work could have been tackled by the group, she looks slightly surprised, considers for a moment and says: 'Well, I've never thought about it. I don't know. Perhaps we could.'

Occasionally a teacher will find himself faced with what looks like a difficult room to teach in, only to find that the very unusualness of the physical setting helps to turn a school-ridden class into a stimulating and quite adult seminar. An English specialist who had had great difficulty in getting her sixth form to talk about poetry when they were in an ordinary classroom, found that they were much easier to teach when they had to have their lesson in a library, where she and they sat round a table naturally as adults. Yet her earlier attempt to reduce the distance between herself and them by sitting on a desk with her feet on a chair had only increased the distance and had had no effect whatever on the quality of the discussion. Again, a man teaching in a boys' school, who had a sixth-form group twice a week for English, found that the lesson when they met in the dining-room, and sat round on benches in a rough oval between two of the tables, was far more lively and productive of ideas than the lesson for which a classroom was available.

This kind of improvisation is comparatively easy with a group of a dozen or so sixth-formers. But what happens when a middle-school class of more than thirty children are deprived of their usual classroom and have to move to a library, or to the dining-room or to a science laboratory? It was hardly surprising, perhaps, that Miss O. was filled with apprehension when she found that she had to take a current-affairs lesson in the junior library, where her thirty pupils would be sitting at small tables in groups of five or six; and that Mr P., a classics specialist, went to pieces when he unexpectedly had to teach his third form in a biology laboratory.

Both these teachers, presented with an unfamiliar and apparently threatening room, reacted, as many of us would have done, by trying to make it approximate as closely as possible to the conventional classroom to which they were accustomed. The current-affairs lesson could have been handled in such a way as to turn the grouping at the small tables into an advantage; but for this to have happened Miss O. would have had to realize that some division of responsibility between these groups was necessary, and—more important—to have had faith in the ability of each group to take on a limited task for the lesson and report its achievement to the other groups at the end. Instead of this she struggled to conduct the kind of lesson she had planned for a formal classroom, and had to use up a good deal of energy in forestalling conversation between the children sitting together in such close proximity at the various tables.

Mr P.—the classics specialist in the biology laboratory—faced a much greater difficulty. He too reacted by trying to do in this room what he would have done in an ordinary classroom. So, not unnaturally, he took up his position behind the master's demonstration bench, thereby robbing himself of all flexibility of movement. The boys, also not unnaturally, sat at the work benches in such a way that about a third of the class had their backs to Mr P. As the lesson went on, they became more and more hostile to him and he gradually lost control, reciprocating their hostility. In this very awkward situation he might have fared much better if he could have improvised a completely unexpected seating arrangement, perhaps collecting all the boys in a wide circle on stools round two of the benches, sitting on a stool at one end of one of them himself, and relying on informality and closeness rather than on formality and separation. By this means he would have emphasized the unusualness of the situation, somehow turning it into something rather pleasant, and drawing his class into a kind of cheerful conspiracy with himself to defeat the feelings of discomfort and deprivation into which their loss of a classroom had temporarily plunged them.

Even given a group small enough to be handled in tutorial fashion, young teachers rarely think of the shape the group makes as it distributes itself about the room. In this situation the problem is one of compression rather than of expansion. The smaller the group the more intimate it can be; the seating should emphasize this difference in the relationship between the members, and it should enhance the possibility of seminar-like methods of work.

On one occasion I found myself in a large airy classroom in a new comprehensive school, watching a modern linguist (Miss Q.) teaching a group of nine rather backward fourth-formers who were making a serious, if belated, attempt to study French. They worked with her for five periods a week, moving about from one free classroom to another. In the particular room in which I saw them, the desks were so arranged that in a large class about half the pupils would have been sitting along three sides of the room, facing the centre, and the rest would have been in rows across the middle. The six girls in this small group had chosen to sit along the window wall, at right angles to the teacher's table, and the three boys were sitting across the room in the second row from the front. Miss Q. therefore found herself in a very curious position in relation to her class, just off the corner of the angle formed by the girls' axis along the window and the boys' axis across the front. The effect of this formation as the lesson proceeded was significant: Miss Q., quite unconsciously, gave the boys more and more of her attention; towards the end of the lesson, the girl at the far end of the girls' axis was beginning to look lost and rather neglected, though she was not inattentive; and the only girls who seemed to get any share of Miss Q.'s attention were the two at her end of the axis, sitting almost level with the boys. Miss Q. was astonished, later, that it had not occurred to her to find a more satisfactory seating arrangement for this rather intimate and earnest little group. She realized, on reflection, that during their wanderings from room to room neither she nor the pupils had ever really paused to consider what might be the most effective way for ten people to sit down and work together.

Such failure to notice the effect of physical grouping on communication and even on the emotional climate of a lesson is not uncommon. I find in my notes, jotted down during students' lessons from time to time, a diagram of a class of fifteen fifth-form pupils, also studying French, scattered to the extremities of a fairly large classroom, presumably occupying the places they would normally have occupied when the whole class was present, and with similarly disastrous effects on the lines of communication.

The problem is, of course, more complex than it looks. Like the girls in the needlework room, these boys were in a sense wishing to keep the teacher at arm's length. And if he had proposed that they should leave their own desks to form a closer group it is more than likely that his request would have aroused immediate resentment, even though the reorganization would ultimately have made for pleasanter and more efficient working conditions. Once again, we are back to the problem of ambivalence which was discussed in the first chapter. The wish to be close to the teacher and to work co-operatively with him is in conflict with the wish to draw away from him and so avoid sharing the responsibility for the carrying out of the task.

There is also another kind of conflict, which, as we have already seen, is always present to some extent in a group—the conflict between the conscious, sophisticated aims of the individual and the unspoken, primitive aims of the group. The fifth formers in this classroom, with an important examination ahead, did not, presumably, want to waste their time. Each must have wanted the best possible working conditions with this teacher; as individuals they must have been well aware of the absurdity of remaining scattered all over the room as they were. Yet the group contrived to keep them in these positions and even prevented the teacher from taking any action to improve the situation.

Sometimes it is one individual pupil who, in the end, suffers from an inefficient classroom grouping. In another lesson, this time with twelve members of a fourth-form class, Miss R. is working orally through a French prose, writing certain phrases on the board. For the most part she is encouraging them to regard this as a trial run through a task which they will be tackling independently for themselves for homework. These pupils are not too widely scattered, and up the middle of the room from front to back, there is a block of desks in threes, which makes for a fairly close concentration in one part of the room. But one member of the group, who is isolated at the back of the room, sits rather huddled over her desk, and although she raises her hand quite often in the first half of the lesson, she gradually gives up signalling her willingness to answer questions as time goes on, feeling apparently that the teacher has forgotten her. The fact is that from the position that Miss R. occupies for most of the lesson this girl can hardly be seen at all, though I, from my seat at the desk level with hers on the far side of the room, am well placed to watch her reactions and the fall in the barometer of her attentiveness. Towards the end of the period a chance move by Miss R. in the direction of the windows brings this girl suddenly into view, and she at last gets her chance to take some part in the lesson.

Interestingly enough, what inexperienced teachers are most often told is that they ought to bring their pupils near the front of the classroom in the interest of control and discipline. This implies that the rearrangement is to be made primarily for the benefit of the teacher; and of course with some classes the need for control will be the most crying need. The notion that a different kind of grouping, even with a well-behaved class, might in fact be pleasanter for the pupils, or that the teacher is seeking a physical grouping in which his own position can be less dominating rather than more so, is seldom given the prominence that it merits.

Merely bringing the group to the front of the room is not really the most important part of the operation. Nor does it necessarily, of itself, solve disciplinary problems if they exist. Another modern linguist, Miss S., trying to conduct oral work with a particularly restless group of eight first-year children, brings them, sensibly enough, to the front of the room, but finds herself with a row of meek little girls in front of her table, flanked on both sides by two pairs of boisterous little boys, who success-fully engage most of her attention simply by demanding it noisily, first from one end of the row and then from the other. In fact, the pair of boys on the left are sitting just behind the girls, while the pair on the right are sitting just in front of the girls. Thus the situation is made even more difficult by the fact that the class, small as it is, is really operating as three sub-groups (the docile quartet and the two noisy pairs) so that Miss S. never has a unified group working with her. This she might have had if she had brought the children together into a semi-circle, or even seated them with her at her own table.

As with younger classes, a changed use of furniture may even help to solve a disciplinary problem with truculent older pupils. This kind of problem is, of course, extremely unlikely to arise in any sixth-form group; but it can very easily arise with day-release classes in technical colleges, where groups of young people in their late teens may react violently against the all too familiar classroom situation that they thought to have left behind when they left school at the age of fifteen. One teacher who was doing a term's practice at a technical college encountered such a group and handled the difficulty in rather an unusual way.

The group consisted of about a dozen young men of about seventeen or eighteen. Their attitude was uncooperative, to say the least: they were noisy and outspoken; and two of them were hostile to the point of rudeness. They were being taught in a small room crowded with desks which could not possibly be moved into any new formation. Accordingly Mr T. obtained permission to move his class into a small staff common room near-by which was not, as it happened, needed by any of his colleagues during that period, and in which there were two fairly large tables. He seated his students round these tables in such a way that the two most difficult members were separated. He himself hovered between the two tables trying to keep some control over the discussion without exerting the sort of school-room authority that would only have increased the hostility between certain individuals and himself. The most significant thing that happened was that the students themselves began to take over the two most difficult members—as they would never have been able to do in the old classroom. By moving the class into a different physical setting, Mr T. had, first, given them more comfortable working conditions; but, more important still, he had shifted the emphasis from the teacher–class conflict to the conflict within the group. Thus the behaviour problem became the group's responsibility; and in deciding how to deal with this, the group had to decide whether they were really in that college to learn and grow or to waste time and deteriorate. The move out of a room that looked like a school classroom into a room that looked like an adult common room may well have had some effect also on the decision they made.

2. RITUAL AND SYMBOLISM

There seems to be little doubt that furniture has symbolic significance as well as functional significance for pupils of all ages. Desks and tables, chairs normally occupied by teachers, chairs normally occupied by pupils—all these stand for certain kinds of ritual and for certain expectations about roles and relationships in schools. Some of these rituals are sophisticated, others are primitive; some facilitate adult behaviour, others perpetuate childish behaviour.

Compare, for example, two school dining rooms, both in secondary schools. One has a high table where the staff eat and two rows of long refectory tables, where the pupils eat; the other has a network of octagonal tables, of which two or three, not easily identifiable, happen to be staff tables. Each of these dining rooms has its rituals. In the first, the ritual may involve frequent orders and reprimands from the high table, echoed by similar orders and reprimands from the heads of the tables on the floor; the majority are expected to obey the instructions of the few; the noise is usually unbearable. In the second dining room, no one appears to be giving any orders; the eight people at each table appear to be jointly responsible for fetching, serving and clearing away the meal, and to have some well-understood routine for dealing with these tasks; the noise is surprisingly low for the number of people in the hall. There is no need to say which of these is the more adult situation, though there is no difference between the numbers of people eating at the same time in the two dining rooms.

Again, the ritual in a classroom at nine o'clock may suggest a benevolent autocracy or a genuine pupil–teacher relationship. Recently I talked to a man who was teaching in a school where a twenty-minute form period was allowed at the beginning of every school day. The conventional image of this form period suggests a form master spending most of his time, if not all of it, sitting at his table, doing the routine tasks of form administration and talking across the table, if time allows, to the class as a whole. This teacher, on the contrary, had been making a point of keeping right away from his own table during those twenty-minute form periods. The boys had their own arrangements for marking the register and collecting the dinner money, doubtless using his table for the purpose. He, meanwhile, would sit in a different part of the room every day, talking with a little group of boys about any subject that happened to be in people's minds, and in this way getting to know his boys as individuals, and also getting to know something about the groups within his class.

Another ritual, described to me by a history master in a boys' public school, had a more direct bearing on classwork. Mr U. told me how he had deliberately used a certain ritual with chairs to symbolize two rather different roles in relation to the same sixth-form group. This was a school which recognized the near-adult status of its older pupils by providing for them a room quite unlike the conventional classroom and furnished with a large table instead of desks. It happened in one year that Mr U. had a sixth-form group both for 'A' level history and for current affairs, and that quite a number of boys were in both classes. In his history periods, which might have been described as directed seminars, he would sit at one end of the table and lead the discussion fairly strenuously. But in the current-affairs periods, which took the form of free discussion on agreed topics, he would sit half-way down one side of the table, and would expect more of the leadership to come from the boys. The boys who attended both these classes easily learned to associate the two chairs he occupied with the two somewhat different roles that he carried. As it turned out, they were also able to react spontaneously, and quite appropriately, to a sudden change of role in one of these situations.

About half-way through the spring term, Mr U. handed over his current-affairs period to a student who was doing his teaching practice in the school and who had been observing this class for some weeks. As an observer the student, too, had sat at the table—on the opposite side to Mr U., near one corner. When the day came for the student to take over, nothing had actually been said about where he should sit; yet, without any pre-planning, Mr U. went over to the seat which had hitherto been occupied by the student, and the student, coming in a minute or two later, went equally naturally to the seat hitherto occupied by Mr U. The boys immediately accepted the student in the role of staff member, and only about half-way through the lesson realized that Mr U. was sitting at the table, quietly observing what was going on, as, up to that day, the student had been in the habit of doing.

By ritualizing the use of these three positions at the table, this teacher had evidently been able to establish a pattern within which behaviour could be flexible because the important roles were clearly understood. He had also made it possible for a student to take over his role in his presence, without having to offer any elaborate explanations which might have weakened the student's position by emphasizing his junior status. The boys were thus able to respond to the student quite naturally, when the master and the student changed roles.

It is not children only who read such meanings into the way

we use furniture to express certain kinds of relationship. The parent in the headmaster's study feels the nature of the interview to be different according to whether he speaks to her from behind his desk or comes over to her side of the room and sits in an arm-chair similar to the one that she occupies. The student in the tutor's room feels the nature of his essay tutorial to be different according to whether the tutor remains at his desk or moves away from it to a chair more like the one he offers the student. The role of the seminar leader is seen to be more dictatorial if he conducts the discussion from a special staff member's chair and less dictatorial if he sits on the same kind of chair as all the other members of the group. On the other hand, a student who is reading a paper to the seminar may feel more confident if he is given the privilege of sitting in a more important-looking chair than anyone else on this occasion. Another may feel this distinction to be threatening rather than supporting and may prefer to sit like the others.

Now however such children may at first dislike and even oppose modifications to the 'normal' use of furniture when these are carried out by their teachers, they make use of symbolic and ritualistic innovations themselves when they wish to communicate with their teachers on an emotional level. The novelist G. W. Target describes a particularly violent form of this kind of reaction in *The Teachers*,[1] where one class expresses its disapproval and disgust against its form master by wrecking the classroom in the most sadistic and objectionable way it can devise. Although no individual or sub-group within the class admits responsibility for the outrage, the message to the master concerned is clear and unequivocal and leads to a considerable amount of heart-searching in the staff group as a whole. This, of course, is a fictitious example. But it has its counterpart in acts of aggression against youth-club premises and, occasionally against school premises. These attacks are often unrelated to any thefts or self-gain, and appear to be directed more against society, or schools, or teachers in general than against any one person in particular. During the war I myself taught in a school that was burgled one night by a group of boys who, as far as was known, had no connection with the school at all. Apart from a few pencils, nothing was stolen, but drawers and cupboards in the headmaster's room were rifled, papers and other objects

1. Target, G. W. (1960) *The Teachers*, Harmondsworth: Penguin Books.

being left scattered all over the room; the housekeeper found that her white overall had been ruined by an ink drawing down the back and a ludicrous inscribed message from 'the Saint'; and a pair of shoes that a member of the staff had left in the cloakroom has been filled up with Harpic and water and made completely unwearable. A meaningless series of pranks, apparently. Yet the gesture must have had some meaning to those who made it.

When these hostile acts are committed openly in the school classroom by children who, at other times, show considerable benevolence towards their teachers, it is important that the adult should try to understand the feelings that give rise to them—perhaps even to tolerate some acting out of such feelings. In the formally structured classroom accommodation of our times, the obvious item of furniture to be used by children in this way is the blackboard. In the first chapter of this book we saw how a group of third-year boys and girls expressed, in an ambiguous message on the blackboard, their confused and highly ambivalent feelings towards the guitar-playing geography master. In the third chapter we saw how a first-year boy expressed similarly ambivalent feelings on behalf of his class by writing 'ABK is mad' first on the blackboard and then on the dusty corridor window.

Now what most of us are tempted to do in moments of crisis like this is to concentrate our attention on the individual whom we know or suspect to have inscribed the message on the board. But here again we may be dealing with a group phenomenon; and it may be that the problem should be discussed at the group level rather than at the individual level. If the action of the one boy is tolerated by the other twenty-nine, it becomes to some extent a public statement. It therefore represents some feeling that is shared and cannot be attributed only to the child who has dared to give symbolic expression to it.

My own memories go back to an even more disturbing occasion when, as a young and still far too shockable teacher, I was subjected to a test-out by a bright, rebellious fourth form in a boys' school during the war. This incident probably left me a good deal more shaken than either the guitar player or the 'mad' teacher quoted above. I arrived in the classroom one day to find on the blackboard a large, crude drawing of a naked male figure. In the general scuffle that greeted my entrance, it seemed to me that one boy only—a boy I particularly disliked —had been out of his place.

If I had been a man, it is probable that the figure on the blackboard would have been female. And we have to recognize that a test-out of this kind will take different forms according to whether the teacher is a man or a woman, whether the class is co-educational or single-sex, and if the latter, whether boys or girls. What, in principle, does the teacher do, faced with this kind of demonstration? Does he express anger, or shock, or pain, and embark on a futile attempt to discover which member of the form is responsible for the drawing? Does he pretend not to notice it or have it rubbed off the board as casually as if it were merely a diagram left up from the previous lesson? Or does he abandon his prepared lesson and try, quietly, and without embarrassment or rancour, to get the class to talk about the feelings or preoccupations or anxieties that give rise to such a demonstration of hostility against an adult?

I wish I could say that I, in my wisdom, had been able to take the third course on that occasion, or even that I had had the presence of mind to take the second. But I have to admit that my reaction was more like the first. I got through the lesson somehow, and in time this class and I did manage to establish a good working relationship. But I believe now that we could have done so a great deal sooner if I had been mature enough to see behind the action of that one boy (whichever member of the form it was) to the more important message the whole group needed me to receive. I believe now that the real protest was against my failure to treat them as adults at a time when a woman who was prepared to make them feel like men could have achieved a great deal with them. If, instead of reacting with panic and anger, I had been able to make them talk openly about the feelings that lay behind this incident—meeting their immaturity with maturity, to use Dr Winnicott's phrase[1]—we might have achieved a more genuine understanding instead of the uneasy armed neutrality that was the immediate sequel to it.

It is rare, in fact, for a whole class to act out feelings of this kind against a teacher. More often one member is left to express the feelings that all, to some extent, share. On the whole, children accept the teacher's rituals fairly unquestioningly.

1. Winnicott, D. W. (October 1962) 'Adolescence', *New Era*, vol. 43.

They obligingly write only the expected words or drawings on the board, and they preserve the normal arrangement of the furniture. In fact, as we have seen, attempts on the part of a teacher to change the conventional arrangement of desks in rows facing the front of the classroom are likely to be met with stubborn resistance. Yet in moments of rebellion or strong hostility, a class (or an individual representing the class) will very often express defiance by breaking some established ritual over the use of furniture.

One example of this is the bizarre situation, perhaps subconsciously dreaded by every teacher, of the class which has turned all the desks round so that they face the back of the room. In fact this situation has been known to occur outside the more hilarious works of fiction about the secondary modern schools; and when it does occur it may be far from hilarious for either the teacher or the class. If the teacher perceives this as a light-hearted joke of the April-Fools'-Day order, the most appropriate action may be simply to prick the bubble by walking to the back of the room and conducting the lesson from there— thus replying with a counter-joke. But if the episode occurs as part of a gradually deteriorating situation between the teacher and the class, it is probable that the feelings expressed by it go very deep; and what the class really needs from the teacher is time to work through the conflicts that are being dramatised. Mere disciplinary action may restore the desks and chairs to their normal positions without touching the underlying causes of the rebellion.

When this kind of impasse is reached in a classroom it may appear that survival depends on quick action by the teacher, summary punishment of the ringleaders and prompt restoration of the usual visual pattern of the classroom. Yet this sequence of events, though restoring the *status quo*, may conceal for ever the real or imaginary grievance that is blocking communication between teacher and class. More important still, the positive elements in the relationship may never have the chance to re-affirm their existence in a spontaneous way. The official action drives the wedge more firmly in, where a pause might have enabled the class members themselves to loosen it.

3. MEMORIES AND ANTICIPATIONS

We have been thinking about the conscious and unconscious uses to which teachers and children put their school furniture. What of the effects of the buildings themselves—their oldness or newness, their datedness or modernity—on learning processes and on the relationships within the school?

The inequalities between schools—simply in terms of buildings and furniture—are enormous. And in looking at buildings and furniture we are looking at more than expenditure or at the gaiety and comfort that money can buy: we are facing inequalities in the kind of educational experiences that are possible for the pupils and their teachers. Schools, of course, are far more than bricks and mortar, or steel and concrete, and we all know that there are many teachers working in cheerless old buildings who are creating for their pupils a concept of education that is very different from that suggested by the school architecture of the last century. And so a child who has learned to love an apparently dreary old building may not, at first, find much compensation for his sense of loss even in a cheerful new building. It is not the surrounding fabric that determines the culture of a school, but the people living in it.

At any time of transition a child is being pulled both forwards and backwards. For the great majority, of course, the most dramatic transfer occurs at the age of eleven, when they move from primary to secondary school. And it is important to realize that a child's feelings about this change are going to be determined as much by what he leaves behind in the old building as by what he finds in the new one. He may have come from a shabby, badly furnished building in the centre of the city, or from a new, well-equipped building on the outskirts.

A moment's reflection is enough to remind us, then, how different in quality these acts of transition must be for the thirty to forty members of any class of eleven-year-olds. Simply to say that all these children are undergoing a move from a primary school to a secondary school is saying nothing at all about the realities of their various experiences. What looks new and exciting to one child may look intolerably dreary to another. What this girl sees as a prison, that one may see as a haven of peace. To one boy, remembering the clump of trees and the slope of grass he could see from his last classroom window, this famous old grammar school may look as dark and sombre as the heavy desk he is sitting at; to the boy next to him, sharing this desk, the situation looks quite different, for he knows that there are playing fields near-by, even if he cannot see them at present, whereas the school from which he has come had nothing but a small, enclosed asphalt yard. To the boys sitting in front, the cumbersome desk is in itself something to wonder at, since they have come from a school where classrooms were furnished with light tables, which could be put together in several ways or could be moved away or stacked against the wall when space was needed for acting, or singing or painting at easels.

And so we could go on. For although these examples are imaginary, they represent aspects of reality and verbalize a few of many possible combinations of past and present experience. In fact, coming to a new school is rather like learning a new language. The difficulties encountered in the new language arise out of the habits formed in speaking the native language: what is difficult for a German learning English may not be difficult for a Spaniard. And so it is with a child learning the language of a new school: he comes to it with habits of thinking and feeling already learned in another school.

In these days of fairly rapid building programmes, it not infrequently happens that a whole school has to move from an old building to a new one. Such a school may be an object of envy to neighbouring schools that see no prospect of escape from shabby old premises. Yet to the staff and children who are involved in such a move, the experience is unlikely to be wholly pleasant. A visitor may expect to find, in the new building, a mood of elation. What he may find, however, is a mood of depression and disappointment, accompanied by a good deal of nostalgia for the (now) loved old building. Complaints about the new one may be legion. The position of the headmaster's room and the office, the narrowness of the staircase, the inadequacy of the locker space, the mistakes in the design of the apparently splendid stage—all these may excite loud comment. Little or nothing may be said about the lightness and airiness of the classrooms, the extended laboratory and gymnasium accommodation, the pleasant views from the windows, the more spacious and attractive hall. And there may even be some envy of the school that has now taken over the old building. Why should this be? What are the new buildings, so often described as 'luxury palaces' by the public, really like compared with the old ones that they are gradually superseding?

Certainly there has been some change in the design of certain rooms—a move away from the old idea of central supervision and towards the idea of group autonomy. Libraries now may incorporate alcoves or private bays, where pupils can sit and work without feeling that they are constantly under the eye of the teacher. The domestic science room has its flat, in which small groups of girls (four or six at a time) can spend a morning, perhaps a full day, perhaps even a week, doing the cleaning, the washing and ironing, the planning, cooking and serving of meals, as these tasks would be done in a well-organized home. Science laboratories suggest less emphasis on demonstration by the teacher and more on experimenting by the pupils. The school hall may be designed so that one end of it can be partitioned off as a drama room, with different floor levels or movable rostra that enable children to work separately in small groups or together in large groups or to perform scenes to one another, either in an arena-type stage or on a raised stage.

On the other hand, the changes are not always for the better. The hall may be open on to a corridor at one side, so that a drama class is constantly subject to the feeling of being overlooked, perhaps disapprovingly, by passers-by. Classrooms in the newest buildings have become more standardized, if anything, as have corridors and staircases. Part of the charm of the better old buildings—the ones that have some of the pleasant characteristics of a rambling old private house—is that nearly every room has its own special size and shape and character. In the old school building that we have left behind, 'Room 8' may have suggested a particular place with a distinctive individuality, rather than a mere number on one of a series of identical doors leading into identical square boxes as it does here in the new building.

We still await the real revolution in school architecture, the kind of revolution that has been foreshadowed in the Newsom Report.[1] We need far greater variety in the size and equipment of rooms than we are yet getting even in the newest schools. The concept of the standard classroom is out of date. We need buildings that include small tutorial and seminar rooms with appropriate furniture for work based on discussion and enquiry,

1. *Half our Future*, op. cit., Chapter 11, 'Building for the Future', pp. 87–97.

along with a variety of workshops and rooms specially designed for activities such as music, film, language work with audio-visual aids and projects that cut across different subjects in the social studies fields. New buildings, as the Newsom Committee pointed out, are still being designed to express current practice, whereas they ought to be designed to meet the teaching needs of the future.

And so it is perhaps not surprising to find that a new building may arouse mixed feelings in those who move into it from a familiar old building. It will have some obvious advantages; but it may prove less radically 'different' as a setting for work than it seemed to give promise of being, and so may fail to satisfy the expectations of its incoming teachers and pupils. Part of this sense of let-down, then, springs from a real sense that the new is not unreservedly an improvement on the old. At the same time, there may be an unacknowledged emotional problem too—one that is familiar to sociologists who have studied the effects of the transportation of families from condemned living quarters to new housing estates. It is not only old inconveniences and discomforts that are lost, but also old patterns of life and ways of thinking and feeling. The community seeks to rediscover its old way of life in quite new and unfamiliar premises, but some things do not fit any more. The old time-table seems unmanageable now that the physical shape of the school is different. Distances from one part of the school to another may be greater. The desks, perhaps, no longer contain books, and so the children have to remember to bring into the classroom all the books and equipment they need for a lesson, and as they frequently forget, new causes of friction suddenly come into existence. The school hall seems to call for a slightly different kind of assembly, the science laboratories for different kinds of science lessons, the new gymnasium for some changes in the planning of P.E. work.

The problem of making an old building a tolerable setting for school work demands powers of improvisation and adaptation. Teachers who are creating a happy and vigorous community in a grey old Victorian building are conscious daily that they are working against heavy odds and can measure their success against the physical disadvantages of the premises in which they work. Faced with a new building—even one that has glaring faults—they can no longer say: 'We are achieving this and this and this in spite of this old building!' They now have to say: 'Our new building offers us chances, at least in some areas of school life, to teach more flexibly; will we be able to use these opportunities, or will we be content to go on working in the old way, as if we were still struggling under the same dis-advantages?'

A change of surroundings is bound to call for some question-ing of old habits, some reformulation of aims and objectives, some willingness to abandon well-marked grooves. But flexibility of this kind depends as much on the organization of time as on the location and arrangement of rooms. Caught up in a sequence of forty-minute lessons, with the incoming teacher almost colliding with the outgoing class, a teacher is likely to content himself with the formal lay-out of desks and chairs, even if he now has furniture than can be moved easily, simply because he feels he has no time to alter it.

Time, like rooms and furniture, has to be distributed among the working groups in a school; and time also, though intan-gible, may come to symbolize strong feelings and may be manipulated by the groups and individuals who unconsciously wish to express those feelings. In the next chapter we will examine this other aspect of school organization, considering, first, how the regulation and disruption of school periods can affect relations between teachers and their classes and the work in which they are jointly engaged, and, secondly, how the whole concept of the time-table may need to be revised in the schools of the future.

CHAPTER SIX

Teachers, Pupils and Time Schedules

I. THE PARCELLING OUT OF TIME

Times and places are interwoven with uncompromising precision in the school time-table, or so it seems. Four or five times each morning, three or four times every afternoon, the shuttling of teachers and classes between rooms takes place, no matter what stage this English lesson has reached, no matter what is just being discovered in that chemistry laboratory, no matter what emotional crisis has just blown up in the classroom at the end of that corridor. Time is what must be chopped up into sizeable pieces and distributed equitably between forms, subjects, rooms and teachers—forty minutes here, forty minutes there, a double period for every form in the science laboratories, a whole afternoon for every year-group at the games field, and so on.

No-one really envies the deputy-headmaster or the senior mistress the job of constructing the time-table, and anyone who can succeed in producing a scheme that works smoothly on the first day of term will—deservedly—earn a round of applause. Yet, in judging the effectiveness of a time-table, is this the only valid criterion—that rooms, subjects and classes, neatly packaged together, should be accurately matched to units of time distributed over the week?

Of course no one will dispute that school time must be rationed. To put the matter in a different way, learning, in an institution of any size, must be held in a stable framework, and time is part of this framework. Many teachers, however, may wish to dispute the assumption that a time unit should be as short as forty minutes (the length of period most generally favoured in schools).

Where time is concerned, no less than where space is concerned, teachers and pupils have two conflicting needs. First, they need stability: they must know when things begin and end, who is entitled to what in the sharing-out process, what sort of commitments about time-keeping must be accepted. Secondly, they need room for manoeuvre: when a class meets with its teacher, they must be able to stay together long enough to warm up to the task, to make mistakes, to experiment, to consolidate. Whether we feel secure or not depends on the stability of the framework; whether we are able to grow and develop or not depends on the flexibility with which the framework can be used. Stability alone easily degenerates into rigidity, just as flexibility alone may degenerate into aimless meandering. Each needs the other if the system is to be kept alive.

To a secondary-school pupil, the process of familiarizing himself with the sequence of lessons that represents his time-table is little more than a sort of conditioning process. It is rare for one phase of learning in his school day to follow logically from another, or for any one of the teachers in the series he encounters to know what kind of lesson he has just come from, unless he and his companions are so hot and flushed that they have pretty obviously come from P.E.

To the visitor in the staff room, the composite time-table spread out on the wall may look like a miracle of administrative efficiency. Whether or not the aid of a computer has been involved, the impression is the same. The more clearly it identifies the five variables (teacher, class, subject, place and time) the more admiration it receives. It is common enough in these times to see in large comprehensive schools extremely ingenious time-tables, which use bands of coloured cardboard to represent the subjects in the curriculum and coloured drawing pins, lettered and numbered to represent teachers and rooms respectively. Thus it is possible, in a school with a nine-form entry and a staff of about seventy, to see at a glance where any one teacher is at any time in the day, what subject he is teaching if he is in a classroom and how many of his colleagues are also free if he is in the staff room.

Control of the total framework is essential if an organism as large as a school of fifteen hundred is to work efficiently. Yet there is something disquieting about the dissection of human knowledge that accompanies this dissection of time. Has not the sum-total of the pieces in the jig-saw puzzle become, somehow, more important than the meaning of the pattern? A displacement here and there, a switching of rooms, even an interchange of teachers may not make much difference to this meaning. Time has been divided up and justly dispensed: that is the great thing.

But has it? Is the system even as tidy as these remarks imply? Despite the efficiency of the formal arrangements found in most schools, fairness is not necessarily ensured. Take a dozen school time-tables and examine them, and all kinds of discrepancies begin to appear. It turns out that a secondary-school period may be anything from half an hour to eighty minutes, if we take into account the effect of doubling periods for certain subjects. Furthermore, some time-tables show a quite arbitrary variation between thirty-five and forty-minute periods, afternoon ones being shorter, or longer, than morning ones; and in some schools the first period of the day is always shorter than any other because assembly, scheduled officially to take ten minutes, always takes fifteen.

Consider what these discrepancies mean. 'Five periods a week of French' may mean two and a half hours a week in one school, three and three-quarter hours in another; this produces a difference, in any twelve-week term, of fifteen hours, about the length of a semester course, carrying one hour of credit, in an American university. Within the same school a form that happens to have all its lessons in the morning, when the periods last forty minutes, will have about twenty-five minutes longer than a form that happens to have all its lessons in the afternoon, when they last only thirty-five minutes; in a whole year, this discrepancy works out at about sixteen hours. Other similar irregularities will readily suggest themselves to teachers. One recently, discussing a student's time-table, pointed out that her particular form, by some curious trick of fate, the reason for which she did not know, had only four instead of the usual five lessons a week in French. This meant that she and her class lost at least twenty hours over the whole year. Again, how much time is lost in a school year by a class which has only two history lessons a week and which regularly loses about ten minutes of one of these because it happens to occur first thing on Monday morning, when school assembly is apt to take even longer than usual? And what about the lesson following P.E. in a system that allows no time between periods for moving from one part of the building to another?

In an educational system as competitive as ours, where a boy's future seems to depend almost exclusively on the marks he will ultimately get for his 'A' level papers, these apparently slight inequalities in the hand-out of time may be having quite interesting effects on decisions made by teachers in their class-rooms. One period a week less than the norm for French may mean the sacrifice of oral work, even though the teacher recognizes that good oral work is the basis of good language usage later; where a form has one of its history lessons foreshortened regularly by morning assembly, a film-strip may seem an unpardonable waste of time; mathematical models may seem like luxuries (or frivolities) in a class that has recently lost three periods because bad weather necessitated sending the younger children home early. For, curiously enough, a teacher who feels that time has been stolen from him by the administrative machine is quite likely to react by stealing from his pupils that part of his teaching programme that he knows they most enjoy, and indeed that he himself most enjoys.

Other small thefts of time, because they are so unpredictable, can arouse even stronger feelings than those which the teacher recognizes at the beginning of the school year and with which he may come to terms. The small thefts are those caused by the boys who bring the milk round in the middle of the morning, the messengers sent along by the school secretary to collect dinner numbers somewhere in the middle of the first lesson, the games master who comes in to read out the names of those required for swimming or cricket practice after school, the producer of the school play who sends round a notice about rehearsals, even the headmaster himself who comes in to give the teacher a message or ask a question.

We have all been guilty in our time of carrying out or putting into effect these predatory raids on time, and have thought little about it. Yet an interruption such as this can easily make a rent in a lesson which cannot be repaired. Someone is reading a poem to the class, after a carefully thought-out introduction, or the pupils are studying it silently and are only about half-way through the first reading; an experiment in the chemistry laboratory has just reached a crucial point and the children are tense with expectation; a music class is singing a song better than they have ever sung it before; a boy is struggling to improve his pronunciation of a French word or to get a construction right, and the whole class is on his side, no longer impatient with him as they so often have been but eagerly willing him to succeed; a discussion about sex problems is going on in a tough fourth-year class, and for the first time the boys are coming out into the open and showing some trust towards each other and towards the teacher. Such situations as these have to be striven for, by teacher and class together, and an interruption just when some objective is being reached robs them of far more than the thirty seconds to three minutes between the moment when the door opens to admit the intruder and the moment when it shuts again as he goes out.

Children actually dislike interruptions and distractions as much as their teachers do. They do not seek variety for variety's sake. A change of scene or a change of activity, far from being inevitably a welcome diversion, may be an infuriating disruption, which prevents them from coming to grips with a task that is just beginning to arouse their interest. Many teachers can still recall the experience of working in the London area during the autumn of 1940, when lessons were continually being interrupted by the air-raid warnings and the all-clear signals. I remember a school whose shelters consisted of sand-bagged cloisters, where the children had to sit back to back on old bus-seats. The repeated moves from classroom to shelter on the sound of a warning produced in the children a reaction not of fear but of irritation, as, paradoxically enough, did the all-clear that sent them back to the classrooms. The staff, who were all noting the same phenomenon, eventually decided that it would be less frustrating to let the children remain in the shelters, even though two or three classes had to occupy each cloister, and to attempt some continuous teaching rather than go on tolerating the repeated interruptions. In these conditions, it seemed, inconvenience in the surroundings was a reasonable price to pay for stability in the timing and duration of each lesson.

It may be, then, that we are quite wrong in assuming that the school time-table should be offering children and young people so much variety in every school day. How can we be so sure that it is better, even for an eleven-year-old, to tackle six or seven subjects between the hours of nine and four, and then do twenty-minute 'homeworks' on two or three of these after he has had his tea? Much of the experience of junior-school teachers would suggest that we are completely under-estimating the child's powers of concentration and completely over-estimating his ability to switch rapidly from one kind of learning to another.

Now it may well be that our devotion to this kind of time-table, with its hotch-potch of subjects packed into every school day, is setting up a vicious circle. It is rather like the problem of the immovable desks. Is it our concept of learning that determines the length of the school period? Or does the length of the school period determine how we think of the learning process? Time seems to be significant here. The shorter the period for learning, the less a teacher dare experiment with his teaching methods; the longer the period the more he *must* experiment. Thus, an unenterprising teacher who never has a class for longer than forty minutes at a time may never discover how much initiative his pupils are capable of taking and how great their powers of concentration can be. Anyone who wants to introduce more self-government into his classroom organization and more personal research and discovery into his pupils' learning, will probably find himself asking for longer units of time—for two double periods, say, rather than four single periods a week.

It is perhaps no mere coincidence that university lecturers, at the beginning of their careers, should so often be warned that the danger point in an hour's lecture—the time when the attention of an audience is most likely to sag—comes about forty minutes after the opening. Is it a sense of some universal time-limit of attention that lies behind our acceptance of the magic formula of the forty-minute school period? Certainly it is easier to get by with a routine lesson when you can dismiss your class after about thirty-five minutes (which is, after all, what most so-called forty-minute lessons work out at) than if you have to keep them for eighty minutes, or even for fifty-five.

Teachers of backward classes often manage to escape from the forty-minute hazard. Having almost continuous charge of their pupils, they are able to organize their day, as good junior-school teachers do, according to the demands of the work they are doing. And so the transitions they effect from one theme to another often make more sense to their pupils than do the time-tables to which their brighter school companions have to work. It is far more difficult for subject specialists to work flexibly within the time-table, as it exists in most schools.

Subject specialists are indeed the most insulated of beings. Within their own specialist groups they usually come to some agreement about what is to be taught in the school, and even perhaps how it is to be taught. But what does Mr X., who takes IIB for English, really know about the work that Miss Y. is doing with the same class in history, or Mr Z. in geography? And what do any of them know about the sort of things these children are doing in the chemistry laboratory or in the domestic science room or in the gymnasium?

Before we consider how these barriers might be reduced, let us look a little more closely at some of the effects of school time-tabling as it is now.

2. TIME-KEEPING AND TIME-WASTING

First, it is important to recognize that people use the time schedules in all kinds of ways.

What is the unconscious motivation behind the habit one member of staff has of continuing to teach for three or four minutes after the end of almost every lesson? What kind of protest, or plea for help, is being made by a child who seems unable to arrive at a lesson on time? What is really happening between the staff and the head when the mid-morning break is unofficially extended by three, four or five minutes, day after day? What do the children waiting in their classrooms read into this lateness of their teacher? Why do teachers so readily go into collusion with their pupils (or pupils with their teachers) by agreeing to hate the first lesson on Monday morning and the last lesson on Friday afternoon?

Different as these situations look, they seem to spring from the same basic confusion—a confusion about the ownership of time. Does it belong to the children? Or to the teachers? Or to some abstract entity known as 'the administration'? First, let us look more closely at the problems listed above.

The teacher who never finishes a lesson on time is always having to rush from one room to another and somehow contrives to look busier than anyone else. Yet his colleagues, far from seeing him as an asset to the community, regard him as a nuisance. He becomes a focus of irritation. His pupils, for whom he is evidently prepared to give up so much time, end by being angry with him too, for he either makes them late for the next lesson if they have to go to another room, or he puts the teacher who is waiting to take over the room into a bad mood. So the community, whose regard he is so desperately trying to earn, comes to have less rather than more concern for him. The more time he steals from them in school hours, the less time people give him outside school hours.

The institution of the school bell merely exacerbates this kind of problem. The bell, it is felt, stands for finality. It must be infallible. If it is 'early' or 'late', everyone is outraged. Oddly enough, it is the bell itself, symbolizing a kind of invisible and omniscient management (or a management that can be blamed if it is not omniscient) that is felt to be depriving a teacher of time, or of condemning him to a longer stretch of time than he was bargaining for. Human fallibility does not seem to enter into this kind of contingency. Moreover, the teacher who mis-times his lesson can always assert that the bell was early or late, as the case may be.

But supposing there were no bell? Schools that do not rely on a bell are, after all, not unknown in this country. I once visited one. Every room had its own clock, and I was assured that there was seldom any problem about changing between lessons. Everyone knew when a lesson was due to end. And the com-munity accepted responsibility jointly for keeping to the agreed times. The school, freed from the imperious summons of the bell, seemed correspondingly quieter, more relaxed and at the same time more at one in its use of time than most schools are. Most significant of all, when a period was about to end, people in the staff room, having come to the end of a free period, would get up and go off to their classes without the irritation and sense of grievance that the sound of the bell so often induces.

A sense of timeliness broods deeply over a school community. We cannot think about time-keeping without thinking about attitudes to lateness, the pupils' attitudes as well as the teacher's. Once time is felt as something that is shared and used by the community for the various tasks it accepts, then lateness be-comes a community problem. If Jack Smith in IIIC regards the period between 10.30 and 11.10 as belonging to Mr Jones, his lateness becomes a personal affront to Mr Jones—a misde-meanor for which Mr Jones must punish him. If, on the other hand, Jack feels that this part of the day belongs to the whole group that contains himself, Mr Jones and the rest of the class, then his lateness becomes something much more complicated.

It is a sort of breach of commitment, something for which his classmates may expect an explanation. It is not Mr Jones's time that he is stealing: it is the group's time that he is wasting. What is more, if he is repeatedly late, the group may come to feel that this is somehow connected with their behaviour towards him, and may in consequence exert a new responsibility towards him as a person.

In the conventionally organized classroom it is not done to admit that a boy's lateness, even if it is repeated, annoys anyone save the schoolmaster. And it is not among younger children only that this conventional attitude of indifference (even, perhaps, of a sneaking admiration) persists. Sixth-formers, conditioned by years of schooling to regard lateness as an offence against the teacher rather than against the group, will automatically address their apologies exclusively to the teacher, if they arrive late to a lesson, even if the lesson is taking the form of a seminar and even if the person who is really being interrupted by the late arrival is another member of the group.

It seems, then, that children and young people are liable to be over-tolerant about lateness where fellow-pupils are concerned. When it comes to a teacher being late, however, they are far from tolerant. The teacher must be infallible. And it is true that lateness on the part of the responsible staff member, whether the class is in a school or in a university, is a breach of dependability; and students, young or old, have a right to regard it as such. The trouble is that the conventions do not usually allow them to be outspoken when such a breach occurs.

A mild form of unpunctuality on the part of teachers is not uncommon in schools where the beginnings and ends of lessons are controlled by a bell. This is particularly so after the mid-morning break, when the staff group may from time to time allow themselves to take an extra five minutes or so over their tea or coffee. What usually happens in the end to break this habit? The head comes into the staff room one day after the end of break and reminds everybody that the children are all in their classrooms; or he raises the matter at a staff meeting; or he puts up a rather curt notice requesting people to make a point, in future, of getting to their classes on time after break. Whichever of these courses he takes, some if not all of his staff are bound to take offence. Yet what else did they expect? It seems that they intended to drive the head to the necessity of taking executive action, thus forcing him to take the role of an authoritarian leader and treat them all like naughty children. As a group they are furious. Yet some of them, as individuals, may recognize that they have manipulated the head into this unenviable position, in this way shifting on to him both their responsibility and their guilt, very much as their pupils manipulate them into accepting the punishing role where a child's lateness is concerned.

To the children waiting in their classrooms, the repeated lateness of a teacher may carry its own message. 'Mr Jones is bored with us. He prefers the company of his colleagues to our company. He doesn't really think that what we are to do in this lesson is either very important or very interesting.' So now Mr Jones is stealing time from the children. They have no orthodox means by which to punish him, as he punished Jack Smith the other day when he was late. Nevertheless they have their own ways of punishing, when Mr Jones eventually arrives. The punishment may not simply take the form of crude misbehaviour. For if there exists a positive regard for the teacher, feelings about his lateness, even on an isolated occasion, will be complicated by a certain possessiveness and a corresponding sense of let-down. So the revenge may take the form of a sudden increasing demandingness; or the class may demonstrate a loss of interest in the subject; or they may find ways of upsetting the time framework themselves.

But it is not individual teachers or pupils only who are guilty of wasting or stealing a group's time. Sometimes teacher and class agree to throw away time—notably in the two lessons placed by chance at the opposite ends of the school week. It is an accepted convention to dislike the first lesson on Monday morning because nobody has warmed up to the week, and to dislike the last lesson on Friday afternoon because everybody is prematurely withdrawing for the week-end. It is therefore very easy for a teacher to enter into collusion with a class that is assuming its right not to use these periods to the full. Concessions which imply that it is impossible to do anything serious on Friday afternoon are really more damaging than they look; for they carry the implication that work is dull and that children tire a great deal more easily than they really do. Anyone who has taken play rehearsals after school on Friday afternoons knows that there is still plenty of energy left for anything that kindles imagination and calls for responsible and self-critical effort. It is perhaps easy for an English teacher to put aside a Friday afternoon for some activity that seems appropriate for the end of the week; the history or geography teacher, on the other hand, who has only one other lesson in the week, may find the situation a good deal more difficult.

There is a reality in the dislike of Friday afternoon. By the end of the week teachers *are* very tired, even if the children are not. And yet, the frustration of the last lesson of the week cannot be put down just to this. An emotional attitude is involved, which makes the situation seem more tiring than it really is. Again, this is really a group problem, to be examined, perhaps, quite near the beginning of term by teacher and class together. Time spent in talking about how everybody is feeling when the first Friday afternoon comes along, may not in the long run be wasted. At the most primitive level, Mr Jones, who has IIIC last period on Friday, will spend most of the year grumbling about it, and it will not take IIIC long to realize that he does not expect much serious work to be done in that period. At a sophisticated level, he will present it to the boys as a problem; and it will begin to dawn on them, perhaps, that if the week were to end at Thursday at mid-day, people would probably have the same irrational feeling about the last lesson on Thursday morning. Through this kind of mutual exploration of the difficulty the boys and their master may find that Friday afternoon, after all, is a workable period, provided there is work that everyone wants to do.

3. THE RIDDLE OF 'IN-SCHOOL' AND 'OUT-OF-SCHOOL' TIME

So far we have been thinking only of the officially scheduled events in the school day. But no one, looking back on his school life, thinks only of successions of lessons from nine o'clock till four. For a child, the most educative part of a school day may be that hour between four and five when he is working with the photographic club or the science club or the historical society. For his teacher, too, certain moments of shared achievement may stand out in his memory far more vividly than any experience he had in a classroom, while some of the best moments from his official 'teaching' periods seem to have had that elusive, 'out-of-school' quality—a quality that goes with voluntariness rather than compulsoriness and seems to involve a kind of fusion between work and play.

Yet in the traditional programme, particularly in the secondary school, it is dichotomies rather than continuities that stand out. Out-of-school activities are expected to be rigidly separated from in-school activities. So on the one hand we have school subjects associated with prescribed pieces of work and leading ultimately to tests and examinations, while on the other we have hobbies and outside interests that are expected to be self-propelling and to carry their own built-in incentives. Within the official time framework we expect to find compulsory lessons, outside it voluntary societies and clubs.

The division between in-school and out-of-school activities inevitably implies the further dichotomy between work and play. And a great deal of tension can be built up in staff rooms over the way people interpret these terms and value or undervalue one another's contributions to the total life of a school. Probably every teacher has a tendency to overvalue his own subject (though not necessarily his own achievement) and to undervalue other people's subjects, particularly when disputes over time arise and 'out-of-school' activities are felt to be encroaching on 'in-school' time. A geography field trip that takes certain pupils from a cross-section of forms right out of school for a whole afternoon may seem a frivolous expedition in the eyes of the English mistress who is reading *Macbeth* with her fourth form and finds she has lost some of her best readers to this expedition; but a few weeks later, when she is having a dress rehearsal of the school play one afternoon, the geography master, who loses some of *his* best pupils as a result, may secretly take an equally uncharitable view of her activities in the school hall. These two teachers may, however, be united in their indignation against the domestic science mistress, who is entitled to withdraw small groups of girls from the third and fourth forms for a whole day at a time, regardless of what lessons they may miss, so that they can have continuous experience of housecraft and cookery in the school flat.

Does, then, the study of geography cease to be work when it takes place in the open countryside where geographical features can be studied directly instead of through books and maps and film-strips? Does the study of literature lose all seriousness when it is focused on the acting out of a play? Does domestic science suddenly deteriorate into 'messing about in a flat' when it is given a home-like context and a time-span something like a housewife's day?

The trouble is not really that we fundamentally disagree about the best methods of teaching. What divides us is the struggle to protect our own allotted in-school time and to grab what we can of the available out-of-school time. As long as the English mistress takes her rehearsals after school time and as long as the geography master runs his field trips on Saturday mornings we will all smile on them. But let them beware of bringing these 'extra activities' into the sacred framework of the time-table.

Now there is reason as well as unreason in this jealous hugging of time, given the sort of work structure that most schools have. You cannot remove members of a class without doing damage to the morale of the group that is left behind. And this group includes the teacher, who is likely to be demoralized by his own nagging suspicion that the children who are left in the class would prefer to be with those who have been withdrawn from it. So perhaps he tries to compensate for his own sense of lost status by belittling the work the absent children are doing, even by hinting that they are not working at all.

How does the teacher feel, for example, when, on a warm sunny day, a section of the class arrives from swimming, about half-way through the lesson, bringing into the room a glow of health and energy and good spirits? Suddenly it seems to him that the other half of the class look strangely pale, listless and unhealthy. And so he may have a momentary feeling of identification with those who have been in the classroom (virtuously) from the beginning of the period, and may indulge in a brief wave of private indignation against the latecomers, even if their late arrival is officially sanctioned in the time-table.

Now those who have been left behind, when certain members of the class have been withdrawn to take part in some other activity, may well be feeling rather demoralized, seeing themselves as people who are never wanted for anything out of the ordinary, the ones who are always left to continue the routine tasks while others are doing more exciting things. And so they may seek compensation (and revenge) by attempting to seduce the teacher into a closer relationship, from which the absentees, when they return, are to be excluded.

In attempting to describe, in generalized terms, these kinds of situations, I may appear to be over-dramatizing. But feelings like this are more insidious than we realize, and can affect our attitudes to one another and even our behaviour to one another in ways that may escape our notice, yet be subtly invading the life of the group and disrupting its work. Whatever the teacher may feel, rightly or wrongly, strongly or only very faintly, about such intrusions into his time with a class, his task is to help all its members to come to terms with their own conflicting —and doubtless unrecognized—feelings about the situation, to help them to repair the breach in the solidarity of the group without resorting to a sacrifice. Above all, he must not allow the children to use him as a pawn in the game. If he allows his own fantasies about the situation to blind him to observable realities, he will only make matters worse.

The kind of demoralization that sets in when some members of a class are away for a whole week or more is much more difficult to combat. I once visited a school on the very day when a contingent of girls from the fourth year upwards had left, a week before the end of the term, for a two-week stay in France. I watched a music lesson in one of the fourth forms which had lost about half its members. The fifteen girls left behind were evidently in a state of profound depression. It did not seem to me that envy was, on that particular morning, the key to their mood, so much as a sense of loss. They were cooperative enough in a listless way; they seemed to be in need of comfort, yet nothing the teacher could do seemed to cheer them up. It was as though the rest of the form had stolen from them something of themselves and that all they could do was mark time, play out time, or kill time.

All this prompts a question about what the schools are going to do when the staggering of works holidays comes into effect and parents are not only allowed but encouraged to take their children away during the summer term. It is evidently being assumed in some official quarters that all that needs to be done is to move the examinations forward, so that there will be no need for children to be at school all through the summer weeks. It seems, then, that teachers may be faced with depleted classes for nearly two months. Are they to put up with the alternations of envy, loss, demoralization and anger that are likely to occur in school classrooms if the conventional time-table is still, in theory, adhered to? Or will they be prepared to devise some totally different pattern of work for these weeks which will recognize and in some way use the comings and goings of the children?

We are back once more to the old dilemma: how can the time-table be made flexible enough to contain these 'out-of-school' activities and special expeditions and events without jeopardizing community agreements about specific units of time? Are the occasional special functions such as plays, concerts and cultural trips to be kept artificially at a distance from the day-to-day life of the school?

Not necessarily. The problem is one of coordination. If a school play or concert is to be a joint responsibility of a particular section of the school—say of the middle forms—then it will not be only the singers, instrumentalists and actors who will be involved. Everybody will have some share in the responsibility. The occasion will not merely be a piece of window dressing in which only the most talented children take part, but a project towards which all contribute in some way. Then, instead of each form being divided into those who are 'in the play' and those who are not, so that special rehearsals during the final week take certain privileged persons out of 'normal' lessons, it becomes conceivable that forward planning can be done so that a coordinated rehearsal involving everybody can take place.

When we consider the actual time-tabling of the regular out-of-school activities, such as team practices, choir practices, debating society meetings, scientific clubs and so on, another problem arises. This is perhaps typified by the predicament of one very able girl in a grammar-school fifth form, who went to her headmistress in the middle of the autumn term to ask whether it would be advisable for her to drop certain out-of-school activities in view of the fact that she was taking her G.C.E. that year. The trouble was, she could not make up her mind what to drop. On Mondays after school she had orchestra practice and she couldn't drop that; on Tuesday afternoon she went to the current-affairs discussions and she didn't want to miss those; at lunch-time on Wednesdays she had choir practice and after school on the same day there was hockey practice, and she couldn't possibly drop either of those; on Thursdays she went to the dramatic society and she couldn't give that up; and on Fridays she had netball practice and she couldn't very well drop that either. What was she to do? In the end she kept all these activities going and still managed to take seven 'O' levels successfully in the summer.

This kind of dilemma is the natural outcome of a school time-table that divorces 'work' from 'voluntary activity' in this way. Questions of choice and commitment are in fact very closely related to problems of timing. In a school system that spreads school societies over the week the objects of choice will really be the outstanding pupils; but in a school system that puts aside blocks of time for 'special interests' (or for self-governing societies, for that matter) the objects of choice will be the activities that are offered. In other words, in the first system, a few pupils will shine in a number of different fields; but in the second system, everyone will have to make a choice, and this spreading of the obvious talent will make it possible for more pupils to develop unsuspected talents. Moreover, no pupil will be driven into the position of having to weigh up strength of commitment to this group against strength of commitment to that group, or to sacrifice one group to another. Once the choice has been made the commitment follows naturally.

There are precedents for this kind of time-tabling. W. B. Curry describes to his imaginary visitor how a balance between freedom of choice for individuals and stability in the teaching arrangements for groups were sought and maintained at Dartington Hall.[1] Gerard Holmes, writing the story of Prestolee, the experimental school in Lancashire, describes how the balance between required studies and optional studies was maintained by stipulating that every pupil had to satisfy certain requirements in 'the primaries' or the three R's before he could embark on his chosen special activity any day, and by providing a series, called 'the lesson for the day', which offered all pupils an assortment of interesting topics from which such choices of special activity could be made.[2] Wyatt Rawson writes of the Dutch experimental school at Bilthoven (now fully recognized by the government) where time-tables are planned for individuals rather than for large groups; the fact that the school now caters for candidates taking external examinations has not, apparently, reversed this policy.[3]

1. Curry, W. B. (1947) *Education for Sanity*, London: Heinemann, pp. 77–92.
2. Holmes, Gerard (1952) *The Idiot Teacher*, London: Faber & Faber, pp. 174–9.
3. Rawson, W. (1956) *The Werkplaats Adventure*, Vincent Stuart, pp. 116–22.

In all these schools, as these authors (headmaster, assistant master and visiting teacher respectively) described them, it was recognized that growth took place as a result of the tension between the opposing states of freedom and order. And this belief was what determined the structure of the time-table in all three schools. Neither order alone nor freedom alone can ensure learning. Unlimited choice in a flimsy framework of activities spells confusion, while absence of choice in a too-rigid framework spells stagnation. The first implies that work is one long playtime, the second that work has no elements of play at all. If these descriptions have given us faithful portraits of the schools they studied, the children in them must have been learning all through their school careers not only how to use rooms and equipment but also how to use time. The author of *The Idiot Teacher* writes:

> Having no rigid time-table, O'Neill's children do not divide their lives into work and play. They are actively busy all day. They come early and they leave when they are shut out. They are sometimes mentally busy, sometimes socially busy, sometimes physically busy: but although they start at 9 a.m., they never start because it is 9 a.m. and they never watch the clock to see when to stop. If they look at all, all they see is 'the time'.[1]

Curry goes further. For him the school day must also offer the child the choice of not working. At Dartington, as described by him, this was done in two ways. First, it was possible for children to opt out of lessons altogether if they wanted to, not by merely failing to turn up, since that would have caused delay for other children and uncertainty for both teacher and class, but by actually putting on record their decision not to go into classes for, say, a week—by committing themselves, so to speak, not to work in that particular way. This privilege was evidently used most often in the middle school, where children would sometimes elect to pursue activities of their own devising (not always easily distinguishable from work) in groups or gangs; but after the age of twelve or so it was used only rarely, by children who were going through a period of emotional disturbance and needed special help.

The second way in which children were given freedom to choose how to use time was through the provision of genuinely 'unplanned time' in the school day. This kind of provision is

1. Holmes, op. cit., pp. 178–9.

seen by Curry to be related to the question of school bounds. In his view it is illogical and even dishonest to say to a pupil: 'You are free in this hour of the day to occupy your time as you choose', if, in the next breath, you add: 'except, of course, that you must not go out of bounds'. At Dartington a pupil over thirteen could use free time, like any adult, to go into town on an errand without asking for special leave. He thus had to learn to decide for himself whether the errand was worth while and whether he could afford the time. Equally, he could choose to spend his free hour simply day-dreaming. This, for Curry, was genuine free time, and he evidently deplored schools in which so-called 'free time' was really time in which the pupil 'must choose between carefully prescribed activities'. How, he wonders, can a child learn to use unplanned time if he never has any?[1]

The conventional time-table divides the day into small parcels of time, regulating everybody's lives, keeping work and play in separate compartments and contriving to imply that no school subject has much relation to any other. Individuals find ways, from time to time, of cirumventing the regulations, frequently riding roughshod over one another in doing so. Time seems to have become a commodity, rather than a dimension of learning. People haggle over its distribution, instead of looking at its total effect on the child's ability to learn.

But supposing that some of, say, the second-year work could be concentrated into half-day sessions instead of being spread over forty-minute periods; and supposing that these larger blocks of time could be handed to a team of teachers to use as they saw fit. If every Tuesday morning were to be labelled 'Language, Literature, History and Music', what difference would this make to the sharing of time? The English, classics, modern-language, history and music specialists (or specialist groups) would now have to look at the second-year work as a whole, as far as this general area of study was concerned. And they would have to work out for the three, six or nine forms a Tuesday morning programme that would make sense to their pupils. It is not inconceivable that the pupils themselves might have some say in how time should be distributed. Nor is it beyond the bounds of possibility that three staff members might occasionally be present in a classroom at the same time during

1. Curry, op. cit., p. 122.

a long session, helping, perhaps, with a project touching on all their specialisms.

In fact such changes are in the wind. In some of the more adventurous schools, experiments that seem to be pointing in this direction are being launched.[1] And whenever a break-away from the old, rigid kind of time-table is being achieved, two other developments naturally accompany the change: teachers begin to hand over more responsibilities to their pupils; and they find it necessary to spend far more time in consultation with each other. Thus rivalry over the appropriation of time gives way to cooperative planning to discover the most fruitful ways of using time.

A structure that leaves more of the detailed organization to groups of teachers will certainly not remove the difficulties from teaching. But it may substitute surmountable problems for mere frustrations. Teachers and pupils may discover that the very act of searching for the real cause of conflict can in itself promote learning—not perhaps about history and music and mathematics as such, but about how to study history and music and mathematics, and also how to live together in a community.

We need to create periods in the school time-table that are long enough for the fusion between work and play to occur more often; periods in which a genuine and flexible choice of activities can operate for any pupil; periods in which teachers work in teams within areas that combine related specialisms; periods in which field trips, excursions and special visits can take their place naturally without disrupting the usual pattern of an afternoon's work; periods in which long-term projects depending on intelligent team-work between pupils become more important than competitive performances in tests and examinations. And perhaps, also, we need to pay less attention to the sanctity of the subject and more to the fundamental nature of work itself, and particularly to the creative aspects of the work that children enjoy doing and can do well.

1. For example, see Rollings, A. and Litton, N. (May 1965) 'The Henbury File', *New Education*.
See also, for an account of similar work in the United States, Shaplin, J. T. and Olds, H. F. (eds) (1964) *Team Teaching*, Harper and Row.

CHAPTER SEVEN

Freedom, Discipline and Creative Invention

I. THE ROLE OF DISCOVERY IN LEARNING

Throughout the first part of this book the emphasis has been on the personal relationship between teacher and class. This relationship is a network of feelings, attitudes and expectations, binding the teacher both to his individual pupils and to his class as a whole. But along with teacher and taught there is always something more immediate: the task that lies between them, often masking but never obliterating the pleasure or the pain of those relationships. In the name of this task we often find ourselves upholding certain kinds of classroom relationship rather than others, allowing 'more freedom' in this lesson and imposing 'more discipline' in that. Is discipline, then, the converse of freedom, or an essential ingredient in it?

First, we must recognize that freedom is not, in itself, an objective and that if we make it our objective, as teachers, we are doomed to failure. For none of us, as members of the family groups, the social groups and the communities in which we live and work can possibly be entirely free. So it is more useful to think of teachers as freeing children to work creatively than to regard freedom in the classroom as a sort of ideal state of affairs without reference to any particular work.

A long time ago, Martin Buber said this about freedom in education: 'It cannot be dispensed with, and it cannot be made use of in itself; without it nothing succeeds, but neither does anything succeed by means of it: it is the run before the jump, the tuning of the violin, the confirmation of that primal and mighty potentiality which it cannot even begin to actualize.'[1] The run before the jump; the tuning of the violin. What, then, is the nature of the jump we want our pupils to take, of the tune we

1. Buber, Martin (1947) 'Education', in *Between Man and Man*, London: Routledge & Kegan Paul, p. 91.

want them to play? What is this 'mighty potentiality' to which Buber refers?

Much of our thinking about the nature of the learning process and about the relation between freedom and discipline in the classroom tends to be clouded by the unthinking way in which we use the terms 'free' and 'formal'. We contrast the 'free activity' period at the beginning or end of the junior-school day with the 'formal lessons' that precede or follow it; the writing of 'free verse' is opposed to the study of 'formal composition'; 'free drama' is seen as something basically different from the 'formal drama' that is tied to the interpretation of a ready-made play; experimental work in the science laboratory, although it would probably never be described as 'free' because of the physical dangers involved, is seen as one kind of lesson, 'formal teaching' or theoretical explanation as another; 'free discussion' is set against 'formal debating'.

A good teacher will always be seeking for links between the two, and he will see the 'free' activities as the bases upon which the 'formal' structures can later be built. Thus an understanding of the forms of language will grow out of exploratory experiences in the use of language in contexts that have significance for the children; understanding of scientific laws will develop from experimental observation in the laboratory; skill and sensitivity in interpreting a scene from Shakespeare is more likely to be demonstrated by children who have learned to portray sensations and emotional experiences in movement and spontaneous dialogue; debating will be more sincere if it is associated with genuine discussion about things that matter.

Perhaps we can explore these questions further by looking at two sets of imaginary classroom situations. Suppose that in one classroom a group of thirteen-year-olds is studying some aspect of a novel; that next door a group of comparable age and ability is engaged in solving a mathematical problem; and that upstairs in the geography room a third group is studying the characteristics of a river gorge not five miles away. In every case, the teacher is imposing on the class his own thought structures. The English teacher is dictating notes on characters and situations in the novel; the mathematics teacher is demonstrating a method of calculation; the geography teacher is discoursing to the class with the aid of charts and maps, pointing out to them what they ought to see. In each room most of the pupils appear to be working industriously, and some of them are showing some interest in what is being pointed out to them. But discovery and communication are minimal. The children, entirely dependent on the teacher, are learning, one feels, little more than empty forms. The class is disciplined but dead.

Perhaps these examples seem a little far-fetched. Certainly, this kind of one-way teaching is more rare now than it used to be. But it still goes on. And probably most of us have taught in this way from time to time and have been able to persuade ourselves that we are doing our jobs quite efficiently. Those of us who lecture in universities and other adult institutions probably do it more than we care to admit. And of course students, young and old, *can* learn something by listening; indeed some kinds of learning can only be done in this way. If we were to rule out all listening activities with one stroke of the pen, we should have to stop telling children stories, or reading poetry aloud to them, or playing music to them, or taking them to theatres or cinemas. Listening is not necessarily passive. There are times when being receptive is perhaps a preliminary to being creative. But in the situations outlined above, merely listening to the teacher does not seem to be particularly appropriate to the kind of learning that is being done. So let us consider what might be going on in these same classrooms if the adults in charge of them were being more adventurous.

In the English room the teacher is now sitting at the back while a group of children, seated round the table at the front, argue over a controversial question about the novel that he has put to them. The rest of the class are listening, and from time to time someone tries to break in and challenge one of the speakers at the front. After ten minutes or so comments on the discussion are invited. The children now search for supporting evidence in the novel for assertions that have been made, and the teacher helps the class to clarify what has been going on. In the last ten minutes everyone writes down his personal opinion about the original question that provided the focus for the discussion, perhaps in the form of an advisory note to the producer of a radio play, or as a critical letter to *The Radio Times* on a televised film of the novel.

In the mathematics room the teacher has presented the problem to the children and is inviting suggestions about possible ways of looking at it, with a view to helping them to discover a key to its solution. In the process they draw upon their experience of solving similar but not identical problems. Promising leads are followed up, and eventually, perhaps by a rather roundabout route, a solution is worked out. The children are then encouraged to re-examine the series of calculations to see whether a more elegant solution can be found, the teacher helping them to perceive new patterns in the material they have been handling.

In the geography room, the children, who have actually taken part in an afternoon's field work in the gorge, are planning with the teacher's help a series of wall charts and diagrams and models to record and classify their discoveries. In the process of deciding how the work is to be allocated, the children are beginning to structure their own thinking about the experiences of the field trip. As they compare the specific examples they saw and the specimens they have brought back of this and that kind of soil, vegetation and rock formation, they begin to discover relationships between apparently disparate units of knowledge, and new concepts begin to emerge in their thinking.

In the second kind of teaching the task is approached in a fashion that allows for creative invention—the kind of invention that children exercise from the very earliest years when they play unsupervised in their homes or in a well-equipped infant school. The urge to make discoveries by using materials in new ways, by experimenting with language and by manipulating physical objects and chemical substances does not die as adolescence approaches. Yet it is far less evident in the work of the secondary school than in good junior schools. Consider how Gardner Murphy describes this urge to learn: 'We reach out toward new experiences, lovingly gloat over them, turn an eagle eye toward fine differentiation among them, modes of grouping and ordering them; put them into hierarchies and systems; look always for new experiences, and new modes of organization.'[1] Is this any less true of the fifteen-year-old, at his most enthusiastic, or even of the adult engaged in new discoveries, than it is of the five-year-old? Is it necessarily any less true of what goes on in a science laboratory or a mathematics classroom than of what goes on in the art room?

For those of us whose work with children has been in the field

1. Gardner, Murphy (1960) *Human Potentialities*, London: Allen & Unwin, p. 178.

of the arts, it is dangerously easy to slip into the belief that it is only through music, art, poetry and drama that the imagination is nourished and the child's creative ability released. But in truth the element of surprise will be present whenever a child, or an older person, is making learning his own. Wherever the learner discovers new and unexpected relationships, he will experience aesthetic delight. It is surely significant that Professor J. S. Bruner, in his 'essays for the left hand',[1] has chapters on poetry and drama, the modern novel, art and mathematics, linked together by philosophical speculations about the nature of creativity and the act of discovery, and that Arthur Koestler in his exploration of the nature of the creative act moves freely and easily between the world of science and the world of the arts.[2] What Bruner describes as 'combinatorial activity—a placing of things in new perspectives',[3] Koestler calls the 'bisociation' of words or ideas that at first sight appear quite unrelated. Such leaps of the imagination are crucial in all creative thinking, whether the thinker is a child of six, a youth of fifteen or a mature adult.

The relevance of this way of thinking is now being strikingly demonstrated at Sevenoaks School, which, although independent, still acts as the only grammar school for the area and accepts about half its pupils on a non-fee-paying basis. The pioneer work that is going on there has been described in symposium form, in a book published jointly by the staff members concerned in the experiments.[4] We are taken into the art room, the technical activities centre and the mathematics classroom; we overhear a discussion between two masters about the real aims of English teaching; we read of self-government in the house known as the International Centre; we follow boys out into the surrounding neighbourhood as they take up various kinds of social work with old people, deprived children and delinquent boys; and we hear the headmaster and some of the pupils themselves commenting on all these experiences. Under-

1. Bruner, J. S. (1962) *On Knowing : Essays for the Left Hand,* Harvard University Press.
2. Koestler, Arthur (1963) *The Act of Creation,* London: Hutchinson.
3. Bruner, op. cit., in 'The Conditions of Creativity', p. 20.
4. White, B., Paterson, N., Talbot, H., Sommerhoff, G., Hoare, G., and Scragg, B. (with an Introduction and Reflection by L. C. Taylor, and contributions by boys past and present) (1965) *Experiments in Education at Sevenoaks,* London: Constable & Young Books.

lying all this work is the conviction of the adults concerned that children can be trusted to use initiative to good purpose when they are given the opportunity to do so. Over and over again we find confirmation of what Bruner and Koestler say about the role of discovery in learning.

My own work as a teacher and as someone now concerned with the education of teachers has only rarely taken me into science or mathematics classes in the schools. I cannot, therefore, draw on first-hand experiences in these fields, and must look to other sources for my illustrations. William James, who brought so much enthusiasm to so many different fields of learning that it took him nearly half his life to decide which one he really wanted to settle down in, provides me with one irresistible example. At the age of eighteen, he wanted to become a painter and in fact spent six months preparing himself to take up this vocation. Between the ages of eighteen and thirty he switched from painting to chemistry, from chemistry to biology and from biology to medicine; and in the end it was as a psychologist and not as physiologist that he made his name. To his brother Henry it was no surprise that William abandoned painting for science. From his recollections of their boyhood days he sketched for us an amusing portrait of the young William, turning every possible situation into a voyage of discovery.

As certain as that he had been all the while 'artistic' did it thus appear that he had been at the same time quite otherwise enquiring too—addicted to 'experiments' and the consumption of chemicals, the transfusion of mysterious liquids from glass to glass under exposure to lambent flame, the cultivation of stained fingers, the establishment and the transportation in our wanderings of galvanic batteries, the administration to all he could persuade of electric shocks, the maintenance of marine animals in splashy aquaria, the practice of photography in the room I for a while shared with him at Boulogne, with every stern reality of big cumbrous camera, prolonged exposure, exposure mostly of myself, darkened development, also interminable, and ubiquitous brown blot.[1]

Against this portrait of the indomitable, inventive young experimenter of 1860, I find myself placing my own impressions of another eighteen-year-old of to-day. I see this boy in his mother's kitchen one evening about four years ago, when he was fourteen, giving me a running commentary on his activities

1. Henry, James (1914) *Notes of a Son and Brother*, London: Macmillan, pp. 115–16.

as he plays about with a bowl of sugar, a long piece of thin wire, a table spoon, a basin of cold water in the sink and a lighted gas burner in the cooker: he tries out this action and that, and discovers that the wire, if heated red-hot, can make a spoonful of cold water give off steam for a second; later he finds, laughingly, that he has made, with these crude materials, a sort of miniature lollipop. I see him two years later experimenting with a ping-pong ball, throwing it up against the wall and mentally calculating the correct angle of incidence to make it ricochet off the wall onto the ceiling, and then calculating the second angle of incidence so that he can catch the ball as it shoots from the ceiling to the floor. I try to recall in detail the numerous mathematical and logical puzzles he has put to me during the past two years and I experience vicariously the pleasure he takes in explaining their solution, his delight in manipulating hypotheses and testing them one after another until he reaches his immensely satisfying conclusion. Repeatedly his behaviour reminds me of the mental activities of other clever children described by Professor Piaget and his colleagues, whose researches disclose how children discover, first through fairly random observations and later through the systematic testing of hypotheses, the laws that determine the behaviour of inanimate objects.[1] And then I remember that this boy I have watched and listened to and frequently been outwitted by, though passionately devoted to science and mathematics, also takes pride in carpentry and indoor decoration and practises these, in his spare time, with considerable skill and artistry.

In this boy the spirit of enquiry has been kept alive, partly through exceptionally good science teaching. But for many adults to-day, real science was killed years ago by teaching that was regimented and sadly unimaginative. The organizer of the Nuffield Physics Project, Professor E. M. Rogers, speaking at the Ceylon Conference in 1963, has publicly lamented this fact.[2] He speaks of the 'wall' that surrounds science for most of us: for some, he says, this is 'a stupid antagonistic wall of ignorance and prejudice'; for others it is 'a wall of mystery and misunderstanding, enclosing the scientist as a magician who knows all,

1. Inhelder, B. and Piaget, J. (1958) *The Growth of Logical Thinking from Childhood to Adolescence*, London: Routledge & Kegan Paul.
2. In *School Science Teaching: Report on an Expert Conference held at the University of Ceylon, Peradeniya*, (1964) London: H.M.S.O., p. 19.

and can do strange things that ordinary people cannot do.' Yet, he reminds us, young children are thrilled with the idea of experiment. If we give a small boy a test-tube, 'his tongue hangs out with enthusiasm'. He wonders what happens to all this enthusiasm. Yet he believes that if science were taught properly, all educated people would maintain an interest in it, and would, moreover, understand the true nature of scientific activity.

In another report on Nuffield Science,[1] Mr W. H. Dowdeswell, the Biology organizer, is quoted as saying: 'We are changing the role of the teacher—that is the most important aspect of the whole exercise. Instead of having him before a class as the fount of all wisdom and knowledge, we are changing his role to be a spur towards wisdom and knowledge.'

What are the implications of these new moves in the field of science teaching? What new strains will teachers who meet the challenge have to learn to accept, as part of this new role? Clearly, there can be no escape into the wrong kind of efficiency —the kind of efficiency that hastens apparent learning at the expense of real learning. The teacher will have to be prepared to tolerate his pupils' confusion and muddle in the initial stages of any new learning. To be sure, he may, as the struggle goes on, have to give a little push here or drop a large hint there; but his interventions must be carefully timed to coincide with the children's readiness to react intelligently to them. Often enough, he may want to intervene too early, to allay his own anxieties, perhaps, about whether he is doing his job properly. We all like to be thought omniscient, and many of us are prone to keep younger people more dependent on us than they need be. A teacher who is able to resist these temptations and can wait for children to discover their own strengths will, in the end, give them something far more durable than the ready-made techniques and formulae which they are not yet ready to understand.

Behind all good science teaching, then, is the urge to help children to discover for themselves the laws that govern the physical world. Similarly, the mathematician wants his pupils to reach beyond the practical uses of calculation to the mathematical ideas in which he himself takes such pleasure. The scientist has the advantage of working with concrete materials and physically observable processes. Some measure of discovery can hardly be avoided in the science laboratory, where changes

1. Eykin, W. van der. (July 1965) "Nuffield Science," *New Education*.

are occurring under the children's very noses. But how can the mathematician who is dealing with the most highly abstract subject on the time-table avoid giving children the concepts before they have tried to perform the operations? He can do this by helping them to use hunch and intuition rather than merely requiring them to follow instructions.

Now I am one of the legion of well-educated adults who emerged from their schooling intellectually blind and emotionally resistant to the pleasures of mathematics. With the approach of the school certificate examination (the old equivalent of 'O' level G.C.E.) I had nightmares about problems on relative velocity, which I perceived as baffling tests of my ability to use a complicated technique which I never really understood. Yet if I now join a class of arts graduates who are being taught by an imaginative teacher, unexpected things begin to happen to me. Where I intended only to observe, I find myself trying to learn. I find that I am being encouraged to use my own intuition in examining a problem in order to find possible ways of solving it; or I am shown a collection of three-dimensional geometrical models and invited to make predictions about the relations between the parts of any one of them; or I am presented with a set of numerical data and helped to turn these first into geometrical terms and then into algebraic terms so that I begin to perceive more clearly than I have ever done before the real relationship between the three kinds of mathematical language; or I am challenged to do a series of calculations, using, not ten, but some other number as the basic unit, and now the number hierarchy I have lived with all these years begins to take its place as only one of any number of hierarchies that might have been selected, and also to take its place beside the binary system that is used to-day in electronic computers.

Bruner's essay 'On Learning Mathematics' contains a passage that describes admirably the quality of this kind of learning experience. 'Intuition,' he says, 'is founded on a kind of combinatorial playfulness that is possible only when the consequences of error are not overpowering or sinful. Above all it is a form of activity that depends on confidence in the worthwhileness of the process of mathematical activity rather than upon the importance of right answers at all times.'[1]

The tyranny of the right answer can inhibit original creative

1. Bruner, op. cit., p. 102.

thinking in any field, not only in mathematics. Sometimes, of course, there *is* only one right answer. Sometimes the child *must* master and store facts. But if the teacher's ultimate objective is to free the child's intelligence rather than merely to give him a stock of ready-made answers, he must not give the child short cuts to knowledge or limit him to safe routes. 'It is only through risk-taking and variation,' says Professor Allport, 'that growth can occur'.[1] What is a teacher's reaction to this doctrine likely to be?

Clearly the scientist's distinction between justifiable and un-justifiable risk-taking will rest on quite different premises from the arts teacher's. In school, 'risk' in a teaching situation is inevitably related to fear of losing control. In a free drama lesson, for example, loss of control may be associated with a rise of the level of noise above the level of tolerance, and perhaps also with the fantasy—not entirely unrelated to possible reality—that aggression may break out and reach physically dangerous proportions. But in the laboratory the risk of physical danger, even with senior pupils, is no mere fantasy; for materials and apparatus are being used which could easily cause physical injury or even sudden death if misused. Safety precautions and specific sanctions are not merely advisable: they are essential. Similarly, certain safety precautions must be taken in a gymnasium where children might, in a completely free situation, undertake feats that they were not physically capable of carrying through.

This is not the kind of risk-taking that Allport is talking about. No teacher has a right to take risks where physical safety is concerned. But if he always plays safe mentally, and expects his pupils to play safe mentally, the learning that goes on in his classrooms will lack any creative surprise. For the most part the responses that occur will be predictable responses.

When teachers stop looking only for the routine responses, what they liberate themselves and their pupils from is the set of academic disciplines that have emerged over the centuries as a result of the work done by scientists and artists on the frontiers of knowledge and creative experience. This is what Cizek was doing in Vienna when he freed his pupils from rules and regulations and set them to paint out of their own imagination.[2]

1. Allport, G. W. (1955) *Becoming*, Yale University Press, p. 66.
2. See Viola, W. (1948) *Child Art and Franz Cizek*, University of London Press, and Munro, T. (1956) *Art Education: its Philosophy and Psychology*, Liberal Arts Press, Chapter 12, 'Franz Cizek and the Free Expression Method', pp. 237–41.

This is what Stanislavski did with his drama students in Moscow when he made them use their own feelings in a situation rather than obey rules of stage procedure and follow theatrical convention.[1] This is what Rudolf Laban was doing when he based his work with dancers on fundamental experiences of movement rather than on techniques learned second-hand from other dancers.[2] This is what Carl Orff was doing with children at the Guentherschule in Munich when he helped them to discover, from the examination of their own speech tunes and rhythms, that melody and metrical patterns were part of their own natural equipment and not mere inventions of the musicologists.[3]

All these revolutions—in the teaching of art, drama, dance and music—were beginning in the twenties. What use have our schools been able to make of these innovations?

2. THE FREEING OF THE IMAGINATION THROUGH THE ARTS

While we must avoid equating art with 'freedom' and science with 'discipline', or implying that art enables the child to be 'creative' while science only requires him to be 'factual', we must nevertheless recognize an important difference between the two kinds of activity. It is by no means easy to define this difference, and perhaps no two people would agree where the difference lies. Mr L. W. H. Hull, with whom I have discussed the question at some length, suggests that 'the essence of the distinction may perhaps be expressed by saying that the sciences are concerned with discovery and the arts with creation'. He sees the scientist's attitude to the world as 'mainly passive and receptive' and the artist's as 'more active': the scientist seeks to understand the world 'by exploring and recording it, and looking for a pattern in its behaviour', whereas the artist seeks 'to alter it by adding something to it'. This is not to say that the

1. Alekseev, Konstantin Sergeovich (pseud. Stanislavsky) (1945) *My Life in Art*, translated from the Russian by J. J. Robbins, London: Bles.
2. Laban, Rudolf, (1948) *Modern Educational Dance*, London: MacDonald & Evans,; Laban R. and Lawrence, F. C. (1947) *Effort*, London: MacDonald & Evans; Russell, Joan (1958) *Modern Dance in Education*, London: MacDonald & Evans.
3. Orff, C. and Keetman, G. (1960) *Music for Children* (English version adapted by Margaret Murray, Books I-III, and by Doreen Hall and Arnold Water, Book IV, with a Teacher's Manual by Doreen Hall), London: MacDonald & Evans.

scientist does not at times use the methods of the artist, or that the artist never uses the methods of the scientist. 'All we can say of a given activity is that it is *predominantly* a science or *predominantly* an art.'[1]

When I try to work out these distinctions in the context of the teacher–pupil relationship in the school, I find myself needing to draw a further distinction between the inner world of the person and the outer world to which the person must relate himself. And so, it seems to me, the role of the science teacher is to present children with objects and materials that they can work on analytically, and then to help them to build up mental constructs of the world, whereas the role of the arts teacher is to enable children to give outward form to their own inner feelings about experience. It is as though the science teacher starts by providing something in the outer world and follows events through to the child's inner world of ideas, while the arts teacher has to provoke something into activity in the child's inner world so that it can take visible or audible form in the outer world.

The importance of the second kind of experience is that it enables the child to explore the relationship between fantasy and reality, both in the world of inaminate objects and in the world of animals and people. Both feeling and thought are involved in the arts, as they are in the sciences. And in art, as in science, work leads to increasing control. But in art the child is reaching towards a greater control of himself as a person rather than of the environment outside himself. Through his poems and stories, his painting and modelling, his participation in drama and movement, he has a chance to externalize and examine his own inner conflicts, to give expression to feelings that are important to him, and so, perhaps, to understand and tolerate these feelings, and the events that give rise to them, better. In its turn, this increasing mastery of his own impulses and desires and fears may help him to control certain kinds of events in the outer world.

Consider, for example, this deeply felt personal statement from an adolescent girl, included in Michael Baldwin's anthology of children's poems[2]—a statement which has the stamp of

---

1. Hull. L. W. H. (1959) *History and Philosophy of Science*, London: Longmans, Green. pp. 2–3.
2. Baldwin, Michael (1962) *Poems by Children: 1950–1961*, London: Routledge & Kegan Paul, pp. 93–4.

originality and uniqueness, and yet speaks for all young people searching for their own identity.

> Who
> are you
> who sit singing
> soft on the marble
> threshold of the house of I,
> the ego, alone and lost, but one
> wailing red, outside the blind
> crystal gateways of
> my mind alone,
> who are
> you?

> 'No-one'
> came back
> the echoing reply
> which lapped the brazen
> pillars of the house of I,
> the ego, alone and lost, but one
> who waited, trembling, inside
> at the golden wealth
> of sound which spilled
> liquidly over me.
> 'No-one'.

This is no mere borrowed set of images, no exercise in the school note-book produced to pattern like any other weekly exercise, but a person dealing actively with what Erikson has called 'the crisis of identity'.[1] How long did it take her, one wonders, to achieve this form of expression of feelings at once so personal and so universal? And what quality of relationship between this girl and her teacher made this kind of self-exposure possible?

The shift from regimented learning to creative endeavour can perhaps be seen in its most striking form in the change that is coming into physical education. In place of the old-style gymnastics many of the schools up and down the country are now substituting the new-style physical education, which originated in Laban's work with dancers and which among teachers is variously named 'free movement', 'modern educational dance' and 'dance drama'.[2]

1. Erikson, E. H. *Identity and the Life Cycle*, op. cit., pp. 88–94.
2. See *Physical Education in the Primary School: Moving and Growing*, (1952), London: H.M.S.O.; Wiles, J. and Garrard, A. (1957) *Leap to Life*, London: Chatto & Windus; Jordan, Diana (1963) 'Movement and Dance', in *Studies in Education: The Arts and Current Tendencies in Education*, London: Evans.

Let us first recall the traditional 'gym' lesson. The class, on entering the gymnasium, would form a column and would march or run round the hall until ordered to stop. Then four, or five, or maybe six teams would take up their positions, and for twenty minutes or so there would be 'free-standing' exercises, carried out strictly to orders from the teacher, who operated in the manner of a sergeant on the parade ground. Each child was expected to do exactly what all the others were doing, much of it to numbers. Then would come the transition to apparatus work, welcome perhaps to most of the class though not to all. For the rest of the period the teams would move round from one piece of apparatus to another, having perhaps five minutes with each. Every child would thus perform, as often as his turn came round, by travelling on the horizontal bar, balancing on an upturned form, climbing ropes, vaulting over a horse or box. If he did this sort of thing well he was constantly aware of being admired, if badly of being pitied or despised. So the natural gymnasts went from strength to strength, the clumsiest pupils became yet more clumsy, and those in the steady average group continued to do some things quite well and other things rather badly. All through these lessons every move was strictly prescribed. There might as well have been lines chalked on the floor to ensure complete conformity to regulation movements for all the scope these exercises ever allowed for individual initiative or imagination.

But now watch a class that has been taught on Laban principles. When you come into the hall, even if the teacher has not yet arrived, the children are already moving about, some fast, some more slowly, all adventurously. They are weaving the most extraordinary patterns with their hands and arms, their legs, and indeed their whole bodies. If you have never seen this before it takes your breath away by its sheer beauty. As you watch you realize that all these children are moving with confidence. You could not put them into an order of merit if you tried. The other striking fact is that although the whole of the floor is being used, although there is clearly no prescribed direction for anyone to go in, and although each seems intent on his own activity, yet they are so strongly aware of one another and so sensitive to one another's movements that no two children ever collide or have to make awkward movements to avoid collision. Sometimes two of them, coming face to face by chance will begin spontaneously to work out a pattern of actions. The pattern may suggest attack and retreat, attack and counter-attack, appeal and rejection, appeal and response. Given time, this kind of interaction can build up into a dramatic sequence. And when the whole class combines to work out in movement a chosen legend or story or to perform a movement theme of their own or the teacher's invention, the results can be astonishingly rich in imaginative power and can make a strong impact on observers.

These children have been freed from their reliance on straight lines, though they can still work in a straight line if this is what is demanded by the situation they are trying to enact. But a class which has only very recently broken away from the old formal gymnastics will, for a while, present a very different picture. You may see these children timidly clustered together, leaving whole stretches of floor space empty; or they will tend to follow each other instead of choosing their own directions to move in; or they may move about in such an undisciplined way that they are repeatedly colliding with each other. Their teacher must constantly be encouraging them to use what is there to be used: 'Find a space for yourself'; 'Look at all the empty space over there!' And so eventually they learn to exercise choice, to distribute themselves over the whole area without having to be told exactly where to go, to share space without having specially allocated pieces of it, to give and take.

Surely this is the kind of emancipation that is needed in all areas of school life. We do not know what new learning will emerge once pupils in the classroom are brought face to face with one another as well as with the teacher, any more than we know what new forms of dramatic expression will emerge once pupils in the gymnasium are brought face to face with one another in more fluid and less predictable patterns of movement. The disappearance of the teams in straight lines, the freer use of space, the new awareness of self and of others—all these have their equivalents in any classroom.

In the junior school this 'freeing of the intelligence' can cut right across subject boundaries. A primary-school teacher can—more easily than his secondary-school colleague—encourage children to explore one central theme in several different media of expression. Movement and dance, painting and modelling, writing in verse or prose, can enrich each other. I would like to illustrate this from some work I saw some years ago in a primary school in the West Riding of Yorkshire. The children (nine-year-olds) had worked on the theme 'Witches Fighting'. I was shown painting and written work which I was allowed to photograph and transcribe; and later, in a movement lesson, I watched the children acting out their fantasies about these witches. They had worked out these dances some weeks before and now recreated them for me to see.

This class included one boy who was considered to be exceptionally bright and one who was backward and had a speech defect. In the movement class, I was told, they always chose each other as partners when work was being done in pairs. At the climax of their 'fighting witches' dance the backward boy lay stretched on the floor as the defeated witch while the other towered over him. Whether this had happened on previous occasions or not I do not know. Apart from any symbolism one may see in the playing of the roles of victor and vanquished, no onlooker could have deduced from the quality of the dance-mime which was the more intelligent of the two. They were as well-matched as any other pair in the room.

Now let us look at what these two boys produced when they turned from the arts of painting and movement to the art of writing. First I print the story written by the very bright boy, just as he wrote it.

The two Witches from Healey Common

One night when the wind was blowing and howling round the trees two witches who were enemies accidently met. They were furious to see each other but they just met in a freindly way. One asked the other one to her cave. So they went, the cave in which were a few old books a cooking pot and a fire, was very cold and drearey. Then one of them poured out drinks. The other one looked at her curiously as though the drink was poisand. She knocked it over onto the floor, then tried to cast spells on one another and laughing a very misterious laugh. Then one of the witches grey eyes shone up againsed her dull wrinkled old face. She went round the other witch with her eyes stuck like glue watching her then she made one sudden dash to a cupbored there in the cupbored was all sorts of things. She reached for a box. The other witch was sat there watching her. The box she had got contained a black sort of powder which was called magic powder. When the other witch wasn't looking she put some of the powder in the drink. The witch turned round and drank, she amediatly fell to the ground with a bump. A couple of hours later she went in and saw that she had turned into a Toad. The Toad went up to her. The other witch had never done this before and she felt ashamed of herself so she sprinkled some other powder on her and she changed her back into a witch. Then they had some thing to eat and remaind freinds for the rest of their lives.

This is unmistakably a child's story—a quaint mixture of timeless fantasy and twentieth-century social realism. It was, in fact, a less vivid piece of writing than many of the others. But there are signs that the experience with dramatic movement is having an effect on his descriptive powers. And I find myself wondering whether the rather touching admission of guilt on the victorious witch's part and the need to make reparation to the defeated fellow-witch has overtones from the experience of acting out a victory over his classmate.

The backward boy's story can be read on two entirely different levels. Judged as a piece of accurate English it could be considered deplorable. But an offering of this kind must, as one teacher puts it, 'be read with the eye of love'. If we allow the evocative description behind this apparently tortured writing to reach us, it becomes astonishingly exciting. This is how the boy actually wrote it:

The witches triumph

Now as the sun rised abuth the twisting forest of the Canadian alpes. The sunlight shone a pone the tree a made the leaves gliter lick silver and in the valley a herd of wild horses just awok from their sleep. The volcano youning and lava cuming out and ball of fire flaming up in fury, and a gust of wind just past by for in mist of the smoke but another witch she blened with the fire and the smoke but another witch came out of the forest she was a trespasser of the enchanted witches ground and she had cum to kill the enchanted witch she scramed up the volcano then they were cuved the lava but ont ones did their eyes wunder. Evey time their eyes were focus on echuther they never blinked a singer eye lash as they fort in the trifice heat of the fire they never stopt for a slingl rest and their bare feet twisting in the bouling lava and their arms twering like a snake but the stones sliped under their feet and they came timbling down lick bares they were flat out. In time they got up. One nootist a stones nere the uther She strock a spell wich made it a loin at ones it slooly crept round the uther one. then it was a black out Smoock filing every were al last the witch dide, and the lion changed into a stone ones more and witch disaperd in the volcano

If, now, we correct his spelling, tidy up his punctuation and re-organize the lay-out of the passage on the page, we find our-selves reading something rather different. Without removing any of the childish crudities of thought, and with only one slight elucidation in line 10, we have in fact a poem of extraordinary power and vividness.

Now, as the sun rose above the twisting forest of the Canadian Alps,
The sunlight shone upon the trees
And made the leaves glitter like silver.
And in the valley
A herd of wild horses just awoke from their sleep.
The volcano yawning
And lava coming out
And ball of fire flaming up in fury.
And a gust of wind just passed by:
For in the midst of the smoke was the enchanted witch.
She blended with the fire and the smoke.
But another witch came out of the forest.
She was a trespasser on the enchanted witch's ground,
And she had come to kill the enchanted witch.
She scrambled up the volcano.

Then they started fighting.
In the boiling lava sometimes
They were covered with lava.
But not once did their eyes wander.
Every time their eyes were focused on each other.
They never blinked a single eyelash
As they fought in the terrific heat of the fire;
They never stopped for a single rest;
And their bare feet twisting in the boiling lava;
And their arms twirling like a snake.
But the stones slipped under their bare feet.
And they came tumbling down like bears:
They were flat out.
In time,
They got up.
One noticed a stone near the other.
She struck a spell which made it
A lion.
At once it slowly crept
Round the other one.
Then,
It was a black out.
Smoke filling everywhere.

At last,
The witch died.
And the lion changed into a stone once more.
And the witch disappeared in the volcano.

For a teacher who had to justify—as work—the kind of activity that goes on in a drama lesson this poem would provide

eloquent testimony. For here was a boy, who in formal situations was inarticulate and nervous, using language with strength
and conviction. The drama teacher, with whatever ideas he
can offer to stimulate his class, is striving to release ideas and to
help children to experience, think about, talk about, and perhaps
write about feelings. The theme may be very mundane—people
queuing up for a bus, workmen on a building site, a family
cleaning a car, a party of people at the zoo, crowds on the pave-
ment during the January sales. It may be drawn from legendary
or literary sources—Arthur drawing the sword from the stone,
Odysseus and his men entering the Cyclops' cave, Perseus
rescuing Andromeda, David Balfour being kidnapped aboard
Captain Hoseason's ship. Or the theme may be the human
reactions to a natural catastrophe such as a flood or a hurricane
or an earthquake. Any of these themes could be dramatized with
or without dialogue. Some would be enriched by music. Some
would be best worked out by the whole class together, with the
teacher continuously offering stimulating ideas; others could be
worked out independently by small groups in different parts of
the hall.

It is becoming obvious that this process of freeing children,
both physically and mentally, from the old regimentation and
predictable orderliness brings new problems in its train. For the
more a learning situation is shaken open to allow for give and
take, not only between teacher and pupil but also between one
pupil and another, the greater the need for discipline. Under the
old régime, when this discipline was largely imposed by the
teacher, emotional experiences seemed irrelevent to the learning
process. But under the new régime emotional experience is part
and parcel of the learning process and can, if uncontrolled,
become a threat to law and order. What, then, is the nature of
the discipline that must evolve from these experiences? Does it
come from the teacher, or from the class, or from the nature
of the task that they share?

3. THE DEMANDS OF THE CREATIVE TASK

Let us look a little more closely at the social situation in the
'free drama' lesson, and consider what demands it makes on the
children and on the adult in charge.

The visitor—or the headmaster—passing through the hall

may perceive the activity as chaos and shudder to think how much time is being wasted on these apparently trivial and frivolous pursuits. And he may turn out to be correct in his judgement. On the other hand, the chaos may be a prelude to new kinds of imaginative concentration and a new release of expressive powers, both in movement and in language. A young teacher recently put his finger on the key problem in this kind of work. 'The line between playing at doing it and really doing it', he said, 'is a razor edge'. He had come to realize, after a very short time, that drama as a learning activity could not be justified merely on the grounds that the children were free of constraints and were enjoying themselves.

Many teachers have an uneasy sense of guilt about using school time for the activities usually labelled as 'free'. They feel that they are not really doing their job unless they are directing or instructing. And indeed there is a genuine dilemma here. For merely standing back is abdicating. A teacher may withhold himself for thirty minutes and do more real teaching in the last ten than he could have done by struggling to impose his own knowledge and ideas all through the lesson. But if he withholds himself for the whole lesson he cannot be surprised if he sees no evidence of growth the next time he watches the class engaged in a similar activity. The effectiveness of his help may depend on the skill of his timing. He may decide to tolerate confusion for three-quarters of an hour: but if the children go away as confused as they came in they will feel, justifiably, that he has abandoned them.

On one occasion I actually saw a teacher holding himself back in this way and timing his intervention, as I felt, perfectly. The class was a small fourth-year group of nine girls who were in their last term in a comprehensive school. They were extremely immature and of very low intelligence. Mr V. had them once a week for drama. They wanted to make up a play to perform to some other classes in the same age-group. They had only two or three weeks to prepare it. At the beginning of the lesson, Mr V. and I listened to a gabbled and incoherent account of what the play was to be about. The characters were four teenagers, the grandmother of one of them, a colonel and his 'posh' son, and a vicar. With sinking hearts we went along to the school hall and sat at the side of the stage while they proceeded to act out this distinctly unpromising material. One of the girls was sitting in the wings on the other side of the stage watching with growing boredom. The girls who were acting were for most of the time sitting or standing at a table, making no use of the space all around them. The dialogue was equally restricted. It seemed that they were unable to get beyond tedious repetitions of the 'Hallo!', 'Where have you been?', 'Have another cup of tea' order. Pointless as it all was, Mr V. refrained, with an effort, from interfering. The girl on the other side of the stage was presently joined by one of the cast. About ten minutes before the end of the lesson the teacher went over to these two. One of them looked up at him and said: 'It's boring, Sir, isn't it?'

He went over to the seven girls at the table, who had by now collapsed into a hopeless silence. He squatted down at the front of the table so that his face was on a level with theirs and said, without irritation or judgement, but as though echoing what they were feeling: 'It's no good, is it?' They agreed at once, and their despair deepened. They gazed at him helplessly. He began to talk to them. He reminded them that they had set out to invent something funny, that would make people laugh. He went on: 'As this idea hasn't worked'—and was interrupted by one of the girls who, looking at him rather sternly, said: 'It's *failed*.' He accepted this correction, and went on to explain that if they wanted to make people laugh they would have to think of a really funny situation and that it must be something they knew about and must be about the kind of people they knew about. They began to recover slightly. One girl said: 'Well, help us, Sir!' In the few minutes that were left he promised he would bring them five ideas the next morning and that they could choose one of these and see what they could work out. At once they arranged that someone would come and see him the next day, and he assured them that if they wanted his help in dinner hours between then and their next lesson with him, he would be willing to give it.

Watching all this from the side of the stage, I felt in a curious way that I was no longer merely an observer but was being drawn into the event. It seemed to me that it had been enormously important that these girls had been able to experience their own failure, and equally important that the teacher should have identified himself with them in their feelings of failure. This was not a teacher projecting his own anxieties into his pupils or breaking in to discredit their efforts; this was a teacher endorsing their own rejection of what they had been doing, and then helping them to realize why they were rejecting it and how they could redeem themselves. This, as things turned out, was what they were able to do. For out of one of the situations he offered to them they succeeded, during the next two or three weeks, in making up a sketch that was sufficiently credible and realistic to keep their audience attentive and amused for over an hour.

These were fifteen-year-old girls of pathetically low ability. Yet they were not without some sense of standards. And we do well to recognize that all children have this desire to achieve, and that the kind of standard we must always be looking for is the standard which our pupils can reach with effort and concentration, given their own limits of ability. What with able children is only 'playing at doing it' may, with backward children, be 'really doing it'. And it is by no means easy to distinguish between the two. Many young teachers, embarking on improvised drama for the first time, report with varying degrees of tolerance and dissatisfaction that the first improvised sketches, particularly with boys, are always full of crude violence. Whatever situation is offered as a theme for a play, it seems to reduce itself to fighting and rolling about on the ground. Some teachers believe that the children must be allowed to work this out of their systems before they are required to do anything more disciplined. Others believe in short-circuiting this by working with the whole class, using running commentaries about everyday situations, continually stimulating the children's imagination by their own evocative descriptions of the scenes they want them to dramatize.

It may well be that there is no clear answer to this conflict. What one teacher feels comfortable with may be intolerable for another. What will work with a class the teacher knows well and sees several times a week may be quite valueless for another class that he sees only once a week. What is stimulating for eleven-year-olds may be embarrassing for thirteen-year-olds. For drama, like all forms of learning, can promote real growth in skill and understanding only if the relationship between the teacher and his class is secure enough for each to trust the other. The children must be able to believe in the integrity of the teacher; and the teacher must believe in the children's basic desire to get better at whatever it is they are doing. And such a relationship takes time to build.

Teachers will sometimes argue that the crude rough-and-tumble of the earliest forms of improvised drama has a cathartic effect, since it allows for the release of hostile, destructive feelings in a fairly harmless way. But I think we must make a distinction here between this kind of cheerful mutual belabouring and the deeply felt, concentrated expression of powerful feelings that we find in children's dance drama. A primary-school class, taught on Laban principles, played out the death of Minnehaha with great tenderness. An hour or so later the same boys performed a series of dances that they had made up in small groups, without the teacher's help. All these dances involved fierce aggression: somebody had to be killed in each one. But also something precious had to be guarded against injury. Now in none of these did one boy so much as lay a finger on another. But there was no mistaking the strength of their identification with the feelings they were trying to portray. Along with powerfully destructive feelings towards the hated object, there was fear of losing the loved object. These, if Melanie Klein is right, are very primitive emotions, echoing our earliest phantasies about our own destructiveness, our own fear of retaliatory persecution, and our own need to repair the loved objects we have damaged.[1] I cannot feel that the other kind of dramatized violence—the kind that is described by teachers as 'fighting and rolling about on the floor'—can be touching anything as deep in the unconscious as this. Mere horseplay is far more a testing out of the teacher—a probing to the boundaries of freedom—than an acting out of primitive feelings. It is social rather than personal.

Nevertheless, a teacher who chooses to work with improvised dramatic sketches rather than controlled (and, paradoxically, freed) movement can achieve a great deal, if he understands why he is tolerating the undisciplined rough and tumble and if he knows what kind of increase in social understanding he is ultimately hoping to bring about. Progress will depend on the right timing of critical comment, not necessarily from himself but from the children as they watch one another's work. For, if the teacher knows what he is about, it will not be long before

1. Klein, M. (1960) *Our Adult World and its Roots in Infancy*, Tavistock Pamphlet No. 2, London: Tavistock Publications.

the pupils themselves will become dissatisfied with mere horse-play. They will soon begin to demand more realistic portrayal of social roles: a policeman must behave like a policeman; an old woman must look and sound old; fathers and mothers must be credible as adults. Once roles take on more meaning, the children begin to think more deeply about the everyday problems of human relationships, and interactions between these impersonated characters become more realistic and credible. Later still the children themselves begin to develop a feeling for structure and form in their plays, and so, by gradual stages, if the teacher is both patient enough and insistent enough, what looks like meaningless play turns into work that has purpose and demands concentration.

The English teacher who is faced with this dilemma in his drama classes—poised as he is between his wish to free the children from the domination of a dramatic text and his wish to bring about increased sensitivity and discipline in movement and speech—is likely to experience the same tension between apparent opposites in his attempts to get vivid, personalized writing from his pupils. Many teachers are now encouraging children to write poetry. And many of them report that they have great difficulty in freeing children from the tyranny of rhyme. Poetry that does not rhyme is, at first, rejected by children. It does not seem to them to be worthy of the name of poetry. As they themselves attempt to write poems many of them will search for words that chime and echo each other, and will twist their thoughts to accommodate these words. But gradually they can be weaned from this dependence. They begin to search for words and phrases that communicate their own personal feelings. They begin to discover other kinds of form.

But now a difficulty arises. In verse writing, any form of words, however 'ungrammatical', is accepted, provided that it communicates a real idea. And so, for a while, other kinds of writing may become rather wild and disorderly. Spelling, punctuation and sentence structure go to the wall: directness is all. Some teachers are therefore suspicious of the freedom of rhyme-less verse as a medium for children to write in, fearing that, having enjoyed this freedom, they will become undisciplined in their more formal writing. Others accept this new carelessness or exuberance as a natural transition from over-disciplined writing to truly involved writing and go on working patiently for the really important developments, believing that sincerity will in the end bring its own technical controls.

Evidence of this new flowering in children's writing can be found, if we take the trouble to look for it, in the various anthologies, with and without commentaries, that have been appearing recently.[1] When we come to the visual arts, the evidence is more prominent, since it is displayed on the walls of art rooms and sometimes in the halls and corridors where even the casual visitor can hardly fail to be aware of it. Indeed, one of the fundamental differences between the visual arts and those like music and drama and poetry is the directness of communication—a point we shall come back to later. Once the paintings are on the walls or the ceramics are laid out on the tables, there is at least a chance that people will look at them and take pleasure in them. And so the child feels that he has created something, not only for himself, but for the community. All art has this shared quality in some degree. And we should not underestimate the importance of the mutual give-and-take in the art room, the exchange of comments and criticisms that helps children to find their own standards and discipline their own work.

Much of the work now undertaken in school art rooms necessitates a very high degree of cooperation in the group. A class that takes on the task of painting scenery for a play, for example, must pool ideas and work as a sophisticated team to arrive at a unified plan and must wrestle with the technical problems that arise in its execution. Similar projects, on a smaller scale, can be devised to encourage children to work together and to learn from one another.

I once saw a young art teacher engaging a group of a dozen second-year grammar-school boys in this way. They had been working individually on square panels that were eventually to be fitted together to form one mural painting. The original painting which was the model for this work had been chosen by the boys out of a large number of designs that they themselves had submitted, and it was displayed on one of the walls for

1. See, for example, Baldwin, op. cit.; Beckett, Jack (1965) *The Keen Edge*, London: Blackie; Clegg, A. B. (ed.) (1964) *The Excitement of Writing*, London: Chatto & Windus; Ford, Boris (ed.) (1960) *Young Writers, Young Readers*, London: Hutchinson; Hourd, Marjorie L. (1949) *The Education of the Poetic Spirit*, London: Heinemann; Hourd, Majorie L. and Cooper, Gertrude E. (1959) *Coming into Their Own*, London: Heinemann.

reference. The mural was not supposed to be a mere enlarged copy of this. The aim was to produce a new composite work of art which would be a different version of the same design. The design itself was extremely complex, suggesting a tropical jungle and full of rich blending colours. The twelve boys had fitted their squares together on the floor and were standing round with their teacher considering what each needed to do to make his work fit better into the context of the whole. As they discussed it they had to try to explain to one another what they were trying to do, relate the whole combined work back to the original painting, incorporate the new ideas and modify the separate pieces so that one boy's intention could be reconciled with another's. As a combination of teamwork and respect for individuals it was remarkable. In fact there was, in this situation, the same kind of balance between individual creativeness and awareness of the demands of the group that I had repeatedly seen when I watched movement classes. The discipline was inherent in the work of art they were striving to create together.

Now if we compare the demands of this piece of group work with the demands made on younger children painting a large mural we see an important difference. At the primary-school level the mural may depict, say, a circus: one child, perched on a stool, will be painting the sky with birds to decorate it; another, crouching on the floor, will be busy painting the faces of the crowd along the lower edge; in between, other children will be working on the tents and caravans, the horses or lions in the ring, the clowns at the side, and so on. Or, if the mural is to represent a strip of coast-line in some luxuriant imaginary land, one child will be responsible for the trees, another for the flowers, another for the animals, another for the sea-shore, another for the fishes in the sea. In this situation, there must be a great deal of physical give and take, but every child can let his imagination run riot through the objects he has chosen to paint into the picture. In the group in the secondary school, on the other hand, the boys were having to cooperate on a more abstract, thinking level. Each boy's perception of his own part of the painting and his perception of the final product had to be tested against the views of the other eleven. The work of art they were trying to create had to look as if it had been painted by one person. To achieve this, all twelve had to look for possible ways of merging their ideas and at the same time search for the inner meaning of the whole picture that was beginning to take shape.

If drama is the most social and group-directed of the expressive arts, painting is perhaps the most individual and inner-directed. Yet we have seen that once drama is freed from the social convention of 'theatre' it begins to find echoes in the deepest layers of the child's personality; and we have seen that through the effort to create a composite painting a group of children can learn a great deal about the social arts of cooperation and mutual give and take. In both situations, heart and head must work together. The freeing of the personality makes for a new kind of social control and a new kind of intellectual communication.

What, then, of music-making, which can be as solitary as painting or as group-centred as drama? The child, when he is practising on his recorder or his violin or his piano, is thrown back on his own resources; but when he is playing in the school orchestra or singing in the choir he must accept the authority of the conductor, who alone knows what the combined efforts of his players or singers should sound like. Is there anything between these two extremes? Can music be produced by a group of children only under the baton of a dictator? Where does creative invention come in?

At this point we must pause and consider what we really mean by 'creative' activity, for already it is becoming evident that we have to distinguish between two kinds of creativeness. The painter and the poet communicate directly with those who receive and try to understand what they have created. But the composer and the dramatist depend on performers—singers and instrumentalists and actors—for this act of communication. True, one can hear a poem being read aloud, and one can study a musical score in the privacy of one's study. But the music cannot be fully apprehended until it is heard, whereas the poem can be. Now the fact is that in the majority of our schools musical activity, unlike art, is almost entirely at the second level: that is, it is the recreation of other people's music that we hear rather than music composed by the children themselves. Generally speaking, music in the schools is still in the position that drama was in before teachers discovered that children were not merely potential actors but also potential dramatists. One notable exception is the work of Maxwell Davies at Cirencester Grammar School, which recently became famous for its performances of works composed by pupils.[1] Nevertheless it has to be admitted that music teachers have not yet advanced far in this new direction. Why should this be?

The music teacher is faced with two formidable difficulties. In the first place, he needs expensive equipment in the shape of musical instruments, and some authorities are unwilling to put money aside for these, as they will for scientific and technological equipment. His second problem is more fundamental. Unlike his art and drama colleagues, he has to enable his pupils to handle a new set of symbols. In fact, his problem is not unlike the mathematician's: for just as the mathematician has to teach his pupils the language of number, so the musician has to teach his the language of music. How is this usually done in the early stages?

Doubtless we can all remember how laboriously we had to learn and memorize the facts about notation, scales, time-signatures, key-signatures and all the rest of it. Kindly teachers gave us amusing mnemonics to help us to remember the letter names of the lines of the treble and bass staves. Gradually it was all drummed into us. But how much did any of us really discover for ourselves in the process? To what extent did 'melody' and 'rhythm' emerge from the sounds we were already using every time we opened our mouths to speak? The answer is, very little. We had to accept the forms of music, as presented to us by our teachers, before we had any basis of experience on which this knowledge could be built.

However, changes are on the way. Today the work of Carl Orff is beginning to revolutionize music teaching just as the work of Cizek revolutionized art teaching thirty years ago. It is strange that the change in music has been so much longer in coming, and that even now it has hardly extended beyond the infant schools. Again the fundamental principle is that the teacher starts with what the child already has and helps him to make new discoveries for himself. Molière's Monsieur Jourdain discovered that he had been speaking prose all his life; but children taught according to Orff's methods discover that they have been speaking music. First their own names, then simple

1. Davies, Maxwell (1963) 'Music', in *Studies in Education: The Arts and Current Trends in Education*, London: Evans.

phrases used in everyday speech, then street cries and nursery rhymes are found to incorporate rhythmic melodies. From this it is a natural step to a more advanced discovery—that when someone makes up a speech tune that is too long and complicated to hold in the memory, he must use symbols so that he can write it down and make it permanent. And so, once again, the formal discipline arises from the necessities of the creative invention itself.

What about harmony? This, too, can start from creative experimenting rather than from imposed rules. A student from Bingley Training College reported in *The New Era* a series of experiments with infant-school children which strongly resembled Orff's methods and may have been consciously based on them. The xylophone and glockenspiel and simple percussion instruments invented by Orff for his pupils in the Guentherschule were used experimentally by the children, first spontaneously at the music table during the free activity period and then in groups with the teacher's help. And gradually, an improvised accompaniment to a song took shape as the children tried out this effect and that, discovering which notes sounded good together.[1]

Is this kind of spontaneous activity appropriate only to the infant school? By no means. It is already being discovered that the same principle can be used with adolescents. It can be an illuminating experience to watch girls or boys of about thirteen or fourteen making music in this way. Perhaps two will improvise a sequence, one playing the glockenspiel and the other the melodica, using the pentatonic scale, in which any two notes will sound well together. The ideas may be very simple, but if the sensitivity to rhythm, melody and tone, and to the effects of changes in volume and tempo, is there, the effect is surprisingly beautiful.

In music, as in drama, creating and performing go side by side, and it is sometimes very difficult to tell where one ends and the other begins. Similarly, the inter-dependence between performing and listening is very close. The more children are actually engaged in making their own music, the more receptive do they become when they listen to others people's. This link between creative activity and appreciative response is not

1. Barker, Elizabeth (1965) 'The Creative Aspect of Music in the Infant School', *New Era*, vol. 46, No. 2.

peculiar to music: children who struggle to write their own poems become more receptive to poetry, and those who experience the joys and difficulties of painting and modelling bring a keener eye to other people's paintings and sculptures. We cannot rigidly separate the two kinds of experience, nor should we try to, for each enriches the other. Even a guitar player in a beat group may surprise us by saying that, as a result of his own struggles to master his instrument and improvise the music he plays with it, he can now enjoy listening to serious music by composers such as Bartok and Stravinsky.

It is easy for us to despise the beat groups. But the fact that young people all over the country are spontaneously forming themselves into groups to create this music should make us pause and consider how the gap between 'school music' and what goes on in the 'caverns' and 'sinks' of Liverpool and Birmingham and other large cities has come into existence, and what can be done to narrow the gap. The creative urge is there. But most secondary schools do not yet know how to use it. Most teachers are painfully aware of the pop groups and beat groups and what they stand for. And even within the schools there is a wide gulf between those pupils who join the school choir or play in the city youth orchestra and those whose interest is limited to pop music.

Some music teachers make little concession to this difference. They expect children against all reason to like what they like. They would feel guilty if they introduced into a music lesson anything less respectable than Gilbert and Sullivan. Many, however, see their role in a different light altogether. But as soon as they depart from the traditional kinds of class singing, theory and music appreciation, they find themselves in the same kind of dilemma as their drama colleagues. What happens when the musician frees his class from the Cecil Sharp versions of folk songs, from the respectable 'classics' and from the toil of learning scales, time-signatures and the rules of harmony and modulation? What happens when he invites them to bring their guitars and their pop songs and show him what they can do within their own musical culture?

I heard of one music teacher in a secondary-modern girls' school who, in despair about her apathetic IVC, took this risk. She sent them off in groups of five or six to arrange a song—any song they knew and liked—for a performance in front of the whole class two or three weeks later. They had to decide how to sing it and they had to improvise an accompaniment. All the groups managed to produce something. Most of the performances were crude; one was appallingly bad; but one astonished her by its vitality and originality. I have often wondered what these girls eventually achieved, once they had been freed from the conventional music lesson and had freed themselves from mere imitation of the pop singers they heard on their transistor sets and record players. I have also wondered how much they were able to learn about rhythm and harmony from their own struggles to produce the sounds they wanted from their instruments.

There is, in the 'modern folk tradition'—as exemplified by such groups as The Liverpool Spinners, The Ian Campbell Group of Glasgow, and The Seekers from Australia—a wide open field for music teachers to work in. But they will have to tread warily. For these folk groups, of which there may be many more than we know about, draw their strength from the fact that they have evolved spontaneously, outside the school walls and without the disciplining hand of the teacher. The adult who merely tries to cash in on it may destroy it. We cannot exploit it: we can only learn to appreciate it and recognize it as a new source of growth.

4. THE TEACHER AS PROMOTER

I have been considering how good teachers—whatever the medium they work in—try to free children to use their own initiative and explore new ideas. Sometimes the results of this are tangible and permanent works of art—paintings or models or poems or musical compositions; sometimes they are ephemeral creations—dances, plays or musical performances, capable, perhaps, of recreation in similar forms, but living only in the memory once the performance is over; sometimes they are mental acquisitions, abstract concepts in the mind of the learner, with no outward sensory form, but with unlimited potentialities for future use and expansion. One characteristic all these achievements share: they depend on the personal involvement of the child in whatever he is doing and on his willingness to discipline his fantasy or his exploration or his experimental activity so that he can give it form and coherence. And this is true whether it is an individual child or a group of children we are considering, and whether the teacher is present with them or not.

It may appear that I have been over-estimating the child's capacity to initiate his own learning and under-estimating the role of the teacher. But the teacher remains the key person in the whole enterprise; for it is he who must create the conditions for this kind of learning, whether it be in a classroom, a laboratory, an art studio or a gymnasium, and whatever the ages and abilities of the class. The apparent chaos of toys and materials and playing children in an infant classroom is really a very carefully planned environment. The hive of industry in a junior classroom where nine-year-olds are carrying out spinning and weaving and dyeing operations in an imaginary society of medieval guildsmen has not sprung into existence by accident, but has been made possible by energetic planning on the part of a teacher. The scene in a science laboratory where a class of twelve-year-olds are engaged in a variety of experiments in an apparently random fashion may be the culmination of weeks of patient investigation by the teacher to discover just what problems the boys are ready to tackle. The exploration and testing out of new forms of language in a French class with the help of tape recorders and film strips are based on a systematic understanding both of the structure of the foreign language and of the amount of new learning that can be attempted in any one period. An apparently unprepared discussion in a group of fifteen-year-olds about the problems of old age may have arisen because a teacher has been providing a diet of reading that is helping them to look at older people, and at their own relationship with them, with growing sensitivity.

The successful teacher helps children to build on their own discoveries and to test their developing skills and awarenesses in a variety of ways. By doing this, he gives them a sense of kinship with the great discoverers and inventors and artists of history, not by pretending that they are cleverer or more gifted than they really are, but by believing in their fundamental desire to learn, even when learning involves struggling with difficulties and experiencing periodic set-backs. Children of all ages can tolerate frustration if they also experience success, and if adults can help them to contain the frustration without being demoralized by it.

Teachers will sometimes imply that the pressure of examinations forces them to cut down or even to eliminate work of a creative or exploratory nature. 'There isn't time,' they say: 'if we don't stick to the syllabus, the standards will suffer.' And often enough their pupils are only too ready to go into collusion with them and to insist even more strenuously than the teacher himself that to go outside the syllabus is an unpardonable waste of time. So we have English specialists who have written nothing of a personal nature since they were children, scientists who have never designed an experiment for themselves, musicians who have never composed any music apart from that involved in exercises in harmony and counterpoint. In invoking the 'standard' demanded by the examination, a teacher may seem to imply that 'standards' are not demanded by the kind of work we have been considering in this chapter. Yet if he pauses to reflect, he will realize that the children themselves set standards when they care about the work they are doing. Carrying out various tests on a piece of metal wire to discover what metal it is, shaping a lump of clay into an imaginary animal, matching a series of rhythmic tunes on a guitar to the words of a folk song, finding phrases and sentences to communicate a frightening experience—all these demand a disciplined attention and the child who experiences a measure of satisfaction in any of these activities will be likely to demand more of himself when he tackles the next task.

Recognizing all this the teacher may well repudiate the examination, in his mind, as an unnecessary prop, and he may even doubt whether the 'results' as measured by the examination bear any relationship to the really important outcomes of the kind of teaching he would like to be doing. Yet he may convince himself that, because of the demands of society, he has to submit to being hamstrung by the examination syllabus, and may try to comfort himself with the thought that if only someone would rid him of it he would be able to teach better than he does.

If we are not to continue using the examination as a sort of whipping boy which can be blamed for everything we fail to do as teachers, we have to address ourselves to the question of what examinations are really for. And this leads us straight into the much more fundamental question of what we mean by evaluation and assessment.

CHAPTER EIGHT

Learning, Performance and Evaluation

I. THE SCHOOL, THE ADJUDICATOR AND THE EXTERNAL EXAMINER

The basic problem of rivalry, first experienced in the family group, is re-enacted with varying degrees of intensity in the working groups that children find themselves in at school. By the time they reach the secondary school this rivalry—at first linked strongly to the need for the affection of an adult—has been absorbed into the less obviously emotional phenomenon we call 'competition'. It has come to be centred on achievement, rather than on the felt experience of being loved.

This competition may be associated with physical, artistic or intellectual rivalry; and it is nearly always linked in some way with the favour or approval of an adult. When the achievements of a number of children are compared by a teacher or by some other adult called in from outside to offer a judgement, the one who wins special recognition is, in a sense, being picked out by the adult for a special, unshared relationship which is denied to the other members of his group. At some level of feeling, probably most children—whether clever or stupid, co-operative or antagonistic, communicative or silent—have a primitive, unrealistic wish to monopolize the teacher, or at least to appear in his eyes as important in some way, if only in a negative way. Even in the most socially cohesive class, this member or that will secretly want to be the pupil whom the teacher likes best; even in the most integrated football team, there will be more than one boy who wants to be the next player to win the captain's approval and be awarded his colours; in a music or poetry-speaking competition nearly every candidate hopes to be singled out for the adjudicator's admiration. If G.C.E. and C.S.E. and all the other proliferations of the public examination system were to disappear overnight, competition would not cease to exist.

How does the school as an institution deal with this problem of rivalry? If we look at sports, cultural contests and public examinations, in that order, an interesting sequence appears. The more closely the outcome of a competitive activity touches a child's personal aspirations, the more carefully does the school (or society) distance the task of assessing his achievement in relation to the achievements of his fellows.

The importance of a school or house match is comparatively ephemeral. For most children, the glory or disappointment of one Saturday morning's victory or defeat is soon superseded by the next. The rivalry is open, physically exhilarating, emotionally exciting, a battle in which the rules are known and in which a staff member or older pupil well known to at least half the contestants can easily be accepted as referee. In fact, one of the obligations on all players is to accept the judgements of the referee. Cries of 'unfair!' are strictly frowned upon. The match is over in a few hours or even less than an hour, and the rivalries subside for another week.

The annual verse-speaking competition is a more prolonged and carefully prepared event, going through phases that may last for several weeks. The ability to shine on such an occasion demands more exposure of the personality and offers less protection in the group. In the last resort, if you are reading or reciting a poem, you have to walk on to the platform alone and rely entirely on yourself. The more formalized and testing a situation this becomes, the more likely it is that the school will call in an outside adjudicator, someone with 'stranger value', someone whose judgement cannot, in the interests of hospitality and good public relations, be for a moment questioned, at least not in his presence. The teacher who has been running the competition, and who may have selected the finalists for that particular afternoon, avoids the pain of naming one child as his or her first choice. By teacher and competitors alike the adjudicator is invested with a sort of magic power to know the best when he sees it.

In fact he has no such magic. As he listens to the performances he is likely to become more and more uncomfortably aware of the inadequacy of his criteria. If he has to hear a set piece spoken by a succession of pupils, he may find himself changing his criteria as the afternoon goes on. If the competitors have been given a limited choice, he may be faced with having to make comparisons between quite different kinds of achievement. If the choice has been unlimited, other criteria have to come into play, and he finds himself making value judgements, not only about a child's performance but also about the piece he has chosen to perform and perhaps about the child's wisdom or unwisdom in attempting to interpret it. The rules of the competition may force the adjudicator to select one, two or three winning entries, yet there may be at least five or six readings to which he finds himself responding equally warmly. So he has to search for a rational justification for awarding prizes to some but not to others.

The adjudicator is really having to cope with two conflicting tasks: on the one hand, he is required to make judgements and put people into an order of merit; on the other, he has to look for growing points and prepare himself to deal with a learning situation that is still going on. For when he faces all the performers at the end of the day his real task is to help them to learn from the experience they have just been through—to learn to look more deeply into a poem, to develop (or control) the range and expressiveness of their voices, to understand the complex nature of what we call 'interpretation'. Perhaps, also, he may wish to help them to look at the role of the adjudicator in a new way, and to see him less as a judge than as another human being with whom each of them has been sharing an experience.

As a visitor he is, of course, in a strongly protected position. However tedious his remarks at the end, or however incomprehensible, he is treated like a V.I.P. The children listen as if his appreciative or critical comments are of far more importance to them than the results they know he will announce at the end. Yet he will probably have the uncomfortable feeling that all they really want to hear from him is his list of winners, and that what they are listening for is some clue that will 'give the result away'. So he feels impelled to make obvious jokes about keeping them in suspense, and he may well find himself wishing that he had defied the usual conventions and got the announcement of the 'results' over at the beginning.

The outside adjudicator may appear only once in any one school. Or he may become a favourite and return again and again to offer his judgements, his encouragements and his criticisms. If he appears frequently, he may lose his 'stranger value' as an assessor and set up in the school a kind of stereotype of 'the adjudicator's expectations'. On the other hand, if he becomes known to the school he may find himself becoming more and more closely concerned with the competition as a continuing and changing activity in the school. In this case his role as an assessor may come to be seen as not, after all, divorced from the teaching role, any more than the teacher's role is really divorced from the responsibility for assessment.

When we come to the public examination, which is closely bound up, not merely with the child's personal aspirations in what will probably always be a leisure activity, but with the kind of career he will take up as an adult, the arbiter of his destinies has to be a much more distant figure—one whom he will never see and who will know him only as a number on an examination script and as a certain kind of handwriting and a certain style of thinking and expression. The assessor is no longer even a person: he is an unknown member of an examining board. How does this fact influence the relationship between teachers and their pupils as the time of the examination draws near?

Young teachers are often greatly troubled by the fear that, in a system which equates success in learning with success in passing competitive examinations, they may be unable to remain true to the ideals with which they are setting out. This fear is based on a genuine concern for the pupils they will be teaching. For the responsibility that rests upon them to 'get their pupils through their "O" levels and "A" levels' is not imaginary. Yet the recognition of the reality of examinations is not unalloyed by elements of fantasy in the way teachers—young and old—tend to regard the whole problem of evaluation and assessment.

The examination is both a threat and a protection. It is a threat because it appears to deprive the teacher of initiative; and it is a protection because it saves him from the necessity of examining his real aims. Small wonder that the teaching profession as a whole maintains a highly ambivalent attitude towards examinations. Small wonder that the new Certificate of Secondary Education, to be entirely controlled by the teachers, elicits qualms of self-doubt.

The doubts are usually rationalized as a modest reluctance to take on the task of making final judgements which will radically affect young people's careers in a fiercely competitive world. But behind this there lurks the irrational desire to preserve the external, anonymous 'them' into whom can be projected the more hostile elements of the teacher–pupil relationship. There has always been something reassuring about the ritual of examination papers arriving in sealed envelopes, not to be opened before the hour of the examination even by the teachers, and of the completed scripts being dispatched to unknown markers without being read, or even so much as glanced at, by the teachers. All this, along with the air of warm protectiveness towards the candidates that pervades the whole school at the crucial time, enables teachers and pupils alike to perpetuate the fantasy that teaching and assessment are distinct and separate functions. Suddenly, the teacher and the pupil are ranged against the examiner; and the fact that examining, in some form, has really always been a part of the teacher's function is forgotten.

Some teachers enter into a kind of open conspiracy with their pupils, explaining to them that true education has to go by the board during the months before the external examination. In the interest of beating the examiner at his own game, they undertake with their pupils to use these months for intensive and quite uneducational cramming. In this way the teacher contrives to shift the centre of the rivalry. It is no longer his own pupils who are competing against each other for high marks in the impending trials; the rivalry is, by implication, between his group and those other candidates—unknown and depersonalized like the examiners—who are being prepared for the ordeal by other teachers. The group, it seems, preserves itself by uniting against those unknown rival groups in the struggle to gain the favour of the examiner.

2. INCENTIVES AND ACHIEVEMENT

We sometimes argue as if the choice between competition and cooperation were an 'either-or' choice of incentive in the classroom, whereas in fact all any teacher can regulate is the balance between them. Every learning situation that involves a group is bound to have elements of both. By emphasizing the learning rather than the results, we tip the balance towards cooperation; by emphasizing the results rather than the learning, we tip it towards competition. But we never reach a state where either wholly excludes the other.

A football, hockey or cricket match will be less enjoyable if the result is a foregone conclusion. The contestants go out hoping for a well-matched struggle. To win is by no means all. Wertheimer's description of the two boys playing badminton illustrates this point well.[1] As long as the older, more skilled player used his strength and talent merely to defeat and demoralize his inexperienced opponent there was no pleasure for either of them. But once he began to send the shuttlecock over in such a way that the younger boy could return it with increasing accuracy, the whole emotional climate changed. By turning the situation into a cooperative enterprise the older boy brought into existence a game that both could enjoy. Paradoxically, he also created conditions in which the competitive excitement had more reality.

Let us return to the school verse-speaking contest, and consider what incentives are operating here. Can we assume that the slender hope of winning a prize, or even the consciously worked up excitement of a house competition, is the main incentive that prompts so many children to undergo the hard work and the nervous strain of entering for these competitions? Would not the feeling for poetry and the wish to learn how to read it with increased sensitivity and with greater technical mastery operate just as strongly in a non-competitive festival, where there were no prizes to win, and where the objective was not primarily to compete but to give one another pleasure?

Now, we must recognize that if a school decides to hold such a festival, it will not be possible to eliminate rivalry, for speakers will still have to be selected to contribute towards the programme, since time must impose limitations on the number that can take part. But suppose each house or year group is given a theme to illustrate, or a group of poems from which to choose; and suppose that committees are set up to hold auditions and to decide what items should be included in the programme. The children are now handling the rivalry themselves, by becoming evaluators of one another's contributions. They have to collaborate in order to make decisions about the kind of programme they want to present. By the time they are

1. Wertheimer, M. (1959) *Productive Thinking*, New York: Harper & Row, pp. 169–81.

listening to an outside adjudicator's appraisal of these programmes—their own and those provided by other groups—
they will themselves have had experience of being adjudicators.
In a festival of this kind the staff, as the sanctioning authority,
can ensure that the competitive elements are held within a basically cooperative framework. By contrast, in the usual kind of
event the framework is competitive, although the children have
to cooperate in certain ways (by agreeing to appear in a certain
order, for example) in order to compete.

This interplay of competitive and cooperative elements in a
group or community enterprise seems to vary according to
whether primitive emotional forces or sophisticated work-
group forces are dominant. I can further illustrate this idea by
examining the culture pattern in the National Music Camp in
the United States, which I visited one week-end. This camp is
held for six or eight weeks every summer in the north of the
state of Michigan, for boys and girls from high schools all over
the country. It provides intensive experience in choral, orches-
tral, operatic and dramatic work for talented children and
young people. It is an honour to be selected to go to it in the
first place. Once there, every student can entertain the possibility of being asked to play in the All High Schools Orchestra,
which draws the best talent from the camp, or of being promoted
to lead an orchestra or a section of an orchestra, or of being
asked to play a solo—perhaps even to be soloist in a concerto—
in a week-end concert or in the culminating concert at the end
of the summer school. For these highly talented young musicians
such competition is stimulating rather than threatening. But it
takes second place to the need to combine together, for always
the music has to come first.

Soon after my return from this visit, I met a high-school
teacher who had once been a student at this camp. She described
an incident that illustrated how self-interest could yield to the
needs of the group in such a work-centred community. The
leader of the orchestra in which she played was a boy, the
deputy leader a girl. One morning the leader arrived two
minutes late for rehearsal. The conductor told the deputy leader
to move up into his place, and indicated to the boy that he had
now lost the coveted position. Nothing more was said. The next
day the girl deliberately arrived two minutes late, and the boy
was reinstated. To her it was more important that the orchestra

should have the leader it needed than that she should enjoy the prestige of occupying his place. 'That,' said my informant, 'was the kind of place we were working in.'

It would be easy to suggest that the week-end performances at this camp represented the ultimate achievements of the students and their teachers. Yet it is unlikely that any of those who have attended it would subscribe to this view. A performance is over as soon as the last note has been played. But the achievement on which that performance rests has an enduring quality. What a boy learns about the structure of a Mozart symphony, about the texture of its orchestration, about its emotional colouring and about the demands it makes on his own skill as an instrumentalist and on the conductor's skill as an interpreter remains with him long after the thrill of the actual occasion has subsided. As a result of having worked at it he will bring to every new hearing of the symphony an informed intelligence and a sensitized ear.

Music, perhaps more than any other activity, needs performance for its very existence. The knowledge that the future contains an audience for whom the music will be played binds the members of a choir or orchestra together in a shared responsibility. The same, of course, is true for a drama group. The challenge of a performance has the effect of making all members of the team feel personally committed to the task and personally involved in the outcome. Yet, if the learning is too much overweighted by anxiety about the performance the really important achievements may be lost. A classroom project—say, a local study based on history and geography—can gain something enormously valuable if the children understand that they are building up an exhibition at which they will be the expert guides and lecturers. But if the teacher loses sight of the real purpose of the learning and becomes over-anxious about the exhibition as a performance that will reflect *his* skill as a teacher, he may destroy the very thing he has set out to create.

In situations like these, achievement can often be confused with performance. Indeed, achievement, in its public aspect, must inevitably have blended with it certain ingredients of performance, and therefore of rivalry. If the teacher allows himself to pay too much attention to his own wish to shine among teachers, through the performances of his pupils, he may lose sight of his true objectives. We need to be sure, both as teachers and learners, which of these two elements is of the greater importance, or the learning process may be seriously distorted.

This was brought home to me once, when I was working with a group of teachers on a course of choral verse-speaking. They had enrolled for this course knowing that the time would be spent, not in talking about how to read and interpret poetry, but in actually doing it. At the outset, there was no thought of a culminating performance. But after a week or so it was suggested to me that I should use this group in a demonstration to which teachers in the area should be invited to come. The group appeared to welcome this challenge, and from then onwards we found ourselves engaged in building a programme.

For a while the thought of the culminating performance appeared to be having no adverse effects. On the contrary, it seemed to be providing us with an additional, unforeseen incentive. But when the demonstration was only three or four weeks distant, I suddenly became sharply aware of a difference that was coming into my own attitude to the task. I realized that I was becoming more concerned that they should acquit themselves well as *my* choir than that they should be learning about the problems and pitfalls, the pleasures and excitements of speaking verse as a group. I found that I was growing anxious and even somewhat irritable in my striving after effects. And suddenly I realized that there would inevitably be moments of achievement that we could share in these weekly sessions that could never be recaptured when there was an audience in front of us, and that this was of no importance whatsoever. I began to realize dimly that I must keep my attention on the essential experiences and not worry too much—or not worry them too much—about the performance that was to come; and I realized that if our work was sincere, the public occasion would produce its own achievements, which would be as much a product of the coming together of choir and audience as of all our rehearsals. Indeed, in order to preserve the integrity of the course as a learning situation, it became necessary for me to renounce the growing idea that these sessions were merely rehearsals for that culminating performance. Once we all recognized what had been happening, we were able to halt the deterioration in the learning situation without abandoning our responsibilities towards the audience we were eventually to face.

3. ASSESSMENT AND TEACHING

A public examination has in it something of the drama and occasion of a performance. No teacher, in preparing his pupils to meet it, is so altruistic as to be unaffected by the hope that they will acquit themselves well, for his sake as well as for their own, for he cannot but be aware that his success or failure will be measured by their results. And so, along with the anxiety lest the examination system should force him to abandon his ideals, there is a desire to 'get good examination results'. The temptation to 'play safe' and prepare the candidates for likely questions rather than educate them in the subject will be very strong for any teacher, all the stronger since he will easily be able to justify his policy in terms of his pupils' needs.

The frighteningly direct statement from a young chemistry master quoted by Jackson and Marsden illustrates the dangers of this attitude all too clearly.[1] This young man reckons that he 'can do A level chem. in four terms—four terms flat out, mind', boasts of the open scholarship, the exhibition and the six places he got last year, and looks forward to becoming head of department in 'a really good school', where he will 'really work those children, tests, tests, tests, and get the results'. He adds, revealingly: 'Get them the results they should have, and that would establish me, wouldn't it? It would get me a reputation. People would know that I could do the job.' As a sop to his conscience he adds that, having 'scrubbed' the teaching methods and 'forgotten' the educational side for ten years or so, he might then 'start looking round and thinking more about the education side'. The tragedy is that he will in the meantime have become incapable of understanding the difference between education and instruction, and that he will have pushed round his sixth-form treadmill a hundred or more young people, many of whom may go back into the schools and teach in much the same way as he taught them.

Few young teachers, let us hope, are as ruthless as this one, or so blind to the real needs of the children they are teaching. Yet most of us have known what it is to feel trapped in the examination system. A child's performance in an examination does not necessarily represent his total achievement in the sub-

1. Jackson, B. and Marsden, D. (1962) *Education and the Working Class*, London: Routledge & Kegan Paul, pp. 36-7.

ject. Few teachers would for a moment believe that it did. Yet we all behave at times as though it did. We have all put up with examination syllabuses which we felt to be constricting and which we knew might block the way to achievements of which our pupils might have been capable. How many of us have ever taken advantage of the clause in the examination regulations that authorizes teachers to submit their own syllabuses and be examined on these rather than on the prescribed ones? It is hard to find teachers who have taken this 'risky' step. Most of us—alas—have preferred to accept the syllabus and grumble about it.

Yet, after all, what is a syllabus? The word has become so emotionally loaded that we have to think quite hard to produce a valid definition. It has come to be regarded as something that confines the teacher within unwanted boundaries, limiting his spontaneity and depriving his pupils of initiative. Yet, in truth, a syllabus is nothing more inhibiting than a formulation of teaching objectives, leaving teachers and learners free to make excursions in any direction they choose in search of fresh material and evidence that will throw light on the general field of study. There was nothing to prevent me as an English teacher from reading round the set books for the English literature paper when I taught my fifth forms. Yet I never dared to do this, although the study of *Macbeth*, for example, would have been greatly illuminated by a few excursions into contemporary studies of political tyranny and the study of *The Trumpet Major* would have been enriched by some further reading of Hardy. Once my pupils entered the fifth year, I 'stuck to the syllabus', and it was some years before I even woke up to the fact that dictating notes was a poor way to equip them for the examination, quite apart from its effect on their own literary tastes.

If I had tried to depart from the syllabus, no doubt my pupils would have put obstacles in my way. For they were probably just as anxious to 'play safe' as I was. Teachers and pupils are very ready to go into collusion with one another over this excessive veneration of the syllabus. Perhaps we have to admit that the confining bounds we so easily complain about are—like the anonymous external examiner—precious to us.

Because of the unnatural separation of the functions of teacher and examiner at the top of the secondary school, it is hard for teachers to accept the idea that if their pupils are mastering skills and concepts through their own discoveries they will be able to take the examination in their stride when the time comes. Indeed, the externalization of the assessment role can affect a school's policy, as well as an individual teacher's classroom methods, in quite fundamental ways.

In School A, a highly selective grammar school, the headmaster feels it his duty to encourage his staff to get as many of their pupils through as many examinations as possible. The boys in one 'fast' stream take several 'O' level papers in their fourth year. The successful ones go straight into the sixth form, where they are faced with specialized studies that they may not be mature enough to tackle; the unsuccessful ones find themselves, at the end of the fourth year, ready to become the discouraged transition group of the fifth year—the bright boys who have failed to accomplish what was expected of them. The rat-race has pushed some people into the sixth form a year ahead of their time, and left others in the fifth form with their own age group, feeling demoralized and humiliated.

In School B, a secondary-modern school, where original, creative work is going on, the headmistress sets her face against any intrusion of G.C.E. examinations. At the same time, she recognizes the claims of society on her brightest pupils and indeed their right to the best possible educational opportunity; and so she takes steps to see that her ablest girls are transferred to grammar schools as soon as they show signs of being able to profit from an academic education.

Thus, each head adheres to the type of education for which, it is supposed, his or her school exists. Ironically, however, the headmaster grudges time for the creative activities that could illuminate and vitalize his pupils' academic studies, while the headmistress deprives her best pupils of the creative experience she believes in by sending them away to other schools where she suspects they may be starved of it. Thus the one head accepts the public examination in his school as a necessary evil, while the other excludes it from hers as an unnecessary evil.

Today, with the advent of the C.S.E. examination,[1] teachers have a real opportunity to revolutionize the whole system of assessment of school learning. Many are already hard at work

1. *Certificate of Secondary Education*, Bulletins I-IV, (1964–5) London: H.M.S.O.

designing new kinds of syllabus that will leave more scope for personal choice and initiative, both on the part of the teacher and on the part of the pupil. The way is open for radical changes. But to take it will demand courage. In the past the most that teachers could do—even the most adventurous—was to design their own syllabuses and submit them to the examining board for approval. Many imaginative and resourceful teachers, without actually taking this step, have found ways of teaching flexibly within the familiar syllabus boundaries. But now they have the chance—if they use the third mode in the C.S.E. examination—to take over the examining role themselves, with the help of external moderators. If they are to use this role to strengthen their own work as teachers, they will need to move towards an entirely new definition of the relationship between the functions of teaching and assessment.

In becoming examiners in the full sense, teachers will have to learn to accept and work with the mutual anxieties of teacher and learner that will inevitably arise. For there is no escape from this anxiety. There never has been. Any junior-school teacher, asked to rate his ten-year-old pupils for the purpose of selection for grammar-school places, has to deal with his anxiety about the validity of his judgements; any university teacher who has to speak for or against a border-line candidate in the degree examination has to go through a great deal of heart-searching as he decides whether to recommend him for a pass or a fail, for a first class or a second class; no tutor in a college or department of education ever finds it possible to dissociate his personal feelings about a student from the evidence that he gives in the examiners' meeting or from the reference he writes for a prospective employer. Personal relationships can no more be divorced from the process of assessment than they can be divorced from the process of educating. And the secondary-school teacher, in accepting this new role of examiner in relation to his older pupils is doing just what his colleagues in some primary schools and in all universities have been doing for a long time. Once the reality is accepted on both sides, the teacher–pupil relationship may be deepened and enriched as a result of it, as I believe it has been deepened and enriched in the colleges and departments of education that use continuous assessment rather than a final examination at the end of the course.

We have been accustomed to think of the G.C.E. examination

as something that is end-stopped, rather than as a logical continuation of a learning process. And this has had its effect on the way in which younger pupils and their teachers regard the various school examinations that are seen to be leading up to it. The ritual of 'going through the papers' after school examinations does little to offset this tendency, although it pays lip-service to the idea that there should be some feed-back to the pupils. Children resist this ritual so strongly that even the most skilful of teachers is apt to feel the foundations of his good relationships with pupils crumbling as he struggles on with the post-mortem. Perhaps what is needed on these occasions is not a post-mortem but a new lease of life. Perhaps we need to learn how to design examination papers which themselves provide new starting points or give rise to group projects that enable the pupils to return quickly from the competitive isolation of the examination room to the interdependent activity of the classroom. For, however strongly children resist the post-mortem, a resolution to transfer attention immediately to some totally unrelated activity, as though the examination has been irrelevant and unimportant, is likely to leave a sense of frustration and dissatisfaction also.

At fifth and sixth form levels the role of the examiner has hitherto been seen as something totally divorced from the role of the teacher. Once the examination script has been written and sent off, the question paper is interesting only as the context from which teacher and pupil together can try to predict a result. No one is interested in using it as a basis for further learning. Lower down in the school, where examinations are internal and marked by the teachers themselves, this determination to keep the two roles apart is already at work. Teachers unconsciously go into collusion with their pupils over this by posting the examination results in order of merit, or even by making a dramatic ritual of reading them out in descending or in ascending order, to the accompaniment of gasps of surprise, pleasure, relief, disappointment or anger, not to mention the unexpressed reactions of the children who simply listen in silence. It is hardly surprising that the task of reintegrating a class after such disintegrating experiences can prove extremely difficult. It is hard to restore a climate in which learning is felt to be more important than establishing one's position on a mark sheet. 'Assessment' has been turned into an annual stock-taking.

The examination results may have little connection with the felt achievements that earned special commendations for particular pupils during the year.

This raises another question—the question of continuity in the assessment procedures. Here again, the new C.S.E. examination offers a significant new opportunity. For now it will be possible for teachers to include in the material that is finally assessed at the end of the course folders of work done by pupils at intervals throughout the course. Now, for the first time in a school examination that has national status, a child will be able to feel that his own initiative and industry and originality in November, or January, or March, will stand to his credit when he faces the more objective test of an examination in May or June. The second kind of test may thus come to be seen as continuous with the kind of work that cannot be 'tested' in the same way, but which nevertheless survives under his name.

Once the two roles of teaching and examining (and of learning and being examined) can be seen by teacher and child as inseparably linked, other kinds of continuity too become possible. It even becomes feasible to think of an examination in which some of the work has to be undertaken by a group of candidates: the group project may arise out of a number of individual projects on related themes; or it may occupy the opening phase of the examination itself, giving rise to individual tasks which are then tackled by the members of the group working independently. Such a scheme could have two important effects on the teacher–pupil relationship. It would make cheating an absurdity, since mutual help would be a legalized part of the whole procedure; and it would make some sort of feed-back, on the basis of cooperative work, a logical and desirable outcome of the testing period, since the pupils would be genuinely concerned to review one another's achievements.

The advent of the C.S.E. examination offers school teachers far greater opportunities than they have ever had before of experimenting with new methods of assessment as university teachers have always been free to do. The very fact that experimentation must go on could bring teachers and pupils more closely together in what is, after all, a joint task.

An examination, whether written or oral, is rather like an interview: its outcome depends as much on the initiative of the examinee as on that of the examiner. Now an interview situation, where interviewers work in pairs or teams, is really a group situation of a very complex kind. For they must come to terms not only with the difficulties of interviewing the candidate, but also with the problems of cooperating with one another. The quality of their own relationship, their willingness to expose facets of themselves to one another, and their fears lest they show up badly in a professional job, will have their effects on their joint personal encounter with the candidate. If they are not relaxed and trusting with each other, the candidate's behaviour will be affected. The more give and take there is between the interviewers, the more likely is it that the candidate will be freed to play his part effectively.

In a recent article on the subject of the C.S.E. examination and its opportunities, Miss Edith Cope draws attention to the need for teachers to face and work with a similar kind of mutual exposure as co-examiners.[1] In the new examination, she points out, 'teachers will be involved directly in questions of judgement and standards under a system of external moderation'. This, she acknowledges, 'can be an intimidating experience'. Nevertheless she urges teachers to accept the necessity for mutual exposure whole-heartedly, and to recognize that such an acceptance is, after all, a necessary condition for full professional responsibility, now at last available to them, as it has always been to their colleagues in the universities.

The discussions that are already taking place on the Subject Panels, the Advisory Groups and the Examinations Committees are evidently going far beyond the mere perpetuation of G.C.E-type examination syllabuses and papers under a new name. They are bringing teachers from different schools face to face in discussions about the fundamental aims of education, about new ways of examining learning and even about the possible recombining of 'subjects' that have hitherto been kept—for examination purposes—in watertight compartments. In fact for the first time teachers are really grappling with the question of what examinations are for, and how they can be used to promote effective learning instead of being regarded as institutions that inhibit effective teaching.

In some ways it is easier to discuss these matters with col-

1. Cope, Edith (1964) 'The C.S.E.—Some Positive Aspects', *Education for Teaching*, No. 65, pp. 41–4.

leagues from other schools than with colleagues in one's own school. The very fact of serving on a committee gives a sort of sanction to enter into controversial questions and to advocate a break with tradition. But the discussions will have to be carried on inside the school staff-rooms too, where tensions already exist and where mutual prejudices abound. It is in the school itself that the greatest exposures will have to be faced and the most important battles won.

The fact is that teachers have to learn to trust each other in these matters before they can begin to trust their pupils. If children are to enter more fully into the problems of self-evaluation, their teachers will have to make admissions to one another about the problems of assessment. For the teacher, as examiner, faces three ways: in one direction he faces those higher educators and employers to whom his pupils will go after they leave his tutelage, and to whom he must give genuine information as far as it lies within his power to do so; in another direction he faces his pupils, and to them he owes honest dealing through the years and the kind of experiences that will train them to evaluate their own work and to see a meaning in his personal assessment of it; and in the third direction he faces his colleagues, with whom he must be prepared to work through the conflicts that will arise once this new role is accepted.

CHAPTER NINE

The Teacher and his Colleagues

1. CLASSROOM AUTHORITY AND STAFF-GROUP MEMBERSHIP

Teachers have often felt themselves to be strangely separated—insulated almost—from their colleagues while actually teaching in their classrooms. This enforces upon them a sense of being out of reach of help, a feeling they may unconsciously build into their membership of the staff group. Paradoxically, the very loneliness of their situation is something they may cling to as a professional right. They will often invoke the sanctity of the classroom to protect themselves from being observed. They can brace themselves to endure the presence of the head at some stage during their first year in a junior post; and from time to time they have to submit to being visited by an inspector or an L.E.A. adviser. But the presence of a colleague is something not to be tolerated. Being observed, for some teachers, is almost synonymous with being supervised, and therefore judged. The more difficult they find it to handle the problems of being the only adult in a group of thirty or more children, the more fiercely will they guard their prerogative of privacy and the more strongly will they resist the intrusion of any other teacher in the classroom.

However, this situation is no longer so typical as it used to be. A physical-education or drama teacher who is working experimentally with movement or dance in the hall or gymnasium, or an art teacher whose work has attracted notice in the school, may be approached by colleagues who want to know more about what he does, and he may—despite his nervousness about being observed—be glad to welcome them into some of his lessons. Or two classes may combine, with their teachers, to use audio-visual material and apparatus, or to organize a project that will relate the studies of history and geography, or of geography and biology, or of physics and mathematics. And sooner or later for most teachers, the necessity of accepting in their classrooms student teachers who take over some of their work helps to break down the natural reluctance to teach with observers present. Along with this general loosening of the taboo on the practice of teachers observing one another's work, there has been a perceptible relaxation of the hostility towards H.M.I.'s, who are now far more often welcomed as helpful visitors than feared as censorious and interfering critics.

Nevertheless it is still true to say that every teacher has to spend a great deal of his time alone with pupils. His sense of personal isolation—as one adult among thirty or more children —is reinforced by the fact that he is constantly face to face with problems of control. People outside the teaching profession have little understanding of the wear and tear of this day-to-day exercise of control. They are ready enough to poke fun at the schoolmaster if he carries 'controlling' behaviour over into his social life. But it is not easy for anyone who has not experienced it to understand the strain involved in being continually in authority over large groups of children, as every teacher is, however democratic his methods and however easily he appears to win his pupils' cooperation. Perhaps even the most successful teacher never quite outgrows his fear that one day he may completely lose control and be at the mercy of three dozen or so rebellious and potentially destructive human beings.

The teacher's image of himself as a person in authority over children is affected in strangely contradictory ways by society's image of what a teacher should be. For society, in trusting its children to the care of teachers, also projects into those teachers quite inconsistent notions about the nature of authority. The school must be a disciplined community, we would all agree. But it seems to follow that if children are unruly and rebellious, the teachers alone must be condemned as ineffective in their jobs, even though the difficulties they are contending with spring as much from lack of parental control as from anything that is being done or not being done in the school. Now teachers are more vulnerable than any other section of society, except perhaps the police, to charges of cruelty or violence. Any hint that a teacher has struck a child in anger reactivates in all of us our earliest fears of punitive and retaliatory parents. Yet corporal punishment, formally administered by a teacher, is still widely accepted as a legitimate means of enforcing order. Thus teachers, unlike any other section of the community, are given sanction to punish other people's children, by inflicting physical pain if necessary. It is as though society's parents both feared the teachers as prototypes of their own punishing parent-figures and looked to them to take over the punishing roles in relation to their own children. They give teachers authority to punish, and both revere and hate them for having this authority.

How, then, does the teacher sustain his role in society without abusing the authority society gives him? Much of the time, his capacity to identify with the child—even with the difficult child—comes to his aid. For in moments of crisis that earlier self that is still part of his inner world and indeed part of his present self may help him to understand intuitively what the child is feeling, so that he can handle the situation sensitively, or, if he has already blundered, change his tactics. An example may make this clear. I remember an occasion when a rather quiet and inoffensive girl of fourteen suddenly aroused my anger by giggling and talking to her neighbour when I was in the middle of reading a poem aloud to the class, rather well as I supposed, in my vanity. I broke off to tell her sharply to see me at four o'clock. She subsided immediately and by the end of the afternoon I had completely forgotten the incident, until I saw her standing by my table looking at me dumbly. Irritated with myself for having prolonged the trivial incident so unnecessarily, I snapped out a rather foolish comment and demanded an apology. She began to look sulky, then collapsed into giggles. I left her to cool her heels while I went to the staff room to have my cup of tea. I drank it in a bad temper, but decided to try more subtle tactics when I returned. Meanwhile, her giggles had turned to open hostility, and when I appealed to her reasonableness she surprised me by bursting out: 'Well, Miss Richardson, I was going to apologize to you at four o'clock, but when you told me to I no longer wanted to.' A sudden mental flash-back to myself at her age confronting a teacher, and refusing to produce the apology demanded of me, restored my sense of balance, not to say my sense of humour. She, I believe was surprised in her turn when she heard me say that I could understand how she felt. The next moment she was admitting that it must have been irritating for me to be interrupted in the middle of my reading, and I left it at that, feeling that honour had been satisfied on both sides. She opened the door for me and said 'good night' with a warm, if slightly mocking, smile, and was on good terms with me for the rest of the two years I taught her. I never again demanded an apology from any pupil, though no doubt there were other occasions when I was short-tempered and impatient.

On this occasion, my sense of kinship with the rebellious pupil in front of me was conscious and therefore, in the end, usable. But who knows how many other occasions there may have been when I merely used a difficult child as a target for my own feelings instead of trying to relate to her as another human being whose feelings I could understand? Teachers, by the very nature of their profession, are peculiarly vulnerable to the unconscious re-awakening of their own most primitive feelings. In a sense, every infant-school teacher faces in her small pupils her own past strivings for autonomy, and every secondary-school teacher faces in his adolescent pupils the residual parts of his own adolescence. And so an emotional clash with a rebellious or distressed adolescent may have a symbolic significance for the teacher as a reminder of some incident or accumulated feeling from his own past, as well as having its own objective reality as an incident in the present. If the distinction between reality and symbol is blurred in the teacher's mind he may misinterpret what is happening and allow unconscious motives to determine what action he takes. He may unconsciously perceive in the child a part of his former self that he disapproved of and deal with the child more harshly because of this likeness; or the incident may reactivate in some half-recognized form some earlier clash between himself and an adult who dealt with him harshly, and he may repeat the process, in reverse. On the other hand, as I have indicated, a conscious recognition of the similarity between the present incident and something from his own past may help him to act more sensitively in the present crisis.

Now we have to distinguish between a momentary identification with a child, which may throw light on the way one is mismanaging a situation, and the sort of generalized emotional identification (particularly with the older pupils) that can sometimes arise when a young teacher feels alienated from his colleagues, perhaps because he sees them as threatening to his self-esteem, perhaps because his subject tends to isolate him from the rest of the staff by removing him from the staff room at times when other people are in it, or perhaps because he cannot find colleagues of his own age who are congenial to him. Moreover, there are certain subjects which, at the secondary-school level, bring teachers of all ages into contact with children in ways that are associated with the home rather than with the classroom and therefore arouse responses—from both sides—of a rather special nature. Teachers of physical education who see children in the changing rooms as well as in the gymnasium and on the games field, and domestic-science teachers who work in the context of home-making, are perhaps particularly open to the rewards of these situations. But the rewards contain hidden dangers. Children may feel that such teachers, whom they can dissociate from the formality of the classroom, are more approachable human beings than some of the other people who teach them. This situation can turn into a kind of trap, for in saying 'We can talk to *you*, Sir', or 'Well, you're young, Miss, so you understand how we feel', a child may also be implying: 'We can tell *you* how we feel about Mr X' (or 'Miss Y'); and before the teacher is fully aware of the danger, the children have begun to treat him as though he were not quite a member of the staff. So he either accepts the compliment of being made a confidant, at the expense of his integrity as a member of his staff group, or he has to withdraw abruptly, leaving the children with a sense of let-down.

In the long run, it must be from the staff group and not from the pupils that a teacher draws his own emotional support. For his staff-group membership represents his commitment to a community task that includes and stretches beyond his commitments to groups of children. It is this that gives continuity and purpose to his work, and makes his necessary detachment from his pupils (and his eventual loss of them) tolerable. Yet the time he actually spends in the staff room in any one day is relatively small. He will probably be lucky if he spends much more than an hour there: he will have ten or fifteen minutes in the middle of the morning, trying to secure and drink a cup of tea, have a cigarette maybe, collect the books or equipment he will need for the next lesson and switch his thoughts from the period he has just been taking; he will probably have twenty minutes or so after lunch to relax and talk to his colleagues; and he may have a free period of thirty-five or forty minutes, when he will no doubt have to make a start on a pile of marking. His own life in the staff room, in fact, is constantly shadowed by the various classes he teaches during the day. He knows remarkably little about what most of his colleagues do in their classes; and most of them know remarkably little about what he does in his.

Despite this, the staff group does contrive to have a life of real significance. The group may be so small that it can function as an integrated team—a face-to-face group in which all the members know each other as persons. Or, in these days, it may be so big that some members literally do not know each other's names, so big that the group life is really going on in well-defined sub-groups rather than in the group as a whole. Both kinds of situation have their own sources of tension.

Some years ago I visited a small junior school of about two hundred and fifty children and a staff, as far as I remember, of eight. All were on Christian-name terms with the headmaster. The atmosphere in the staff room seemed very relaxed, and one did not have the impression that people were in ignorance about the nature of one another's work, as one so often feels in a large secondary school. There was a similar absence of artificial barriers between the teaching staff and the auxiliary staff. The school secretary drank her mid-morning cup of tea in the staff room; and I was taken to the school kitchen and introduced to the two women who cooked and served the school lunches. Now we must not imagine that this staff group was blissfully free from tension and difficulty—that the situation was all love and no hate. Emotional misunderstandings can be greater in a small face-to-face group than in a large amorphous group, for in a large group tension can, most of the time, be more easily dispersed and reduced. Nevertheless there was probably, in that small school, a very real sense of identification with a community task that could be felt as a unified task; and it must have been less easy than in a large school to go on avoiding the necessity of working through emotional and functional disagreements when they did arise.

The larger the staff group, the more complex the hierarchy: this goes without saying. Formal divisions are built into the structure. There are vertical divisions that correspond to parallel functions within the total task, and horizontal divisions that correspond to levels of leadership. Beneath this formal pattern of roles and relationships there are informal, largely emotional groupings in existence also, and all kinds of built-in attitudes and personal prejudices that affect people's behaviour towards one another and their ability to work together as a cooperative group. And so, before we look more closely at the consciously designed pattern of roles and relationships, let us take a look at some of the unconscious mechanisms that may be working underneath the surface. We shall find that some of these group mechanisms spring from the anxieties of teachers as individuals, working in the relatively isolated conditions I have been describing.

2. BONDS AND TENSIONS IN THE STAFF GROUP

In trying to throw light on the difficulties that arise between individuals or sub-groups in the staff room, I must not underestimate the importance of the bonds that are forged through the sharing of responsibility for the education of the young. And these bonds can be very close. They may come into existence as a result of the accident of proximity: the sharing of a laboratory, or the joint responsibility for a library, may lead to a genuine partnership through community of interest; two teachers whose form rooms are separated only by a thin partition may, if they are basically compatible people, develop a mutual tolerance and understanding in spite of, or perhaps because of, this inconvenience. The pooling of responsibility for some voluntary project, such as a concert, or a play production or a school camp, can either come about as a result of a friendship between two or more staff or may, itself, bring such a friendship into existence. These relationships can often cut across the formal boundaries between senior and junior members of staff, and be mutually beneficial.

However, this is only one side of the coin. For where there are in-groups there are also likely to be out-goups, and the warm solidarity that exists between certain members of the staff may have been purchased at the cost of other people's loneliness and sense of rejection. It is not among children only that the problem of isolation exists. There may be an isolate in every staff room, for all we know. And as long as others can convince themselves that he or she is 'irritating' or 'pompous' or just plain 'ineffective', they will continue to keep such a colleague at arm's length. The teacher in question may, indeed, be any of all of these things. Yet such a label is never a true description of anything so complex as a human personality. Why is it, then, that a collection of adult persons, aware of their mutual dependence for support and understanding in the work they do, dismiss so easily the positive values of the group member who attracts this kind of hostility or contempt? Why do we work—unconsciously, maybe—to keep people fixed in the roles we have ascribed to them? Can it be that we all—whatever kind of institution we work in—use our colleagues in this kind of way so that we can externalize the conflicts we have to handle in ourselves?

Every teacher must learn, as time goes on, to face his own inconsistencies. There will be times when he feels able to handle his pupils wisely and can feel a measure of success in teaching them; and there will be other times when he feels he has little skill in human relations and little talent for arousing enthusiasm for the work that he wants his pupils to do. In other words, we all have to learn to temper our own experiences of success with a realistic awareness of our failures, and to sustain ourselves in moments of failure with the assurance that we can at times do better.

But it is not easy for us to face in ourselves the good and the bad schoolmaster, the strong and the weak classroom personality, the perceptive and the blind student of human relations. We therefore look for mirror images, not of our total selves, but of the irreconcilable parts, the bits we claim and the bits we reject. And so, as members of staff groups, we are liable to associate ourselves unconsciously with certain mechanisms employed by the group for dealing with these ambivalent feelings, both towards the self and towards others.

In any working group certain members may have to carry for the rest these best and worst aspects of themselves. In our memories, the staff rooms we have worked in seem to have contained certain individuals who had to accept certain kinds of labels for the rest of us. This man was 'known' to be a poor disciplinarian; that woman was 'known' to be a bit of a martinet; someone else was revered as a perceptive and skilful teacher, always in control of even the most unruly class, yet never asserting a merely punitive authority—the prototype, in fact, of the kind of teacher we all wanted to be. In this way, the members of a staff group try to deal with their own internal conflicts by splitting off the good and bad parts of themselves. They can all identify with the good teacher into whom they have projected their own best qualities, and use him or her as a sort of ego-ideal or ideal self. At the same time, they get rid of their own in-effectiveness by projecting it into someone who seems less com-petent than they feel themselves to be, using him as a scapegoat to carry their burdens.

Now it is very difficult for anybody to resist this compulsion to accept, or 'introject', the qualities placed in him by the com-munity. And so the teacher who has been invested with every-body's good qualities will probably, in fact, go from strength to strength, while the one who is given the role of scapegoat goes further into the wilderness, badly in need of help, perhaps, yet not knowing quite how to ask for it. All this may sound far-fetched. After all there are good teachers, mediocre teachers and bad teachers; and inevitably we relate more easily to some of our colleagues than we relate to others. But we do tend to label people; and often we do so without realizing—or acknowledging—that the labels, particularly if they are un-complimentary ones, may also be describing parts of ourselves. As I recall the colleagues who, in various schools, excited my ridicule, or my dislike, or my anger, I can see in them various aspects of myself as teacher that I hoped other people did not perceive. One, it seems, personified my own inadequacy in relation to two forms I was having difficulties with; another represented my own tendency to be over-possessive with the forms I particularly liked; a third symbolized my own wish to glorify my subject at the expense of other people's; and so on. Yet my image of the way these teachers related to their classes was probably based on my own fantasies about their behaviour rather than on any real evidence about it.

This tendency, to which, probably, most of us are prone at times, sometimes takes another form. Instead of projecting our own good and bad characteristics into other individuals, we project them into sub-groups. Why is it, for example, that men are so often said to be less conscientious than women, and that older teachers are assumed to be less willing to experiment with new techniques than younger ones? Women do not really have a monopoly of conscientiousness, nor do the young have a monopoly of originality or adventurousness. Yet statements such as 'Well, of course, he's a man, so he can shrug it off and not worry', or 'She's too old to try anything new' go unchallenged. However, the negatives have their corresponding positives: for we also hear people say that male teachers are more cool and level-headed in a crisis than female ones, and that the older members of the staff provide stability in a school. Yet the truth is that men, as well as women, can act hysterically on occasion, and that an emotional upset in a staff room may arise as easily from the behaviour of an older teacher as from the behaviour of a younger one.

Today most schools are having to deal with a comparatively new source of tension—the split between the married women and the unmarried women on the staff. The proportion of married women teachers is steadily rising and many of them are working only on a part-time basis. Inevitably, perhaps, they are coming to be regarded as the 'nine-to-four' teachers, who avoid commitments after school and refuse to allow professional obligations to interfere, beyond a certain point, with their family responsibilities. Now it is easy for a married woman to exploit her role as wife and mother, so that her contribution to school life is minimal. But who is to say where the line should be drawn between adequate and inadequate contribution to the total task of the staff group? And who is to say how much of what looks like self-sacrificing devotion to school interests is really providing personal satisfaction to the teacher concerned? The middle-aged, unmarried woman may be more envious of her married female colleague than she realizes; and because of this envy—particularly if she is unable to acknowledge it to herself—she may be inclined to see her own greater involvement in the life of the school as a virtue rather than as a natural result of her condition as a single woman. Moreover, it is not only feelings about the demands of out-of-school activities that must be faced and dealt with; for the married woman, if she has young children, will inevitably have to put her family before her school, even during the statutory school day, in times of illness or crisis in the home. The burden of carrying the regular classes is therefore likely to fall more heavily on the unmarried woman, and this, in a girls' school especially, can very easily give rise to strong, though often unexpressed, resentments. All this can precipitate a great deal of mutual hostility—mutual, because the envious feelings of the unmarried woman are, more often than not, matched by the sense of greater worthiness enjoyed by the married one, and, for that matter, by her envy of the single woman's freedom to come and go as she pleases, enjoy holidays abroad, and so on.

To some extent the youngest women on the staff contribute also to this *malaise:* for, to the older woman, aware of her young colleagues' preoccupation with the likelihood of early marriage, it seems that young women generally are less whole-heartedly committed to the job of teaching than she herself was in her early twenties.

This is a relatively recent staff-room problem, and within a couple of decades it may have disappeared. In due course, as the pattern of employment changes and the single professional woman virtually disappears from the schools, it will be men in general who will have to exercise, towards their female col-leagues, the tolerance and understanding that the unmarried women are now being called upon to exercise in relation to the married women. Perhaps, indeed, the increasing scarcity of single women to take the major burdens in the girls' schools will provide the most unanswerable argument we have yet had in favour of co-education.

I have been discussing the dangers of stereotyped thinking about the nature of people's commitments and about the images of one another that different sub-groups carry around with them. What, then, of the way in which science and arts teachers view each other's roles in the school? Is the two-culture problem as acute in the schools as it is said to be in the universities and in society at large?[1] There is in the secondary school one very important link between the scientist and the artist: the fact that they teach the same pupils. This fact must help to narrow the gap and to increase mutual respect and understanding, as, in some colleges and departments of education, the fact that science and arts specialists share the same tutor or seminar leader helps to narrow the gap. Yet mutual mystification can still arise, and false images can still persist, even where arts and science specialists are not separated by faculty boundaries as in a university. We still hear it said that the scientist is concerned only with facts and—by implication—that he cares little for aesthetic and moral values; and we still hear it said that the arts man is concerned only with ideas and opinions and is careless

1. Snow, C. P. (1959) *The Two Cultures and the Scientific Revolution* (Rede Lectures), Cambridge University Press. See also Bronowski, J. (1964) *Science and Human Values*, Harmondsworth: Penguin Books, pp. 12–19.

about objective evidence. This kind of mutual stereotyping is rather neatly illustrated, in a different way, by Professor Bronowski, when he writes: 'I have had of all people a historian tell me that science is a collection of facts, and his voice had not even the ironic rasp of one filing cabinet reproving another.'[1] This kind of splitting has arisen from the fragmentation of human knowledge in an advanced state of civilization, and from the consequent confusion about what we mean by a well-educated man or woman. It is as though the division between the two cultures were echoing a deeper disunity in the educator, whether artist or scientist—the split between himself as a person concerned with children as growing persons and himself as a subject specialist concerned with educating his successors in that subject.

But the split between the artist and the scientist, where it exists, has emotional roots of another kind, too. Both suffer from guilt: the artist because he is hard put to it to prove his utility in a society that depends more and more for its survival on science and technology; the scientist because he is equally hard put to it to prove that he is concerned with aesthetic and moral values. And so, each may try to defend his own ego by building up a stereotype of the other which represents only a fraction of what he really is. The artist may feel that the scientist's work does not really involve any creative originality, at least where his contacts with children are concerned, while the scientist may feel that the artist's work lacks discipline and objectivity. It is by no means easy for a teacher of physics or chemistry, who has to impose restraints on his pupils lest they create dangerous conditions in the laboratory, to understand what is really going on in the school hall when these same pupils are being 'let loose' in an orgy of noisy and apparently undisciplined dramatic activity; and even if the drama is obviously being well controlled, it may seem to him to be more concerned with meaningless fantasies than with hard reality. Equally, it is difficult for the drama teacher to appreciate that, behind the formal controls in the laboratory, there is creative, experimental work going on and a kind of excitement that is appealing to the aesthetic and emotional side of a child's nature.

I have been using the term 'artist' in a general sense, to refer to those teachers whose bias, as scholars, has been towards the

1. ibid., p. 20.

arts rather than the sciences. But the secondary school system creates a further division between the teachers of the 'academic' subjects and those whose concern is with the fine arts, physical education and the so-called 'practical' subjects. In England this division has a special significance, since those who teach the 'non-academic' subjects are not, for the most part, graduates. The cleavage between these two sub-groups is given visual emphasis in some schools by the wearing of academic gowns. The sense of inferiority suffered by non-graduates, even when their preparation for entry to the teaching profession has been just as long and arduous as any graduate's, is deep and bitter. It can create small, defensive sub-groups within the staff community—groups who meet what they believe to be the contempt of their colleagues by setting up a counter-image of themselves as the teachers who are closest to the real needs of children. The terms 'academic' and 'non-academic'—meaningless though they really are in any educational setting—become loaded terms. In the eyes of the art, domestic-science or physical-education specialist, 'academic' may come to be synonymous with 'out of touch with children's needs', while in the eyes of their colleagues, 'non-academic' can come to be synonymous with 'unconcerned with standards'.

Sometimes the defensiveness can work in another way—the musician loading the syllabus with 'academic' content, to prove his respectability, for example. An article in *The New Era* pleading for the recognition of the art of movement as an academic subject is perhaps another indication of the seriousness of this cleavage in the teaching profession.[1] The controversy that raged in the pages of *The Observer* in the autumn of 1964, following Sir John Newsom's article on the education of girls, illustrates in another way how easily sectionalism gives rise to defensive and highly irrational arguments. In the upsurge of anxiety about the hard-won rights of women to be admitted to the highest professional posts, Newsom's words were given a significance they were never intended to have. He was accused of advocating a sort of neo-Victorian subjection of women, though what he had advocated was an education for girls that did not lose sight of the special role of women in society. His plea for the reintegration of emotional and intellectual values in

1. Redfern, Betty (1965) 'Physical Education as an Academic Discipline', *New Era*, vol. 46, No. 2, pp. 37–40.

education was misinterpreted as a kind of anti-feminism, felt to
be all the more dangerous because it seemed to be lurking
behind an apparently pro-feminist campaign.[1]

The truth is that when the values we uphold seem to be
threatened, we are apt to disown other values that we really
cherish too. For the staff group in any school the essential thing
is that important issues should constantly be debated in the
context of policy-making. This requires leadership of a very
sophisticated kind—not a leadership that imposes ready-made
views and pushes for quick decisions, but a leadership that can
take a long view and allow time for people to probe beneath each
other's superficial thoughts and defensive opinions to find the
solid common ground on which they can really work together.

3. LEADERSHIP, CONSULTATION AND POLICY-MAKING

If we are prepared to accept the idea that the school is an open
society, then it follows that we must regard leadership as a
'boundary function'.[2] I have been suggesting this, in somewhat
different terms, throughout this book, in emphasizing the in-
evitability of tension between the teacher's in-groupness and his
out-groupness in relation to his pupils. If he moves too far away
from the group, he loses vital contact with its members and can
no longer lead; if he moves too far into the group he becomes
swallowed up by it, loses touch with the surrounding community
and therefore with the group task, and can no longer mediate
between the group and the community.

The headmaster has this same problem in maintaining his
position on the boundary between his school as a total institution
and the community (village, city or county) of which it is a part.
He has both to be aware of current policies at regional and
national levels and to maintain his school's autonomy within
the framework of these policies. This means that he has to
differentiate between those community restraints that have to be
accepted and those that can be questioned and modified within
his school. He must in other words, act as a kind of mediator,

1. 'The Education of Women', *Observer*, 6 September 1964 (and correspondence on 13, 20 and 27 September, followed by Sir John Newsom's reply on
11 October).
2. Rice, A. K. (1963) *The Enterprise and its Environment*, London: Tavistock
Publications, p. 15, and (1965) *Learning for Leadership*, London: Tavistock
Publications, 4, pp. 20–3).

interpreting the outside world to the inner world of the school, and interpreting this inner world to the one outside the school. Since he cannot fulfil the second function without the active help and cooperation of both staff and children, reason demands that he carries out the first by consultative methods rather than by issuing instructions and limited information.

In small schools, much of this leadership can be exercised informally. That is to say, the head feels close enough to his staff to be able to consult them continuously without calling special meetings to do so. But now that schools are becoming steadily larger, the role of the head is changing, even though the function of headship is not fundamentally different. As his area of responsibility expands, it becomes increasingly difficult for him to be in personal contact with all the members of his school and increasingly important that he should decide where the priorities really lie.

In the past, heads of schools have prided themselves on knowing all their pupils at least by name; some still boast that they have no pupils who are not known personally to them by more than name. But what does the word 'know' really mean in these contexts? How reciprocal is this knowing?

Few people below the level of the sixth form in a grammar school, even, are likely to feel that they know much about the headmaster as a person; and even for the sixth form the kind of knowing experienced by those who are actually taught by him will be of a very different order from the knowing experienced by those who do not see him in this other role. This almost unavoidable distance between headmaster and pupil is well described in a novel by Jeremy Brooks, where, towards the end, the boy who plays the title role in the story is asked to call on the headmaster one morning, only a couple of weeks or so after he has left school. As he hurries to the school in response to this request, he realizes that he is feeling 'the usual flutterings which any schoolboy, or only just ex-schoolboy, must feel in the circumstances'. And, in telling the story, he pauses to reflect on the tenuous nature of his relationship with this man, tenuous despite the five years spent in his school:

I had never had much to do with the Head. As Chemistry master for the upper forms he had brushed briefly against me; and on one occasion, for I forget what offence, Epsom and I had to present ourselves in his study for what was known at the school as a 'whipping':

that is, a whipping from his tongue. But he was a kind, humorous man; I think he must have had a vocation for teaching, for he could keep order without either inspiring fear or forfeiting respect.[1]

For most of us, when we were school children, the 'headmaster' or 'headmistress' was bound to stand for a certain degree of remoteness, even of unapproachableness. We knew the head as the person who appeared on the school platform and took assembly, the person to whom we might be sent if we committed some especially serious offence or simply became too much for a teacher to cope with, the person from whom, if we ever aspired to sixth-form status, we might one day seek advice about the future. The head seemed to represent for us a set of roles which we associated with a sort of ultimate authority within the school. Only as we ourselves approached adult status could such a figurehead begin to emerge as a personality with whom it was possible to have a genuine human relationship.

In the large schools of today, it seems unavoidable that the head's first obligation is to know his staff. The emotional satisfactions of really knowing the children must, surely, be relinquished to those who actually teach them or carry other roles in relation to them. Some people deplore this, fearing that the heads of the future will be at best remote, inaccessible creatures and at worst dictators, turning schools into efficient factories. But we must not fall into the error of simplifying the issues in this way. Nostalgia is a profitless and rather foolish pastime. It is far too easy to romanticize the small school at the expense of the large one, and to allow our thinking to be dominated by the popular mythology about what happens to schools once they pass the magic number of five hundred.

What right have we to suppose that the head of a large comprehensive school is any less approachable, in the eyes of his most junior staff members, than the head of a small country grammar school, or to assume that he will interpret his role as the giving of orders rather than as the seeking of opinions? A teacher who is by nature authoritarian will turn a school of two hundred into a dictatorship if given the authority to do so, whereas one who believes in self-government will find ways of nurturing freedom and engaging a staff-group discussion even in a school of two thousand. It is not size in itself that determines the quality of a school's emotional life any more than it is the

1. Brooks, Jeremy (1960) *Jampot Smith*, London: Hutchinson.

existence of senior executive roles that determines how these roles are played.

The positions of leadership that are occupied by the head and his or her deputy expose both to certain kinds of emotional exploitation by their colleagues. The group, when it is acting on the basic assumption of dependence, needs a good leader to idealize, and, when it is acting on the basic assumption of fight–flight, a bad leader to oppose. From these needs, at the primitive unconscious level, comes the tendency—common in many kinds of institution—to project loving and kindly qualities into one authority figure and vindictive and punitive qualities into another. If you talk to prison governors or Borstal governors, you very often get the impression that this kind of defence is being used so that people can avoid coming to terms with liking and disliking the same person. Thus the governor may be regarded, by the prison officers and by the inmates, as an amiable person who has everybody's welfare at heart, while the deputy governor has the reputation of being out for everybody's blood. If the projections are reversed it will be the deputy governor who is seen as benevolent while the governor is seen as the terrifying, ultimate big stick. In this way people try to cope with their conflicting feelings about the institution, which can be seen on the one hand as punitive and on the other as rehabilitative. The stereotype of the sergeant in the army who is expected to bully and shout at his men, while the officer in charge behaves like an understanding and always gentlemanly father, is another familiar example of the same thing. Similarly, the matron of a hospital is often expected to take the role of the demanding, intolerant mistress of the house whom everybody wishes to defy, thus freeing the doctor—any doctor doing the rounds of the wards—to receive everybody's adulation. The kind of splitting and projection I discussed earlier is a defence against facing and dealing with the conflicting parts of the self; but this kind of splitting arises from the difficulty of reconciling one's conflicting feelings towards a person in authority, carrying as they do all the overtones from similar conflicts in relation to powerful parent figures.[1]

1. For an analysis of the problems of splitting and projection in the nursing profession, see Menzies, Isabel E. P. (1960) 'A Case Study in the Functioning of Social Systems as a Defence against Anxiety: A Report on the Study of the Nursing Service of a General Hospital', *Human Relations*, vol. 13, No. 2, pp. 95–121.

The trouble is that there are people in positions of leadership who are only too ready to accept such roles. Aggressive, even punitive personalities are attracted to the kinds of post that enable them to behave, officially, in an aggressive and punitive way. They have a need to dominate and perhaps to punish. Running a prison, or a Borstal institution, or even a school or hospital will give them plenty of opportunities to do this. Equally, the role of headmaster may attract the kind of person who needs to be benevolent, to be revered as a sort of kindly god, and who shrinks from any recognition that his subordinates can feel anything but affection towards him. And so once again we have a collusive process: the staff group goes into collusion with the punitive headmaster by maintaining him in the role he chooses to adopt, and sets someone else up as the benevolent alternative leader; or they sustain the kindly head as the recipient of their affectionate loyalty, and unconsciously nominate someone else to be the recipient of their own aggressive dislike.

A good headmaster takes steps to avoid being placed in either of these extreme roles. He creates opportunities for the open expression of disagreement, even of hostility, in the work situation. He ensures that his deputy has opportunities to deputize for him in the full sense of the word, and guards against the temptation of giving the deputy the tasks he himself prefers to avoid. He does not only give vigorous leadership himself: he also delegates authority to others, and frees them to use initiative and make decisions in their own spheres of operation. It is no use appointing sub-heads in the upper, middle and lower schools without empowering them to hold their own staff meetings, or creating a house-tutorial system without empowering house masters and mistresses to hold meetings with the tutors in their houses. What is more, a wise head will see that time for these meetings is built into the school time-table, along with times for consultations within and between special subject groupings. One way in which a head can show his sincerity in handing over real responsibility to his senior staff is by doing a little teaching himself and accepting a subordinate role in the department he is qualified to join. This situation tests both the head's ability to change role and the ability of the department-head concerned to deal with his own fears of being observed in action by his headmaster. Both must go into this situation with their eyes open to its possible danger. But if the dangers are met and overcome, each may learn a great deal from the occasional reversal of leadership roles.

The role of the deputy head demands a corresponding integrity. But because he has to accept the discomforts of operating as a leader on the external boundary of the institution, without enjoying the full status of headmaster, the temptations he is subjected to are considerable. To escape from the frustrations of the role, he may perceive himself either as protector of the staff against the head or as protector of the head against the staff. If he continually fights the head, he becomes less and less capable of identifying with him and deputizing for him when the necessity arises; if he continually fights the staff, he is considered to be 'in the Head's pocket' and becomes less and less capable of mediating between the staff and him and keeping the channels of communication open. Clearly, to adopt either of these extreme positions is seriously to damage and undermine the leadership functions that he and the head must fulfil together.

It can often happen, particularly in the smaller single-sex schools, that a fairly young head has to work with a deputy head who is not far off retiring age. This can create a situation of painful tension, particularly if the deputy head is still mourning for the retired head or is regretting his or her own lost opportunity of securing a headship in earlier life. But it can create a situation of great strength in a school. If the inevitable feelings about the situation are understood and tolerated, a genuine relationship of mutual respect and affection can develop and the cooperative work of giving leadership to a vigorous staff group can go forward, as anyone who has had the benefit of this kind of joint leadership knows.

The problems of leadership do not begin and end with the head and deputy head. In the large comprehensive school, the status symbols that come with appointed leadership can either facilitate or mediate against true consultation and shared responsibility. The house master's private room is a necessary condition for the work he has to do, in relation both to the tutors and to the children in his house; the subject-department head's private room can be a useful retreat if a junior member of his department wants to discuss a teaching problem with him, and it can facilitate regular meetings of the department to thrash out departmental policy. At the same time, these rooms can cut their owners off from the staff group as a whole, and can arouse considerable feelings of jealousy, deprivation or loss. This is particularly so when promotion from within occurs. Suddenly, after a summer holiday, a colleague with whom one used to do the crossword in the dinner hour has become a house master or has taken over the science department, and one finds that he is no longer so available—no longer, perhaps, quite so much a personal friend as he used to be.

Part of the trouble is that the gap between teaching and administrative functions is widening, and our understanding of the problems of consultation has not yet caught up with this development. No teacher, even in a small school, entirely escapes from administrative duties, and few administrators, if they continue to work in schools, entirely abandon teaching. Yet as the schools become more complex the two roles tend to drift apart, so that the young teacher at the bottom of the hierarchy may feel out of touch with those who make the decisions, while the experienced teacher at the top of the hierarchy may feel out of touch with the realities of teaching.

A man or woman who changes role after promotion to a senior post may cease to experience at first hand the effects of the actions for which he or she now becomes responsible. Regulations and practices which used to be questioned now come to be accepted as indispensable to the smooth running of a school. The present deputy head, a few years ago, would have thought twice about reading a particular notice out to his form, knowing what its effects on certain pupils might be; yet he now thinks nothing of reading similar notices out to the whole school, even perhaps on the intercom, or of sending one round to be read out to classes by whichever teachers happen to be with them. He used to protest in the staff room about the evil effects of streaming for ability; now he must allocate unknown children to high, middle or low streams as though he had never had these doubts. In the past he expressed disapproval of the practice of giving prizes to selected pupils; now he must organize the school prize-giving as though he believed in it enthusiastically. To his colleagues who have not been promoted it must seem that organizational efficiency has come to be more important to him than the basic principles on which the system is built. It is rather like what is often said about politicians—that whichever party is in power moves impercept- ibly towards the established norm of government.

What can be done to reduce this gap between the administrators and the general body of the staff? Clearly, a formal structure is needed that makes possible a continuous interchange of opinions and evidence and genuine decision-making in which everyone can have a voice. Furtive comments in corners of the staff room can achieve nothing: they merely feed anxiety and build up emotional crises. Open—even heated and acrimonious—argument in a task-centred meeting is a very different matter. And fortunately there is a very strong force operating in any staff room, as in any working group, to promote this kind of discussion. We are back to Bion's 'work group'.[1] Much of this chapter has been concerned with the primitive and largely unconscious mechanisms that affect the attitudes of staff members to one another. But if this were the only kind of behaviour to be found in staff rooms, no school would survive. Staff meetings would have no objective content and there would be no real cooperation in the task or educating children.

It is through the continuous work of the smaller groups of teachers that the sources of friction and conflict in a large school can be identified and the difficulties tackled consciously and openly on the level of work rather than in disguised and largely unconscious ways on the level of the basic assumptions. Time spent in this kind of discussion is never time wasted. Where a continuous work-through of problems is going on at all levels in the organization, change and development become possible. Everyone, down to the most junior member, feels implicated not only in the day-to-day running of the school but also in the making of future policy. It is this feeling of personal involvement and personal significance that gives a school its vitality.

4. THE STAFF GROUP AND ITS STUDENT TEACHERS

As if the task facing the staff group were not already sufficiently difficult to perceive as an entity, it is further complicated for nearly all schools today by the presence of a training function. In this respect the school is rather like a teaching hospital. The primary task of a hospital, it seems clear, is to care for and, if possible, cure sick persons; but if it is a teaching hospital it must also accept the responsibility of training future doctors and

1. Bion, *Experiences in Groups*, op. cit.

nurses. Similarly a school must reconcile its task of educating children with another task that sometimes appears to be in conflict with it—the task of helping to train future teachers. Most schools have to take a number of student teachers for a total of about fifteen weeks in the year. It is not enough that this should be seen as an obligation, met by the regular teachers in the school to oblige the college or department of education. It must be accepted as a task that is shared with the training institution.

In many schools the student from a college or department of education is welcomed on two counts: first because he affords some much-needed relief to certain teachers by taking over, temporarily, some of their classes; and secondly, because he brings new ideas into the school and strengthens the link between the school and the training institutions. Yet, even if the social climate is warm enough for him to be absorbed without too much difficulty, his presence is bound to create tensions. If he is successful, there will be some natural fear lest the regular teacher's relationship with his classes will be impaired in some way. No teacher can avoid feeling anxious if his student appears to be teaching his classes better than he can himself, even if he genuinely wants the student to succeed. If, on the other hand, the student runs into serious difficulties, the staff, with some reason, find themselves torn between their recognition that the student must be allowed to live with his mistakes and be given the chance to correct them, and their protective feelings towards the children. Which, now, they wonder, is the primary task: to educate the children or to educate the future member of the teaching profession?

These two aims are not as distinct and separate as they might appear to be. Most children are being taught well some of the time and badly some of the time, whether there are students in the school or not. And, being remarkably resilient, they survive. The experienced teacher who is able to help the student without jeopardizing the pupils has not forgotten the mistakes he himself made when he first began to teach. Instead of reacting by rejecting the earlier self he can see in his student, he trusts him to grow by experience as he himself did, and trusts the children to play their part in a mutually educative process.

The presence of students in a school calls for a supervisory function that is different in some respects from that exercised by

heads of departments over their specialist teams, and, in schools
that use a house-tutorial system, by house masters over their
teams of tutors. For the student is a member of another institution and liaison must be maintained between that institution
and the school. A large school may have, in any one year, as
many as thirty or forty students, perhaps from five or six
different institutions. To meet this problem of liaison some
schools are now building into their organization a permanent
tutorial function concerned with the special needs of this
changing sub-group within the staff room. This arrangement
has obvious advantages for the student. But it brings new
problems of relationship into the staff group which need to be
carefully examined.

The role of tutor to students in training, if it exists, needs to be
clearly defined. The tutor has to work out with the heads of
department concerned a series of time-tables which both meets
the needs of the students, as interpreted by the training institutions, and is acceptable to the teachers whose classes must be
handed over. If difficulties arise over a student's work, he may
have to mediate between the school and the college or department. In exercising these functions, he will be fortunate if he is
not at times used as a scapegoat, not only by his own colleagues
and by the visiting supervisors, but even by the students whose
interests he is trying to safeguard. For when a student finds himself caught between the conflicting expectations of school and
training institution, as he often will, he will look round for somebody else to unload the burden onto. Who better than the general
tutor to students whose role exposes him to the recriminations of
both parties to the disagreement? On the other hand, a member
of staff with this responsibility has a great opportunity to work
with the students as a group, not by shouldering their burdens
for them, or by becoming authoritarian or over-protective, but by
opening up the problems in discussion, so that they can help one
another to face the difficulties realistically. Thus he can perform
for these temporary members of the staff group a similar leadership function to those exercised by the house masters in relation
to their tutors, by the heads of subject departments in relation to
their specialist assistants, and by the headmaster himself in
relation to his senior staff.

It is arguable, indeed, that some kind of continuing forum for
members of a staff group who are taking up their first posts

would be of enormous value during this critical transition period when the teacher, though no longer technically a student, is still relatively inexperienced and, indeed, still officially in his probationary period of service. It must be recognized that all teachers take time to grow into their jobs. The occasional disquieting news that a young man or woman who did reasonably well in the education year and received a creditable grade on his practical teaching, collapses and fails during this probationary year, prompts the question: what kind of support is given by the staff group to its youngest and most vulnerable teachers? In some schools, it appears, they are left to sink or swim. The great majority get the support they need and do learn to swim quite quickly. But there are some who, quite unexpectedly, sink. Some of those who sink are people whom the teaching profession can ill afford to lose. It may be that the young teachers who flourish in their first posts do so partly because they find themselves working with a staff group in which continuous discussion and consultation about the problems of running a school are built into the fabric of the organization. The individual grows and develops in proportion to the group's concern that he should so develop.

I have been arguing, it seems, as though the children in the school were merely pawns to be pushed here and there, taught in this way or that way and organized into various kinds of groupings without regard to their own feelings or powers of decision. But what is true for their teachers is surely equally true for them. They, too, need a measure of autonomy in their group and community life. And the more vigorous and reality-based are the consultations of the staff as a group, the more account can they take of the opinions and criticism of those they teach. It is not enough, then, to examine the nature of the roles and relationships within the staff group, or within any one class-room: we must also consider the problem of the inter-group relationships in the school, and particularly the nature of the relationship between the staff as a group and the whole body of pupils in the school.

CHAPTER TEN

The Social Organization of the School

1. THE IDEA OF 'DEMOCRACY' IN EDUCATION

Most English schools today would claim to be democratic institutions. Yet the contrast between a school like Dartington Hall, with its councils, committees and election procedures, and a conventional grammar school, with its form captains, house captains and school prefects, is surely very marked. Teachers from the two kinds of school might find themselves talking in two quite different universes of discourse. What seemed like a democratic community to the more traditionally trained teacher might look like a benevolent autocracy to the teacher from Dartington Hall. What the former might perceive as anarchy, the latter might understand as 'self-government'.

Now we really have two different problems here—two problems that are separable, although they should be treated together. On the one hand, we have to consider how the separate social units, such as forms or tutorial groups, elect or appoint their official leaders; on the other hand, we must ask how relations between groups are handled and how the problems of delegation and representation are tackled in the institution as a whole. Most schools do something about the first; comparatively few do anything serious about the second.

Some years ago a London headmistress, contributing to a symposium on comprehensive schools published by the National Union of Teachers, made the rather surprising statement that most secondary schools now have a school council, senate or parliament.[1] In the same year an American educator from the College of the City of New York, Samuel Everett, published a book describing his impressions of the English secondary school

1. National Union of Teachers (1958) *Inside the Comprehensive School*, Schoolmaster Publishing Company, p. 82.

scene.[1] He had sought the advice of London County Council administrators, education officers up and down the country and educators in the field of teacher training and had been sent to the schools where the 'best practice' could be observed; he spent, it would seem, a day or two in each. In only two of these schools, apparently, did he find a school council of any sort. One of these was a London comprehensive school, whose headmaster contributed to the N.U.T. symposium; the other was a secondary modern boys' school, also in London. Dr Everett's book is full of compliments about the high academic standards in our grammar schools and full of warm praise of the evidence he found in all kinds of schools of exciting creative work. But here and there in his book, and particularly towards the end of it, he allowed himself to make some cautious criticisms. He was surprised to find that the running of out-of-school activities was largely in the hands of the teachers; the prefect system, it appears, puzzled him, and he was mildly shocked to learn that prefects were, in many schools, appointed by the head (with or without the cooperation of the staff) rather than elected by the pupils. All in all, it is evident that this visitor from the United States found our schools deficient in social training in comparison with good American high schools.

'Social training' is a rather loaded expression. To some teacher critics it spells a sort of phoney democracy in which children are encouraged to vote for the sake of voting. But for others it spells something rather different: a recognition that the school is a complex social unit as well as a place in which adults teach children or adolescents, and that within this social unit problems of relations between groups inevitably exist, and can be used as material for learning. For many of us, it spells a bit of both: we advance and retreat, our feelings about this facet of the educational process fluctuating according to the different ways we experience it in different places and at different times.

Now this ambivalence is not peculiar to the English teaching profession. Dr Everett himself shows it all through his book. At the time when he visited this country, American educators were still in the post-sputnik mood of guilt and concern over the wastage of intellectual ability at the top of the high schools. They were also barely recovering from the pre-sputnik lashing

1. Everett, Samuel (1959) *Growing Up in English Secondary Schools*, University of Pittsburgh Press.

they had received in the mid-1950s from such books as Arthur Bestor's *Educational Wastelands*, Hilda Neatby's *So Little for the Mind*, and Mortimer Smith's *The Diminished Mind*, whose contents more than fulfilled the aggressive intentions of their titles.[1] Rightly, however, the upholders of what was best in the Dewey tradition did not want to see the high schools abandoning social education completely in the frantic search for intellectual enrichment of the curriculum. And so, Everett, while urging his compatriots to take notice of the high standards of academic achievement he had observed in English schools, was also at pains to point out that we, for our part, might have something to learn from the American practice—in particular from the devices used in American high schools to help young people to grow up socially by taking on adult responsibilities in the running of their own extra-curricular activities.

However, we have precedents in our own educational history for this kind of experience. The first of the 'New Schools', as Boyd and Rawson point out in the recently published history of the New Education Fellowship,[2] were founded in England towards the end of the last century: first came Cecil Reddie's boys' boarding school at Abbotsholme, and then J. H. Badley's co-educational boarding school at Bedales. Both these schools are included in the symposium on the independent progressive schools edited by H. A. T. Child[3] and published in 1962, just four years after the appearance of the N.U.T. symposium on the new comprehensive schools.

Mr Child's contributors speak with a relaxed serenity of the hard-won achievements of the middle decades of this century. This is not to say that they are resting content with what has already been done or implying that all questions have been answered. But they are secure enough in their small, well-established schools—most of them boarding schools and only one with as many as 600 pupils on its roll—to speak with an

1. Published in 1952, 1953 and 1954 respectively. See also, for a British educator's comment on and an American educator's reply to these challenges, Holmes, Brian (1956) *American Criticism of American Education* (Bode Memorial Lecture), Ohio State University Press, and Conant, J. B. (1959) *The American High School, a First Report to Interested Citizens*, New York: McGraw-Hill.

2. Boyd, W. and Rawson, W. (1965) *The Story of the New Education*, London: Heinemann.

3. Child, H. A. T. (ed.) (1962) *The Independent Progressive School*, London: Hutchinson.

easy authority and a sense of personal independence. Each school emerges from this gallery of portraits with very distinctive features.

The contributors to the N.U.T. volume, by contrast, are speaking to the uncertain future rather than from the settled past. They, too, speak with authority, but they are more defensive about their schools. It is a collective defence that is being offered; the purpose of the book is not so much to offer portraits of individual schools as to offer, from actual experience, examples of different solutions to a number of central problems of organization in large day schools. The schools represented are very large: only one still had as few as 600 on its roll when the book was being compiled, and by now it probably has about 1,200. All the schools are day schools, and most of them are situated in heavily populated urban areas. The two main preoccupations of the teachers in these schools during the first years of their existence, were, first, how to cope with the problem of size, and secondly, how to refute the predictions of the jeremiahs that they would not be able to do well, academically, by their brightest pupils.

It is hardly surprising, therefore, that whereas Mr Child's contributors seem to move from the children as individuals to the school as a community, the comprehensive-school heads seem to move in the reverse direction. It is rather like the difference between the approach of the social (or even the clinical) psychologist and that of the sociologist. It is significant that the N.U.T. volume contains only one reference to the existence of school councils, whereas thirteen out of Mr Child's contributors mention systems of self-government, one only to reject them, the rest to give varying amounts of detailed explanation about the way they work.

What we have to ask ourselves is whether these small, independent boarding schools—the 'first-generation progressives', as they are sometimes called—have any messages about the problems of self-government that are relevant to the needs of our newest and largest day schools. One striking similarity that emerges from the two books I have been discussing is that, in both, the authors are at pains to point out that there is no blueprint for successful social organization. Many different patterns of school council emerge from the independent boarding schools; and at least three different systems of differentiation (by house groupings, by year groupings and by lower, middle and upper school groupings) emerge from the new comprehensive schools. What evolves in one will never be identical with what evolves in another. Indeed, this kind of freedom given to English teachers to conduct their schools in the way they think best is one of the qualities of the English education system that Everett most admired.

Kurt Lewin once said: 'Democracy cannot be imposed upon a person; it has to be learned by a process of voluntary and responsible participation.'[1] What, then, are the fundamental problems that teachers and pupils must face if they try to turn their schools into places where democracy can be learned? What emotional and interpersonal difficulties lie behind the procedures that are commonly used for electing form leaders, school-society committees and representatives to school councils, where these exist? How much interest are teachers prepared to take in this side of their pupils' growing up?

Dr Pedley, in *The Comprehensive School*, concludes, rather sadly, that teachers are 'not much interested in this question'—the question, that is, of training young people in democratic procedures and responsibilities. 'Their attitude', he says, 'is merely negative, not obstructive; they are happy to see children from different streams and different kinds of homes mixing socially. Only a few have thought out a philosophy and, arising from it, methods designed to produce an actively cooperating society and the conditions which would make comprehensive schools vehicles of a communal culture.'[2]

The truth is that we still know far too little about the emotional conflicts that are stirred up within and between groups of adults, let alone children, when we set up the various social structures in an institution. For we are not dealing only with 'social' events, in the usual sense of that term: we are often dealing with people's inability to test out their fantasies about other people's behaviour. This problem is complex enough when we are only concerned with inter-personal behaviour; it is even more complex when we are dealing with inter-group behaviour. It is not primarily because they are not 'interested'

1. Lewin, Kurt (1948) *Resolving Social Conflicts*, New York: Harper & Row, p. 39.
2. Pedley, R. (1963) *The Comprehensive School*, Harmondsworth: Penguin Books, p. 118.

in helping children to cope with democratic procedures that teachers hesitate to embark on elaborate procedures of self-government. It is rather that they are uncertain what forces will be released if they do.

Few schools succeed in avoiding, or indeed try to avoid, some experience with these problems. How, then, can teachers build on the traditions they already have and make more conscious use of such voting and decision-making as are already common in the schools? What new developments of thinking and action could arise from these beginnings?

2. FORM-ROOM LEADERS AND THEIR ELECTORS

One of the conventions that teachers use for giving adult sanction to the exercise of leadership in the classroom is the holding of 'form-room elections' at the beginning of every new term. These rituals are generally regarded as fairly simple matters, to be settled in ten minutes or a quarter of an hour. Children are expected to be sufficiently sophisticated about their struggles for leadership to come to quick decisions in choosing 'form captains' and to abide by these decisions peaceably for the rest of the term. Yet the task is not an easy one even for a form that is well up the age and intelligence scale.

For a large, newly constituted group of children—say, thirty eleven-year-olds in their first term in a secondary school—the task must be baffling. In the first place, even if a week or two are allowed to elapse before the children are asked to carry out this election, it is very unlikely they they will be at all clear about the role that is to be assumed by the elected member. Different children will bring to the task different notions about the role—notions stemming from varying experiences of authority and responsibility in primary schools and in homes and in the informal society of the streets and public parks. In the second place, the group may be using the election for emotional purposes quite unrelated to the needs of the community and to the assumptions of the form teacher about it. In the third place, emotional conflicts are almost certain to be stirred up by the whole process of the election—conflicts which may affect the behaviour of the form for weeks and even months to come.

What is the usual procedure? Perhaps the teacher leaves the field open, using a kind of sociometric method, asking each child to write two or three names down in order of preference; perhaps he uses a more elaborate procedure, asking for nominations, listing these on the blackboard and then conducting a secret ballot; or perhaps he favours a more public avowal of preference, merely asking for a show of hands as each name is called out. Who can say which of these methods is the more painful, which the more truly educative, which the more democratic? The sociometric method may preserve the appearance of total secrecy for the voters, at the same time yielding interesting data for the teacher, who may regard the resulting sociogram as evidence about the distribution of potential leadership within the form. But how many children afterwards will discover, by insistent probing and questioning, just how many of their classmates voted for them? And how many will be haunted by the fear that no one voted for them? The method of voting only for previously nominated members limits the pain of exposure to a handful of children, who, in any case, have had the distinction of being nominated, and if the ritual demands that the candidates close their eyes or leave the room while the voting is going on, the decencies are established, feelings are gently pushed below the surface and the teacher goes home assuming that the children have learned a new lesson in democracy.

But have they? What is this role of 'form captain' which one member is to take for the next fourteen weeks or so? The role may indeed prove an unenviable one, despite its romantic associations with the idea of being captain of a ship or skipper of an air crew. Often in the course of the term, it may seem to the incumbent that he has merely been set up as a sort of scapegoat—the person who will be blamed by the staff for all the misdemeanours of his classmates. If a teacher arrives late for a lesson and finds the class in an uproar, the form captain will be taken to task for failing to keep order. If someone's book has not been handed in at the right time, he may be blamed for not making sure it was there when he collected the others. If he is ever late for school he will be rated soundly for not setting a good example. And if he does try to assert his authority when the form is left without a teacher he may find himself howled down by his resentful classmates.

Sometimes the choice of form captain may be quite consciously and ruthlessly made to coincide with the appointment of a scapegoat. The form elects a rather quiet diffident member and then leaves the victim to carry the blame for everything that goes wrong. It is as though they want to make sure that the individual they place in authority over themselves is somebody who will be incapable of exerting that authority. Alternatively, the form may elect one of its more aggressive, troublesome members, perhaps in the hope that this one will be able to lead the fight against the staff instead of acting as a kind of deputy to the staff. Surprisingly, however, if the form teacher trusts the elected child to behave responsibly, his or her attitude may change completely. The fight–flight leader may, to everyone's surprise, carry the new office with sophistication and wisdom, being neither a puppet of the staff nor a tool of the form group that has elected him.

The feelings of the elected captain, whatever motives he attributes to his electors, are bound to be complex. For he is now operating on the boundary between the form-room group and the rest of the school. He must accept a certain obligation towards the staff group as well as towards his form-mates. To some extent he now shares the teacher's predicament, in that he is partially outside the group, though still in most respects a member of it. Inevitably the complexities of his new role will tax his ability to reconcile his allegiance to the form with his loyalty to the staff. He has to recognize, moreover, that the quality of his leadership will affect the kind of image his form presents, not only to the staff group, but also to other forms in the school.

Despite the pains and discomforts of the office, however, it is on the whole a coveted position, giving rise to considerable rivalry between the strongest claimants and to considerable loss of self-esteem in those whose claims appear to be beneath consideration. We must surely recognize, therefore, that the kind of election that teachers usually conduct with their forms at the beginning of the term will not be without its effects on the internal life of the form in the weeks that follow. It will be surprising if there is not at least one frustrated candidate for every victorious one. As for the victorious candidate, he is likely to feel some need to share his power with his defeated rival; for it seems that the burden of power is too frightening to be carried alone, and that the burden of guilt for having won this power has to be assuaged in some way. Hence, perhaps, the emotional

safety device in the custom of electing not only a form captain
but also a vice-captain, or even, in some schools, of blurring the
distinctions by electing two form prefects with equal status. Yet,
even if we provide the safety devices, we should not under-
estimate what it is we are asking children to do.

At the same time, we should not under-estimate the capacity of
children—even quite young ones—to discuss these problems and
even to examine their own motives for behaving as they do in an
election process. Let us consider, for example, the procedure
described in *The Werkplaats Adventure*, Wyatt Rawson's account
of the famous school at Bilthoven in Holland, already mentioned
in an earlier chapter.[1]

Here, we are told, children from the age of seven are encouraged to talk openly about the conflicts that lie behind form-
room elections. Rawson describes a meeting in which a group
of twenty-five boys and girls between ten and twelve years of
age conduct the business of electing officials. Nine posts are
filled—the form leader and deputy leader, the chairman and
secretary of the meeting, the librarian, two representatives on
the programme committee of the Monday-morning assembly
and two editors of the wall newspaper. In the course of the
meeting one girl who wants to be form leader is turned down
because 'she doesn't work hard enough' and no one 'would ever
listen to her': when she protests she is told that she may get the
post later on, but not this time. A big boy who wants to be chairman of the meeting has to accept a decision against him, because
'he's always laughing and talking'; but he eventually gets a
share of the responsibility for the wall newspaper. All this is
conducted, not by the teacher, although she is present and takes
part in the discussion, but by the retiring chairman.

Here, then, is a kind of election process that combines voting
with self-nomination: children volunteer for posts, and the
group decides which volunteers to appoint, sometimes by discussion, sometimes by taking a vote, sometimes by drawing lots.
Thus there is at least an attempt to bring feelings out into the
open. If a boy is turned down because he is too noisy and
frivolous to be a group officer, he knows the reason for his
rejection and has some idea what he must do to qualify himself for acceptance the next time. If anyone is eager to have
some responsibility, however big or small, the group will

1. Rawson, op. cit., pp. 27–30.

probably give him some special role in the end. And since, in this particular system, there are evidently nine possible posts each term, it is unlikely that any member of the group will go through a whole year without having had experience in at least one of them.

And there is another important development. Posts that involve executive leadership are separated from those that involve chairmanship or secretarial duties in a form discussion. The form leader and the deputy leader are not *ex officio* chairman and secretary of the meeting: it is recognized that these roles are different and must be handled by different members of the form. It therefore becomes possible, in a form meeting, for the leader and his deputy to be taken to task if it is felt that they are failing to carry out their executive functions. There is a system of checks and balances. Furthermore, there are other positions which carry specific functional responsibilities: these are, in industrial terms, 'service functions'. The librarian and the editors of the wall newspaper, having exercised this kind of responsibility, may gain experience which they can apply later to the other forms of leadership.

Clearly what Rawson describes here is only one segment of a complete community structure in which children have many responsible roles to play, including representative roles in inter-group situations. The Werkplaats community, in fact, empha-sizes self-government as part of the learning experience of being in a school. What happens in form and tutor groups, therefore, is a reflection of what is happening in the school as a whole, with its school council, its 'order committee' and its special committee to deal with serious behaviour problems. In such a community, relationships between groups as well as between persons are recognized as part of the raw material which child-ren must use as they struggle to grow up into sensitive, thought-ful adults.

3. THE SCHOOL CLUB, ITS STAFF SPONSORS AND ITS PUPIL COMMITTEES

So far, we have been looking mainly at the classroom. But in most schools there are activities officially going on outside the classroom and outside school hours which are regarded as important opportunities for children to learn. I am referring, of course, to school clubs and societies. Sometimes we find that these are strongly directed by staff members; sometimes we find that they are being run by puppet committees whose actions are really determined by staff; and sometimes we find that they are genuinely self-governing. One thing they all have in common: they are voluntary. Thus support for them may wax and wane, and enthusiasm among the steady supporters may itself fluctuate.

The very efficiency of clubs of this kind, when they are staff-dominated, may be masking problems of human relationships (including, perhaps, problems of pupil–teacher relationships) and preventing children from learning from their own mistakes and discovering for themselves what kind of responsibilities leadership should carry. Conversely, a club in which children are allowed to take major responsibilities will almost certainly run into trouble; yet it may offer a more genuine learning experience than the smoothly organized one in which catastrophes never happen. Sometimes, in such a club, the original purpose seems to get lost in the struggle to cope with the social difficulties. Given new responsibilities, children may test staff intentions by electing a committee that proves incapable of controlling any situation. If, following such an election, the adults in the community can tolerate the results of it, the children themselves are likely to take steps to change the leadership. Thus, within the framework of an adult sponsorship that enables the group to work through its aggressive feelings, a more stable set of relationships may eventually be set up by the children themselves.

Some years ago a student in one of my classes (Mr W.) described in some detail an experience he had had of running a junior debating society, with the help of a woman colleague, for the children in the first and second years of a mixed grammar school. He had brought this into existence, watched it change dramatically, both for the better and for the worse, over a period of two years, and finally left it, as a natural consequence of leaving the school.

The two teachers started the whole venture by putting up posters, inviting first and second year pupils to attend a free discussion one Friday afternoon on the subject 'Education in England'. To their amazement, about a hundred children turned up, and they had to move out of the classroom they had booked into one of the laboratories. Here Mr W., taking the chair, found himself facing a horde of children, sitting on benches, stools, floorboards and window-sills. They spent most of the hour 'firing somewhat insulting comments' at him, as he told us, which he, as the representative of the teaching profession had to accept without retaliating. Clearly, such a horde would be quite unmanageable as a debating society. And so, Mr W. and his colleague devised a selection procedure. They issued quite elaborate application forms, hoping to frighten a few off. But, again to their amazement, sixty or so children eagerly filled the forms up and handed them in. From these debating aspirants, they selected thirty—fifteen from the first year and fifteen from the second. And so, a few weeks after the opening of the spring term, the Junior Discussion Group was born.

This child of the selection procedure devised by the two teachers turned out to be a healthy, if somewhat dependent, baby. During the first term of its existence Mr W. and his colleague made all the decisions, choosing topics for discussion, persuading children to speak or take the chair and generally organizing the weekly meetings. By the end of the term— despite all their efforts to promote some learning about the procedures of formal debating—they were not able to feel that they had really taught their members anything. Nevertheless, the group had acquired an astonishing stability. Although the children were very nervous about public speaking and although they did it badly, there was only one occasion when a member who had promised to speak failed to turn up. Within the membership three sub-groups gradually appeared: the 'enthusiasts', who were prepared to speak or take the chair, the 'willing helpers' who would not speak but would help by getting the room ready, and the 'listeners' who gave no help at all but always turned up faithfully to listen.

And then, like all healthy offspring, this one began to show signs of impatience with the parents who insisted on doing everything for it. One day, about half-way through the summer term, five of the enthusiasts appeared at the staff-room door asking for Mr W. They told him that, although they very much enjoyed being members of the Junior Discussion Group, they felt that they did not have enough control over events. Mr W. encouraged them to make suggestions to remedy this: and they announced that they wanted to elect officers to perform the functions that had hitherto been performed by the two staff members.

Mr W. met this demand by calling a special meeting before the next debate. And a committee of three officers—a chairman, a deputy chairman and a secretary—were elected. The trouble was, of course, that no one was at all sure what these offices were meant to be, apart from the chairman's. And the immediate effects of the election were disastrous. The newly elected chairman found himself quite unable to control the meeting, and the staff felt obliged to cut it short. The next week things were even worse, and the meeting was ended even earlier.

The sequel to this was that three of the enthusiasts came to the staff-room the following Monday, nearly in tears, saying that the group must be reorganized and appealing to Mr W. to call a special meeting and ask the elected officers to resign. As it turned out, the committee, who had evidently been having a rough time, were only too thankful to relinquish their responsibilities, and a new committee was elected. The three who had come to the staff-room had not been seeking election themselves, interestingly enough, and resisted attempts to make them take over. In the end one of them—a girl—accepted nomination and was elected chairman. She and her two elected colleagues (a girl and a boy, both quiet, unassuming members of the group) ran the society very competently and almost without staff help as the term went on.

During this phase, it is interesting to note, the resistance to the idea of abiding by debating rules was lowered a little and the standard of speaking improved. And then about four weeks before the end of the summer term, the staff began to notice a growing restlessness. Members would arrive late or leave early, and requests were made for outside speakers and for visits to places of interest in the neighbourhood. Although the staff met these requests, the restlessness continued. And as the term ended, the Junior Discussion Group fizzled out.

The story really continues for another year, but I want to concentrate on this one year, as it shows us some extremely interesting fluctuations of mood and activity.

Mr W. had begun by unconsciously calling into existence a very aggressive fight–flight group, with the emphasis, not on running away, but on a frontal charge. Not unnaturally alarmed by the outcome of this first invitation, he proceeded to ensure that the permanent group he brought into existence should start life in a very dependent relationship to himself, by making them a specially selected *élite* who had every reason to feel grateful to him for allowing them to exist at all. He himself, when he described this whole experience to us, said that he had become aware, later, how much he had depended on this group to enhance his status in the school. Even more interesting was his own comment on his original action in offering a free-for-all on the subject of 'Education in England': in a sense the fight against convention, as expressed in the educational system within the school, was his own fight against the staff, but by projecting it into the children he unwittingly turned himself into the target.

The acknowledged task of the discussion group was to learn techniques of debating. Indeed the suggestion that the group should be formed had come from the headmaster, who was concerned about the low standard of debating in the upper school and wanted someone to train the children while they were still young. But it will be remembered that during the first phase, when the staff were running the whole thing, the members remained very resistant to this learning. They accepted the dependent culture, but refused to do the learning which the culture existed to promote. But once the children were running the show, they began to lower the resistances to this learning. Once the staff members had delegated leadership to the children, their teaching functions in the enterprise were accepted; even though they were taking little part in the activities except as members of the audience, the earlier attempts to teach the members began to bear fruit.

What, now, about the events at the end of the summer term? Well, it was known that this society was open only to first and second year pupils. Consequently, the group was inevitably going to lose half its members when the term ended. As their leadership structure included no provision against loss of continuity, it was hardly surprising that as the end of the term approached the members should grow restless and dissatisfied and start looking outwards, away from the familiar group that was bound to die, or at least to suffer mutilation, as the term ended. In a way, this was the basic assumption of flight taking over, perhaps very appropriately since, when something ends, flight is the only sophisticated course to take.

Now, this club was not functioning in a social vacuum. Both in the staff room and in the school as a whole it was, consciously and unconsciously, projecting an image of itself. Events at the beginning of the second year revealed a rather startling fact about this image. As an *élite* group, selected by the staff sponsors out of double the number of applicants, it turned out to be less attractive to newcomers than might have been supposed. When the posters went up the following September inviting first-year pupils to apply, scarcely anyone responded. The exclusiveness of that first year was evidently taking its toll. The surviving foundation members, now senior members of the club, found themselves having to court the younger children to entice fifteen of them to join. It appeared, then, that news had got round about the fifty-per-cent rejection the previous year, and that very few of the newcomers had felt inclined to subject themselves to the possibility of a similar rejection. One is reminded of the situation at the top of the school, where able boys and girls shut their minds to the idea of a university education rather than face the possibility of failing to win a place.

Was the junior discussion group described by Mr W. a failure, then? He himself presented it as an example of a group project that had failed. But the students who listened to his story were unanimous in their feeling that his club members had done a good deal of learning, not about debating techniques, it is true, but certainly about the problems of leadership and representation and the real implications of voting. And perhaps these less tangible gains were of far more importance than those the staff had had in mind at the beginning of the venture. Indeed it was hardly surprising that the 'learning' about formal debating had not progressed very far, since this activity was, in itself, a quite inappropriate one for children of this age. Their lack of satisfaction in the activity itself doubtless played some part in the ultimate breakdown. What was significant was that the children themselves had been able for a while to transform the situation into one that enabled them to learn something about their own relationships. And Mr W. was in no doubt, as he looked back on the whole experience, that he, as a teacher, had learned a good deal about the democratic processes he had brought into play when he met the first aggressive move from the children, not with counter-aggression, but with a wise partial withdrawal from the position of leadership he had first assumed.

Now these two teachers, in running this school society in the way they did, and in allowing themselves to take intelligent risks in this way, were encountering in miniature many of the problems that a headmaster and his staff will encounter if they decide to substitute some form of self-government for the established system of school prefects, house captains and so on. In fact this junior discussion group with its thirty members was not much smaller than two of the school communities (Summerhill and Kilquhanity House) described in Mr Child's symposium. And many of the other schools represented in that volume, like the Dutch Werkplaats, started life with equally small numbers. How, then, do schools meet the new problems that come with increasing size? And what general principles emerge from their experiences that are of use to schools that start life as large institutions and have to cope with complexity right from the beginning? Perhaps we can tackle this question by examining the prefect system and the school-council system side by side, in the context of the fundamental problem of relationships between adults and adolescents in an institutional setting.

4. DELEGATION AND REPRESENTATION IN THE SCHOOL COMMUNITY

It is somewhat disconcerting to find Dr Everett, the American visitor already referred to, making the following statement about the prefect system, as he saw it at Harrow, Rugby and a large number of state grammar schools: 'The prefect system in English secondary schools is as responsible as any other social institution for inculcating those characteristics of intellectual and personal honesty, individual courage and gentlemanly behaviour which have made up the code of the English aristocrats.'[1] One wonders whether he wrote this with his tongue in his cheek. But this was evidently not so, since he repeatedly assures us that these exalted persons were universally respected by younger children because of the authority invested in them. And again and again we find references to the perpetuation of the 'aristocratic' tradition through these, for the most part,

1. Everett, op. cit., p. 63.

'teacher-chosen' leaders. Is it that Dr Everett was projecting his own stereotype of the English school into what he saw? Or does he force us, through his apparently naïve descriptions, to see our own school customs as they really are?

Dr Pedley, writing in 1956, denounced the prefect system in round terms as out of date. He felt that teachers in the middle fifties were too preoccupied with the idea that sixth formers and prefects must be 'leaders' and wanted to see them create opportunities for far more pupils to be 'active members' of the school community, 'capable of assuming responsibilities *ad hoc*, as occasion arises.' He wished to see the end of the tradition which enabled a minority of powerful older pupils to dominate the majority and so to perpetuate an 'increasingly narrow and pretentious hierarchy'.[1] He too, relates the institution of the prefect system to our aristocratic tradition, but not quite with the reverence shown by Dr Everett. Seven years later, in *The Comprehensive School*, Pedley had to report that, of the hundred schools of which he had enquired, no fewer than ninety-six still had prefects. However, there were, he felt, some gleams of light. Here and there the concept of 'prefect' was changing. Responsible roles were being given to children as far down as the third and fourth years, instead of being reserved for the near-adult pupils at the top.[2] Yet even in these schools, the essential difference between the idea of 'prefect', whether appointed by staff or elected by pupils, and the idea of elected representatives remains. What is the difference?

The prefect system rests on the idea of authority delegated from the headmaster or headmistress (or possibly from the whole staff group) to a selected band of pupils. These people, though still in fact pupils of the school, are expected to act at times as delegates of the staff, empowered to carry out their wishes. The extent of this delegation varies from school to school. In some, the prefects merely enforce—or try to enforce—an existing set of rules, the origin of which most people have forgotten; in others, they may be expected to suggest modifications of these rules; and sometimes one hears of a prefect body taking an initiative not unlike that taken by Mr W.'s young debaters, and demanding more say in the making of school policy than the adults have thought fit to give them.

1. Pedley, R. (1956) *Comprehensive Education*, London: Gollancz, p. 79.
2. Pedley, *The Comprehensive School*, op. cit., p. 117.

The assumptions underlying the idea of a school council are quite different. Here there is full recognition of the fact that there is a boundary between staff and pupils. Even the oldest pupils, by the very fact that they are still at school, are not yet accepted by society as fully adult. It is therefore pointless to pretend that, at certain times of the day, this boundary has been obliterated by the handing over of pseudo-adult roles to certain selected pupils. The staff must rather create a situation in which they and their pupils (young and old) can confront each other. The adult cannot, and must not try to, escape from the conflict of such confrontations. He must be prepared to accept opposition, and must help his pupils to come to terms both with the ultimate authority that belongs to the staff and with the responsibilities that are within their own grasp. And so, instead of appointing certain boys and girls as delegates of the staff, the head and his or her colleagues make it possible for the various groups in the school to elect their own representatives or delegates to a central governing body or to committees for dealing with special problems and activities.

It is important to recognize that a boundary is not the same thing as a barrier. A boundary is something that can be crossed at the right time, but a barrier is intended to keep people out. The move towards lowering barriers—artificial ones—between teachers and pupils has been fairly universal in the schools of this country, and has been particularly strong in those schools that are generally considered to be 'progressive'. But when barriers between teachers and pupils are completely removed, the existence of the boundary between adults and adolescents is, paradoxically enough, less easy to ignore. And so one of the crucial questions that must face any headmaster and his staff group, when moves towards the setting up of a school council are made, is the question whether or not staff members have seats on the council. Opinions on this range all the way from the belief that self-government is meaningless unless teachers and pupils risk a genuine confrontation in public to the belief that not even the head should attend pupils' meetings.

Mr Kenneth Barnes, writing about Wennington School, emphasizes that the relationship between children and their teachers must include opposition and difficulty. 'The struggle that I believe to be necessary and good,' he says, 'is one in which we—the adults—have to be prepared for whatever may

come, to like being the people against whom the children batter
themselves and try out their powers.'[1] He is not speaking only
of school councils and committees here; but it is obvious that
such committees give one kind of opportunity for children to
bring out their aggression against teachers and learn to use it
constructively.

At the opposite pole, almost, is the view of Mr J. H. Simpson,
formerly the first headmaster of Rendcomb College. In his first
account of this school in *Sane Schooling*, where he calls it 'Churnside', he stated categorically that he did not consider that adults
should attend either the General Meeting or the Council.
Eighteen years later he published *Schoolmaster's Harvest*, in which
his experiences at Rendcomb took their place in the sequence
that included being pupil and master at Rugby, teaching under
Howson at Gresham's School, working for three years as a junior
inspector in a northern industrial town and being principal of
a Church-of-England training college. In this later book he
expressed the same views in exactly the same words, lifting them,
in fact, bodily from the earlier one. His argument was that
children could not be expected to discuss controversial questions
openly in the presence of adults who were also their teachers,
and that they should not be put under the strain of either
hearing their teachers disagreeing in public or suspecting that
they were concealing their true opinions in the interests of staff
solidarity. Having tried, first, having all the staff present and,
later, sending his own personal delegate, he ended up by keeping
all his staff out of the meetings. Strangely enough, he continued
to attend them himself, usually adopting the role of a casual
observer with half his mind on his correspondence, and sometimes giving information or offering his opinions.[2]

Now it is clear that his boys did have genuine work to do in
his general meetings, mainly because he instituted a system of
accountancy that enabled him to hand over to the General
Meeting a good deal of legislative control over the spending of
school funds. Also there was a network of special committees,
elected by the General Meeting, including a Council which
acted as a judicial body. Yet one feels that by keeping his staff
out, he was showing a failure of trust, both in their ability to

1. Child, op. cit., p. 167.
2. Simpson, J. H. (1954) *Schoolmaster's Harvest*, London: Faber & Faber,
pp. 156-9.

learn how to cope with their own aggressions and in the ability of the children to learn how to negotiate with adults. Fearing that they might all fall into the error of pretending that staff and pupils were 'equal', he and his staff avoided the task of talking and conferring about school policy across the child–adult boundary.

The position taken up by the Quaker schools on this question shows a similar reluctance to face and come to terms with the issue of adult–adolescent conflict, although their school councils do not appear to have been deprived of staff representation. Two of the schools included in Child's symposium are Quaker schools: the Friends' School at Saffron Walden, the very earliest to be founded, dating back to 1702, and Leighton Park, designed on public-school lines, founded in 1890. Mr Nicholson of Saffron Walden dismisses the question rather summarily, saying that his school does not 'spend a lot of time on elaborate forms of self-government like a school council'. Earlier in his article he points out that, having accepted an annual intake of about twenty county scholars, the school has to 'concentrate on being a good grammar school'.[1] We are left with the impression that education through social responsibility is having to yield to the pressure of anxiety about examination results.

Mr Ounsted, the head of Leighton Park, refers to his school council with a good deal more warmth, though he too confines himself to a very brief reference, offered, by implication, as a footnote to the full description of the school's policies which his predecessor, Professor E. B. Castle, published in 1954. Mr Ounsted's almost laconic assurance that 'the normal activity for left-wing-minded boys' on the Council is 'to reform its constitution, usually for the better and in a direction remoter from staff control'[2] may be taken as an answer to the honest doubts expressed by Professor Castle in his book. What he says there about the whole issue of self-government is worth quoting, as it illustrates once more the conflict all teachers have to face in deciding whether time spent on this kind of thing is time well spent or time misguidedly stolen from other more important activities.

In my present remoteness from direct responsibility for running a school I am inclined to think that the staff legislated too much and the boys too little and that I often failed to apply the logic of my

1. Child, op. cit., pp. 59 and 57.   2. ibid., p. 102.

convictions in this respect. But, from my impressions of schools where self-government was in full flood, I formed the view that, valuable as real self-government was, its processes demanded so much time that if we instituted it at our school it would be at the sacrifice of other activities that we regarded as equally precious.[1]

The somewhat ambivalent feelings of these three headmasters towards self-government as an institution appear to bear out Professor Campbell Stewart's views on the attitude of Quaker schools generally to the problem. Despite the fact that most of them now have a school council of some sort, operating side by side with a prefect system, Professor Stewart does not appear to feel, on the evidence of his researches, that the real problems of consultation on the boundary between the adolescent society and the adult society have been faced in these schools. His general conclusion is that 'the Quaker compromise here has been, with a few notable exceptions, to give cautious place to such bodies as a patch on the fabric of the existing hierarchy'.[2]

In view of the liberalizing influence of the earlier Quaker educators, this revelation is surprising. But we must beware of attaching labels too unthinkingly. Not all the Friends' schools have Quaker headmasters; and some schools that do have Quaker headmasters, including some of the most forward-looking, are not in the list of official Friends' schools. It may be that the reforming spirit of the Quaker educators has a better chance of flourishing in a school that is outside the official 'Establishment', just as schools that are outside the 'Establishment' in its broader sense have a certain freedom to be revolutionary that most schools feel they lack.

It is perhaps worth taking up in more general terms Professor Stewart's reference to 'the fabric of the existing hierarchy' in the school. The word 'hierarchy' here is important, as it is in Dr Pedley's reference to the prefect system which was quoted earlier. For, as soon as a school council is introduced two very crucial questions arise. The first—whether there should be staff representation—we have just been considering. The second is whether it is logical to maintain a prefect system alongside as a kind of executive arm of the staff group. It is surprising to find that many of the older schools accept the

1. Castle, E. B. (1954) *People in School*, London: Heinemann, p. 76.
2. Stewart, Campbell (1953) *Quakers and Education*, London: Epworth Press, pp. 254-7.

compromise without discomfort. Mr Simpson, for instance, justifies the existence of both on the grounds that 'the organization at Churnside was emphatically a dyarchy, both as regards in-school hours as opposed to out-of-school hours, and as regards the province of headmaster and prefects as opposed to the practice of the General Meeting'.[1] Where, one wonders, do the staff fit into this dyarchy? Professor Castle also believes in the prefect system, although he thinks it wrong 'to give responsibility to a small group of senior boys while denying even minor responsibilities to the rest', and although he is no longer so sure that prefects should be appointed by the staff rather than elected by the boys.[2]

In some schools we find a slightly uneasy compromise: the prefect role is retained, but in modified form and sometimes under a new name. At Badminton[3] prefects are elected by the girls and serve on the council *ex officio*; at Frensham Heights[4] and Wennington,[5] they are appointed, but are called 'counsellors' and are given little punitive power; at St Christopher, Letchworth[6] they are found only in the senior boarding-house, where they are elected and are called 'servers'.

From Sevenoaks School comes an example of a more unusual compromise between the old system and the new.[7] Here, with financial backing, a 'Sixth Form International Centre' has been set up alongside the existing all-age houses as an integral, but uniquely organized, part of the school community. Into this House come senior boys from all over the world, together with English boys (making up not more than half and not less than one third of the total number) who are moving up into the Sixth Form from the lower part of the school. In his account of this experimental venture, Mr Scragg, the House Master, suggests that the prefect system is one of the features of English school life that older foreign boys find most difficult to accept. He himself, like Dr Pedley, appears to deplore the 'rigid hierarchy of power' that is symbolized by the prefect system, with its underlying assumption 'that those not called to high office are irresponsible'. The members of the International

1. Simpson, J. H. (1936) *Sane Schooling*, London: Faber & Faber, pp. 112 and 170–2.
2. Castle, op. cit., pp. 80–1. 3. Child, op. cit., p. 27.
4. ibid., p. 69. 5. ibid., p. 161. 6. ibid., p. 134.
7. Scragg, Brian. 'The International Centre', in White, *et al.*, op. cit., pp. 94–109.

Centre in fact include some boys who are school prefects; but, inside the Centre, all the privileges and authority associated with the office are 'shed'. In place of the usual house captain and prefects, there is a committee of three, which is elected twice a term to put into effect the decisions about house organization and discipline that are made by the whole community in its weekly house meetings, and to act as 'provokers' of new ideas or projects. Mr Scragg gives an example of a conflict that arose in one house meeting over the question of television viewing, and describes how this argument, at first quite flippant, developed into a serious debate about the much more fundamental problem of how the House would deal with members who persistently opted out of community decisions. 'Painfully,' he says, 'but in the end intelligently, the boys themselves arrived at a conclusion which might easily have been imposed upon them at the outset by the authorities'. In fact, they decided for themselves that in the event of a boy's flagrantly continuing to ignore committee warnings, to the point of disregarding a formal vote of censure against him, the housemaster would have to be brought in as the authority ultimately responsible to the headmaster and to the rest of the school for the conduct of the Centre.

The Sevenoaks experiment seems to be something more than a 'patch on the fabric of the existing hierarchy'. There is some indication that developments in the International Centre are being watched attentively by the school community, and that there is some hope that it will prove to be a spearhead of further experiment along similar lines. But one wonders how the boys who are both school prefects and members of the international in-group manage to reconcile the roles they take outside the Centre with the principles on which their life inside it is based.

W. B. Curry, with his characteristic refusal to compromise, saw no place in his school for prefects, which he regarded as 'more analagous to gauleiters appointed by the Führer' than to leaders in a democratic community.[1] It is evident from the Dartington Hall contribution to the symposium of 1962 that his successors, Mr and Mrs Child, share his views. The prime need of the adolescent, in their view, is for 'self-determination'. And, so, in the senior house, the Council, or Moot, is regarded as an open legislative body in which teachers and pupils share

1. Curry, op. cit., p. 25.

responsibility for making and remaking the rules and for dealing with any problems arising out of them. From time to time this body also elects *ad hoc* committees, from volunteers who are prepared to undertake organized tasks for the community as a whole and are allowed to exercise authority in the specified and limited areas which they have been appointed to look after. Thus all these older pupils, like the members of the International Centre at Sevenoaks, are learning what they most need to learn —'to take authority into themselves'. In return for this, the staff feel that 'the efficiency of a school world run by prefects and monitors is well lost'.[1]

Now it is easy to be lulled by these imaginative and persuasive writers into the assumption that we have only to accept the principles underlying these various procedures of self-government and all will be well. But a little reflection is enough to remind us that, even in a tiny school of thirty to sixty members, such as Summerhill, Kilquhanity House or Monkton Wyld (all represented in Child's symposium) it takes a great deal of courage and skill and a considerable understanding of group behaviour to handle the emotional conflicts that must arise in these open discussions we are told about. Even in a small group of ten or fifteen the emotional undercurrents are extremely powerful and at times very frightening. In a group of thirty or fifty or a hundred we are dealing with even more explosive feelings, in which sub-groups as well as individuals are involved.

In the large group no child can be sure that his friends who urged him to raise a particular matter will support him; no one can quite predict how the sub-groups will form when everyone is there together. The child who can be bold enough in the informal exchanges in the dining-room, or out in the playing fields, or in the changing rooms, may suddenly feel isolated and insecure in the big, formal assembly. It is easy for a group to find itself being manipulated by one powerful, thrusting member and to become involved in acts of cruelty by silent consent. Nevertheless, the situation can still be contained in one large meeting, where at least everybody's outward behaviour is there to be observed by others and when the need for reparation has a chance to assert itself. Here, at least, there is a chance for members to test reality by raising questions, challenging other people's opinions, opposing (or supporting) adults, trying out

1. Child, op. cit., pp. 47–9.

their powers of persuasion and argument, testing social strategies.

But once the community expands beyond the size where general meetings of this sort are feasible, a new problem arises. Groups must now communicate through their representatives. Once the representative has gone to the council meeting, the group left behind finds itself a prey to all kinds of fantasies about what he is saying and how he is conducting himself. The representative, for his part, finds himself among relative, or complete, strangers, perhaps not as certain as he thought he was about the opinions of the group he represents, and thrown back on his own resources when unexpected questions arise in the council. Clearly, the election of the representative is only the first step in a whole series of unexpected outcomes. It is not enough for the group to sit back and leave everything to the representative as though he could know by a sort of magical intuition just what his group would expect him to do in any emergency. They must find ways of maintaining some kind of communication with him, yet they must make him feel that they trust him to do the best he can for them in the circumstances in which he finds himself. This trust is a two-way matter. The representative needs the emotional support of his electors; he will lose confidence if they appear, at one extreme, indifferent to what he does on their behalf, or, at the other extreme, full of suspicion and distrust. The group need to feel that he can function effectively in their absence, and that he can both carry his own internalized group into the committee on which he serves and carry the internalized committee back to the group. To the extent that he and other representatives can do this, as they move backwards and forwards between their own groups and the council, so far will it be possible for the members of the whole community to go on struggling with the never-ending process of testing fantasies against reality.

The kind of machinery that is set up in the larger schools for handling these problems is therefore of great importance. At St Christopher, Letchworth, for example, where there were in 1962 about four hundred children on the roll, each 'Company', or tutor group, is represented on the Council by its Staff Adviser, its Sub-Adviser (a sixth-former) and its elected Councillor; and in each of these companies the agenda for every council meeting are fully discussed before that meeting actually takes place.

Thus all Councillors (staff and pupils) go to the meeting knowing the views of the Companies they represent and knowing that they will later be reporting back to an informed and interested group.[1] At Wennington the system is rather different. Here, members of the school are free to attend and watch the proceedings of the Senate (the representative body) from a gallery; and after every meeting duplicated copies of the minutes are distributed around the school.[2] Again, at Dartington Hall, where the Moot, or general meeting, has now taken the place of the Council and Cabinet interaction described by Curry, there is now an Agenda Committee of six, which meets with the Heads and draws up plans for the fortnightly meetings so that discussion is directed towards some definite aims.[3]

Perhaps the most important part of the self-governing process is the work that goes on all the time, if the consultation is genuine and decision-making realistic, on the staff–pupil boundary. Every time a pupil challenges a staff member, either in a general meeting or in an elected council, two kinds of test are being made. First, the sincerity of the adult decision to let pupils have a say in the conduct of their community affairs is being tested. And secondly, the integrity of the staff group as the responsible adults in the community is being tested. Together these add up to the complex question: what is the capacity of the teacher as a person and of the staff as a group to accept the opposition of pupils without letting them collapse into anarchy? When a teacher is challenged or opposed by a child, what will he do? Will he retreat into authoritarianism and merely crush the child? Will he submit weakly to the child's will and let him— and the group—make a foolish and perhaps dangerous decision? Or will he oppose the suggestion, not as an outraged teacher, but as an adult who has relevant information and evidence to put at the group's disposal, thus turning the clash between himself and one member into a genuine problem for the group as a whole to thrash out?

The third course of action is clearly the most educative of the three, and indeed the only one that is consistent with the underlying principles of self-government. But we have to pause here, and distinguish carefully between community decisions that are merely foolish and will lead to inconvenience or discomfort and decisions that are dangerous and put the physical health

1. ibid., p. 134.　　　　2. ibid., p. 162.　　　　3. ibid., p. 47.

and safety of the pupils in jeopardy. This is where the necessity of the head's veto arises. The staff group, including the head, may quite often decide to allow a foolish decision to go forward, confident that they can, in due course, help the community to learn by the mistake and readjust itself to the demands of reality. But the head must accept the final responsibility of deciding whether or not to exercise his veto if the school is really heading for danger. Curry left his imaginary visitor in no doubt about the reality of this right of veto, which he maintained must not only exist but must clearly be seen by all the members of the school to exist, even if it never has to be exercised.[1] With this ultimate control in the background, a wise and skilful staff group can act in such a way, in their task of sharing authority with their pupils, that the group sees the danger for itself and averts both the dangerous decisions and the necessity for the final veto to be used.

All the schools described in Child's book, as the Head of Bedales says of his school, 'grew', not merely numerically, but emotionally and intellectually. For the two kinds of learning go forward together.[2] As emotional crises are faced and dealt with, so concepts about the problems of living and working together are taking shape in children's minds. A school is an organic community and its methods of self-government must grow as the school grows. It is hardly surprising that the large comprehensive schools of today, with their five or nine form entries, some starting from the amalgamation of two or three schools, with all the inter-group problems arising from such situations, others—more fortunate—building themselves up gradually from the first-form entry, have on the whole clung to the well-tried and once appropriate prefect system, or preferred a compromise between that and a school council. For what a St Christopher or a Dartington Hall or a Wennington can gradually evolve in a community that will not expand beyond about 400 pupils cannot simply be taken over by a large day school with very different conditions of work and a very different kind of school population.

We shall have to wait for a long time, perhaps, before the large schools that are already experimenting with these ideas can make their experiences available for teachers to study. On all sides one hears that these experiments are going on. Interest-

1. Curry, op. cit., pp. 18–19.   2. Child, op. cit., p. 34.

ingly enough, in one of the new comprehensive schools the prefects themselves, I am told, went to the headmaster and suggested that they should be liquidated, since their existence as a prefect body seemed to them to be incompatible with the new ideas about representation and shared responsibility that were taking shape in the school at the time. And so, in that particular school, the prefect system has now been abolished, not by edict of the headmaster and his staff but by the senior pupils themselves in collaboration with the headmaster and his staff. Even more interestingly, these pupils were only in their fourth year at the time, in a school that was growing upwards from an initial first-year entry and started its life with no senior pupils at all.

When accounts of such experiences reach the light of day, we may find that the basic discoveries of the small progressive schools still have relevance. Or we may find that we are only at the beginning of a new series of investigations into the conscious and unconscious behaviour of interacting groups in the large school community.

CHAPTER ELEVEN

Teaching and Living

THE INSTITUTION, THE ROLE AND THE PERSON

The school is ever in a state of flux. Along with the changes in society that inevitably affect its way of working, it experiences within itself an endless cycle of loss and renewal. Every summer it may lose some of its teachers and must lose many of its pupils. Every autumn the new influx of first-formers pours in, accompanied probably by a trickle of new teachers. The community must continuously be adapting itself to new people, new ideas and new problems. Even the most conventional of schools cannot be static.

Yet to those who are about to embark on a teaching career, it must seem that 'the school' as the institution they have known changes very slowly. To many, as they prepare to re-enter it as adults, the way forward looks distressingly like a way back. For the teaching profession, in placing upon every new member this necessity to return—symbolically, if not literally—to the scene of his childhood or adolescence, makes heavy demands on his newly acquired maturity. Society, as Dr Bryan Wilson has pointed out, offers him no clear message about what his role as a teacher is to be;[1] yet it throws him into an institutional situation in which the role seems so fixed and immutable that he may see little prospect of doing anything save conform to what the school appears to expect. And if he goes back into a secondary school he finds himself at the receiving end of pupil attitudes that look painfully—perhaps ludicrously—akin to those he himself was conscious of only three or four years ago.

For some young teachers, it is true, this return to an institution that is held together by familiar rituals and routines may on the whole be reassuring rather than unnerving. Becoming a teacher

1. Wilson, B. (1972) 'The Teacher's Role—a Sociological Analysis', *British Journal of Sociology*, vol. 13, pp. 15–32.

may be almost too inevitable a sequel to being a pupil. But for others—an increasing number, I believe—this second embracing of the world of school, so soon after the adolescent escape from it, is felt to involve an emotional risk that is hard to identify or describe. A student who is in genuine doubt about whether to take the final step and seek a teaching post may say something like this: 'Well, it isn't that I don't like teaching: I do. And I enjoy being with children. But I don't want to spend the rest of my life in schools.' Even an appointment to a school that is obviously forward-looking, that is full of opportunities for a young, energetic and imaginative teacher, one, moreover, that has all the advantages of a good up-to-date building and an enlightened head, can leave a young man feeling that a trap door has suddenly closed down on him. His heart, he may say, dropped into his boots at the very moment when he was joyfully accepting the post.

What kind of phenomenon are we observing here? Are these doubts irrational, in the worst sense of the word? Or are they healthy efforts to come to terms with a natural, even inevitable ambivalence towards the teaching profession? If the latter, it may well be that the very teachers who go forward into the schools trembling lest they may find that they have merely gone back into them, will turn out to be those with the most positive and constructive attitudes. Perhaps periodic despair is a necessary accompaniment to creative innovation in the schools. Perhaps what Mrs Jean Floud has called 'the occupational hazards to teachers' personalities'[1] must be squarely faced by the teacher himself if they are to be overcome.

Because of the weight of their own memories of all the teachers who have taught them over the years, young teachers are very often oppressed by the thought that they will always have to act artificially in the classroom. The 'role' in the sociological sense becomes confused with the 'role' in the theatrical sense. There is a fear that 'taking the teacher's role' will deteriorate into 'playing the part of a teacher' and losing one's identity in the process. 'How can I be myself,' they will ask, 'yet still be an effective teacher?' In a tutorial discussion someone recalls how he found himself simulating anger over an incident in the chemistry laboratory when what he really wanted to do was

1. Floud, Jean (1962) 'Teaching in the Affluent Society', *British Journal of Sociology*, vol. 13, pp. 15–32.

laugh. Another, with considerable distress, confides to the group suddenly her fear that she is becoming a nagging teacher—a 'schoolma'm' in fact. A third describes how he had to 'stop being friendly' with one class and start putting on a show of coldness and indifference because the boys were beginning to take advantage of him. Another admits to a tendency to be too sugary and over-pleasant towards her pupils, and wonders why she cannot be more natural and casual with them, Can the teacher's own identity survive the rituals of being a teacher?

These are real anxieties to those who are entering the profession. And yet perhaps it is not the young only who experience this concern about the tension between the demands of the role we have to take and the need to be ourselves in relation to our pupils. I believe that we all live through again this sense of artificially 'playing the role' of the teacher every time we embark on a new teaching relationship. For, at the first encounter with a strange class or group, we meet again, head-on, as it were, the built-in expectations of the class about how we are going to behave as teachers. And so we may have the uneasy feeling that we are acting the part that is expected of us (or deliberately not acting the part expected of us) instead of simply reacting spontaneously as persons to a developing situation that contains other persons. The gradual relaxation from merely 'playing' the role to 'taking' it in one's own personal way, as the formal encounter with the new class deepens into a real relationship, is perhaps one of the recurrent rewards of teaching. The acceptance, in oneself, of the strains that are inherent in the role is one of the continuing costs.

I have been trying to explore in this book some of the conflicts that the teacher has to learn to contain in himself as he tries to give the appropriate kind of leadership to immature yet steadily maturing human beings. The authoritarian teacher avoids these conflicts; the weak, *laisser-faire* teacher is overwhelmed by them. Most of us manage to escape from them a good deal of the time, by pretending that they do not exist. But if we can recognize and tolerate them in ourselves, we have a chance of helping our pupils to learn by their own efforts and thus to experience both the pain and the joy that accompany learning that is personal.

Most of the situations I have described could have happened in any kind of school—large or small, public or private, co-educational or single-sex. Many of them can be seen as funny from one angle and disturbing from another. Some show teachers in a good light, others in a poor light. Yet it is easy for all of us, probably, to imagine ourselves caught in these situations, the unflattering ones as well as the flattering ones, and reacting in much the same way.

I cannot claim that the illustrations I have used amount to 'evidence' in the strictly scientific sense of that term. They suggest rather a way of reading events—a search for patterns of behaviour that seem to point to certain kinds of predisposing causes.[1] What I have tried to do is to reinterpret my own experience, as a teacher in schools and as someone now in close touch with young teachers learning their job. I have done this partly in the light of studies of group behaviour and partly in the light of what we know about the growth tasks of the adolescents who inhabit our secondary schools.

One of my central themes has been the necessity for the recognition of feelings. This is not anti-intellectualism. It is a plea for the reintegration of the life of the emotions and the life of the intellect. All teachers are engaged in helping their pupils to deepen their rational understanding of the world they live in— the material world of objects and the social world of other human beings. We cannot do this by ignoring the irrational elements in their behaviour. We cannot strengthen their hold on reality by disregarding the power of fantasy.

At all levels in the educational hierarchy, from the lowest form in any school to the top administrative level in the local government offices (and we need not stop at the local ones) feelings are influencing action in largely unrecognized ways. Yet it is perfectly possible for such groups to act as if the persons engaged in the enterprise, whether it be classroom learning, staff discussion or administrative planning, were quite un-affected by such feelings—as though intellectual discussion were somehow, by its very nature, insulated against feeling. I have suggested repeatedly that it is part of the school's work to help children and young people to recognize and control these emotional forces, and that the task of a group will be tackled more effectively, whatever it may be, if we have the courage not to ignore feelings or pretend that they do not exist.

1. Support for this way of looking at evidence can be found in Cheshire, Neil M. (1964) 'On the Rationale of Psychodynamic Argumentation', *British Journal of Medical Psychology*, vol. XXXVII, No. 3, pp. 217–30.

If, as Professor Ben Morris points out, education is an 'enterprise' between teachers and pupils and not something that is done to pupils by teachers,[1] then the actual problems of working and thinking together in groups are part of the materials of learning. Yet in many books about education the problem of the group's internal life is by-passed. Studies of groups as such are felt to be of clinical rather than of educational interest. It seems easier to assume that the attitude of the teacher to his class has to be basically authoritarian, though we all hope that it can be benevolently authoritarian and that it will include more than a dash of democratic idealism. I have been suggesting that the teacher, while never denying his leadership or abdicating his ultimate responsibility for what happens in his classroom, needs to go further than this, if he is really going to help his pupils to grow up. And one of his most important tasks is to help them to recognize this conflict without resorting to defensive mechanisms such as splitting and projection, displacement or withdrawal into silence and apathy.

I believe that teachers need to know about these things and that we may come to feel that some exploration of their own conflicting feelings in relation to authority and leadership is a desirable, perhaps even essential, part of their own education as teachers. For the teacher himself—even the head of a school—stands on a boundary between those for whom he takes a leadership role and those to whom he in turn looks for leadership. And, standing on this boundary alongside him, are his colleagues, with whom he must actively and strenuously learn to work.

1. Morris, Ben (June 1958) *The Study and Practice of Education*, Lyndale House Papers, University of Bristol Institute of Education.

Bibliography

ALEKSEEV, KONSTANTIN SERGEOVICH (pseud. Stanislavski), (1945). *My Life in Art* (transl. from the Russian by J. J. Robbins), London: Bles, (reprint from 1942 edition).

ALLPORT, G. W. (1955) *Becoming*, Yale University Press.

AUSUBEL, D. P. (1954) *Theory and Problems of Adolescent Development*, New York: Grune & Stratton.

BALDWIN, MICHAEL (1962) *Poems by Children 1950–1961*, London: Routledge & Kegan Paul.

BARKER, ELIZABETH (1965) 'The Creative Aspect of Music in the Infant School', *New Era*, vol. 46, No. 2.

BECKETT, JACK (1965) *The Keen Edge: an Analysis of Poems by Adolescents*, London: Blackie.

BESTOR, A. E. (1953) *Educational Wastelands: the Retreat from Learning in our Public Schools*, University of Illinois Press.

BION, W. R. (1961) *Experiences in Groups*, London: Tavistock Publications.

BONNEY, MERL E. (1947) 'Popular and Unpopular Children: a Sociometric Study', *Sociometry Monographs No. 9*. New York: Beacon House.

BOYD, W. and RAWSON, W. (1965) *The Story of the New Education*, London: Heinemann.

BRONOWSKI, J. (1961) *Science and Human Values*, London: Hutchinson. (rev. ed. 1964. Harmondsworth: Penguin Books.)

BROOKS, JEREMY (1960) *Jampot Smith*, London: Hutchinson.

BRUNER, JEROME S. (1962) *On Knowing: Essays for the Left Hand*, Harvard University Press.

BUBER, MARTIN (1947) *Between Man and Man*, London: Routledge and Kegan Paul.

CASTLE, E. B. (1954) *People in School*, London: Heinemann.

CHESHIRE, NEIL M. (1964) 'On the Rationale of Psychodynamic Argumentation', *British Journal of Medical Psychology*, London: XXXVII, iii, pp. 217–30.

CHILD, H. A. T. (ed.) (1962) *The Independent Progressive School*, London: Hutchinson.

CLEGG, A. B. (ed.) (1964) *The Excitement of Writing*, London: Chatto & Windus.

COPE, EDITH (1964) 'The C.S.E.—Some Positive Aspects', *Education for Teaching*, No. 65, pp. 41–4.

CONANT, J. B. (1959) *The American High School To-day: a First Report to Interested Citizens*, New York: McGraw-Hill.

C.R.E.D.I.F. (1958) *Voix et Images*, Paris: Didier, p. xxx.

CURRY, W. B. (1947) *Education for Sanity*, London: Heinemann.

DAVIES, MAXWELL (1963) 'Music', in *Studies in Education: the Arts and Current Trends in Education*, Evans for University of London Institute of Education.

DOUGLAS, J. W. B. (1964) *The Home and the School*, London: MacGibbon & Kee.

ELVIN, H. L. (1965) *Education and Contemporary Society*, London: Watts.

ERIKSON, ERIK H. (1960) *Childhood and Society*, New York: W. W. Norton.

(1959) *Identity and the Life Cycle*, New York: International Universities Press.

(1964) *Insight and Responsibility*, New York: W. W. Norton.

EVANS, KATHLEEN (1962) *Sociometry and Education*, London: Routledge & Kegan Paul.

EVERETT, SAMUEL (1959) *Growing Up in English Secondary Schools*, University of Pittsburg Press.

EYKIN, W. VAN DER (1965) 'Nuffield Science', *New Education*. July.

FLEMING, C. M. (ed.) (1951) *Studies in the Social Psychology of Adolescence*, London: Routledge & Kegan Paul.

FLOUD, JEAN (1962) 'Teaching in the Affluent Society', *British Journal of Sociology*, vol. 13, pp. 299–308.

FORD, BORIS (ed.) (1960) *Young Writers Young Readers*, London: Hutchinson.

FREUD, S. (1921) *Group Psychology and the Analysis of the Ego*, London: Hogarth Press, vol. 18 of the Complete Works.

FROMM, ERICH (1942) *The Fear of Freedom*, London: Routledge & Kegan Paul.

GOLDING, WILLIAM (1958) *Lord of the Flies*, London: Faber & Faber.

GRAINGER, A. J. (1965) 'The Bullring', *New Era*, vol. 46, No. 9.

HALMOS, PAUL (1952) *Solitude and Privacy*, London: Routledge & Kegan Paul.

H.M.S.O. (1963) *Half Our Future* (Newsom Report).

(1963) *Higher Education* (Robbins Report).

(1964) *School Science Teaching* (Report of an Expert Conference held at the University of Ceylon).

(1964–5) *The Certificate of Secondary Education*, Bulletins 1–5.

HOLMES, BRIAN (1957) *American Criticism of American Education* (Bode Memorial Lecture), Ohio State University Press.

HOLMES, GERARD (1952) *The Idiot Teacher*, London: Faber & Faber.

HOMANS, G. C. (1951) *The Human Group*, London: Routledge & Kegan Paul.

HOURD, MARJORIE L. (1949) *The Education of the Poetic Spirit*, London: Heinemann.

HOURD, MARJORIE L., and COOPER, GERTRUDE E. (1959) *Coming into their Own*, London: Heinemann.

HULL, L. W. H. (1959) *History and Philosophy of Science*, London: Longmans Green, (reprinted as paperback, 1965).

INHELDER, BÄRBEL, and PIAGET, JEAN (1958) *The Growth of Logical*

Thinking from Childhood to Adolescence, New York: Basic Books.

JACKSON, B., and MARSDEN, D. (1962) *Education and the Working Class*, London: Routledge & Kegan Paul.

JAMES, HENRY, (1914) *Notes of a Son and Brother*, London: Macmillan.

JENNINGS, HELEN H. (1950) *Leadership and Isolation*, New York: Longmans Green.

(1959) *Sociometry and Group Relations*, Washington D.C.: American Council for Education.

JERSILD, A. T. (1957) *The Psychology of Adolescence*, New York: Macmillan.

(1952) *In Search of Self*, Bureau of Publications, Teacher's College, Columbia University.

JORDAN, DIANA (1963) 'Movement and Dance', *Studies in Education: The Arts and Current Tendencies in Education*, Evans for the University of London Institute of Education.

KLEIN, MELANIE (1960) *Our Adult World and its Roots in Infancy*, Tavistock Publications, Tavistock Pamphlets No. 2.

KOESTLER, ARTHUR (1964) *The Act of Creation*, London: Hutchinson.

LABAN, RUDOLF (1948) *Modern Educational Dance*, London; Mac-Donald & Evans.

LEWIN, KURT (1948) *Resolving Social Conflicts*, New York: Harper & Row.

MARSHALL, SYBIL (1963) *An Experiment in Education*, Cambridge University Press.

MENZIES, ISABEL E. P. (1960) 'A Case Study in the Functioning of Social Systems as a Defence Against Anxiety: a Report on a Study of the Nursing Service of a General Hospital', *Human Relations*, vol. 13, No. 2. pp. 95–121.

MORENO, J. L. (1961) *Who Shall Survive?* New York: Beacon House, (reprinted in revised form from earlier edition of 1934).

MORRIS, BEN (1958) *The Study and Practice of Education*, University of Bristol Institute of Education.

(1965) 'How Does a Group Learn to Work Together?' in NIBLETT, W. R. (ed.) *How and Why do we Learn?* London: Faber & Faber.

MUNRO, T. (1956) *Art Education: its Philosophy and Psychology*, Liberal Arts Press.

MURPHY, GARDNER (1961) *Freeing Intelligence through Teaching*, New York: Harper & Row.

(1960) *Human Potentialities*, London: Allen & Unwin.

MURPHY, LOIS B. (1962) *The Widening World of Childhood*, New York: Basic Books.

N.U.T. (1958) *Inside the Comprehensive School*, London: Schoolmaster Publishing Co.

NEATBY, HILDA (1953) *So Little for the Mind*, Toronto: Clarke, Irwin.

NEWSOM, J. (6 September 1964) 'The Education of Women', *Observer*.

NORTHWAY, MARY L., (1953) *A Primer of Sociometry*, University of Toronto Press.

(1947) 'Personality and Social Status', *Sociometry Monographs*, No. 11, New York: Beacon House.

ORFF, C., and KEETMAN, G. (1960) *Music for Children*, London: MacDonald & Evans, (English version adapted by Margaret Murray, Books I-III, and by Doreen Hall and Arnold Waters, Book IV, with a Teacher's Manual by Doreen Hall).

PEDLEY, ROBIN (1956) *Comprehensive Education*, London: Gollancz.

(1963) *The Comprehensive School*, Harmondsworth: Penguin Books.

PETERS, R. S. (1964) *Education as Initiation*, (University of London Institute of Education Studies in Education), Evans.

RAWSON, WYATT (1956) *The Werkplaats Adventure*, Vincent Stuart.

REDFERN, BETTY (1965) 'Physical Education as an Academic Discipline', *New Era*, vol. 46, No. 2.

REID, L. ARNAUD (1965) Review Article on Peters, R. S., 'Education as Initiation', *British Journal of Educational Studies*, XIII, ii, pp. 192–205.

RICE, A. K. (1963) *The Enterprise and its Environment*, London: Tavistock Publications.

(1965) *Learning for Leadership*, London: Tavistock Publications.

RICHARDSON, ELIZABETH.

(1951) 'Classification by Friendship' in Fleming, C. M. (ed.), *Studies in the Social Psychology of Adolescence*, London: Routledge & Kegan Paul.

(1963) 'Teacher-Pupil Relationships as Explored and Rehearsed in an Experimental Tutorial Group', *New Era*, vol. 44, Nos. 6 and 7.

(1965) 'Lateness, Absence and Withdrawal', *New Era*, vol. 46, Nos. 9 and 10.

(1965) 'Personal Relations and Formal Assessment in a Graduate Course in Education', *Education for Teaching*, May; No. 67.

ROGERS, E. M. (1964) 'The Aims of Science Teaching in Schools', in *School Science Teaching* (Report of an Expert Conference held at the University of Ceylon, Peradeniya), H.M.S.O. London.

RUSSELL, JOAN (1958) *Modern Dance in Education*, London: MacDonald and Evans.

SHAPLIN, J. T. and OLDS H. F. (eds) (1964) *Team Teaching*. New York, Evanston & London: Harper and Row.

SIMPSON, J. H. (1936) *Sane Schooling*, London: Faber & Faber.

(1954) *Schoolmaster's Harvest*, London: Faber & Faber.

SMITH, MORTIMER (1954) *The Diminished Mind: a Study of Planned Mediocrity in our Public Schools*, Chicago: Henry Regnery Co.

SNOW, C. P. (1959) *The Two Cultures and the Scientific Revolution* (Rede Lectures), Cambridge University Press.

STEWART, W. A. CAMPBELL (1953) *Quakers and Education*, London: Epworth Press.

TANNER, J. M. (1961) *Education and Physical Growth*, University of London Press.

TARGET, G. W. (1960) *The Teachers*, Harmondsworth: Penguin Books.

TRIST, E. L., and SOFER, C. (1959) *Explorations in Group Relations*, Leicester University Press.

VIOLA, W. (1948) *Child Art and Franz Cizek*, University of London Press.

WERTHEIMER, M. (1959) *Productive Thinking*, New York: Harper & Row.

WHYTE, W. F. (1943) *Street Corner Society*, Chicago University Press.

WHITE, B., PATERSON, N., TALBOT, H., SOMMERHOFF, G., HOARE, G. and SCRAGG, B. (1965) *Experiments in Education at Sevenoaks*, London: Constable Young Books.

WILES, J., and GARRARD, A. (1957) *Leap to Life*, London: Chatto & Windus.

WILSON, BRYAN, R. (1962) 'The Teacher's Role—a Sociological Analysis', *British Journal of Sociology*, vol. 13, pp. 15–32.

WINNICOTT, D. W. (October 1962) 'Adolescence', *New Era*, vol. 43.

Index